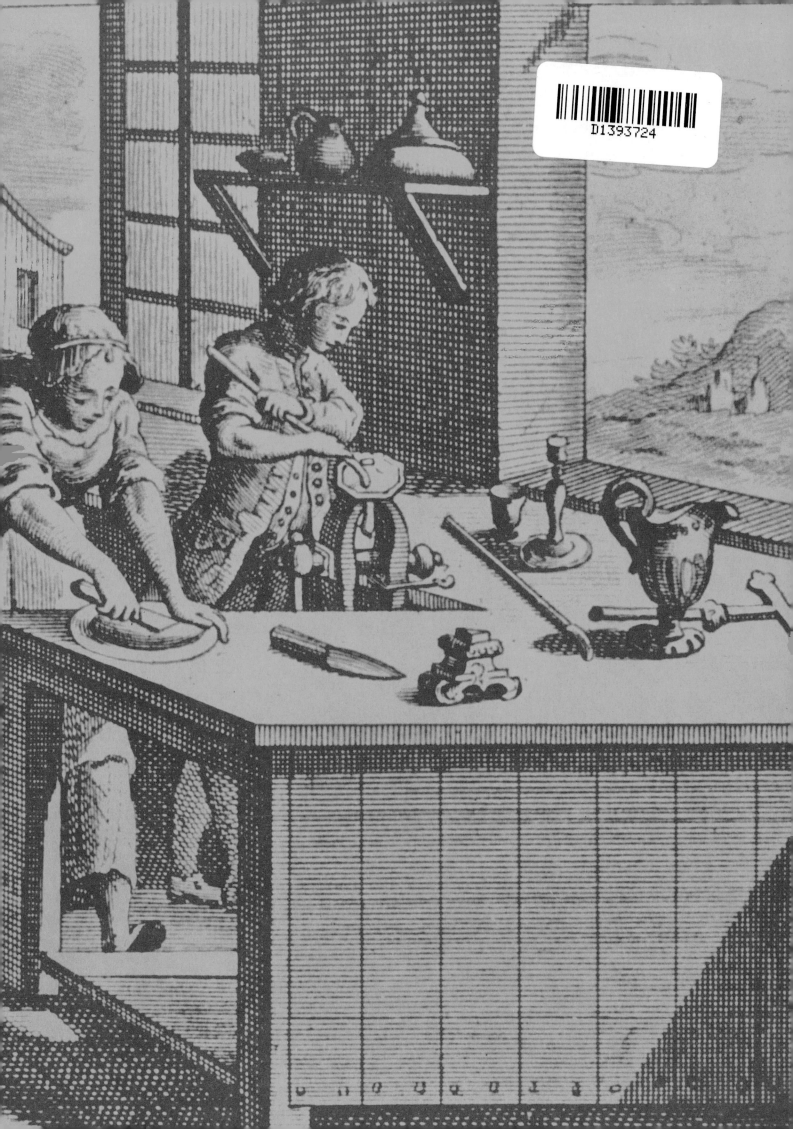

A History of Jewels

A History of Jewels

By J. Anderson Black

With an Introduction by
Edward Lucie-Smith

ORBIS PUBLISHING · LONDON

Introduction

Jewellery, as a thing to write about, hovers in a kind of no man's land. How are we to discuss it? From the technical point of view, perhaps – the secrets of casting and chasing, granulation and soldering? Or are we to speak of jewels in their archaeological and anthropological aspect, as evidence of vanished civilizations and the customs of primitive men? Or in terms of what is called 'romance' – recalling the extraordinary adventures which have befallen certain stones, such as the Koh-i-noor, as the result of human covetousness or carelessness? Or are we to talk of the jewel as a piece of sculpture on a small scale, a miniature work of art? Or else in its role as an amulet, a focus for magical power, a means of imposing a pattern favourable to ourselves upon random circumstances? All of these approaches to the subject are legitimate; none, in itself, offers a complete picture.

Let us go back to the beginning, and look at matters very simply. I am lying on a beach, the sun beating down on my bare back. It is almost time for lunch. Still drugged with heat, I begin to arouse myself, to lift my head, open my eyes. As I open them, something slowly swims into focus. An arm, golden brown, with fine golden hairs. Clinging to it are a few grains of sand, and a few little pearls of water. And clasped around the wrist is a bracelet, intricately patterned, made of gold, with a few coloured stones. As my glance travels down the arm, it is suddenly arrested by this ornament. The sensual shock is tremendous. Suddenly, I become a thousand times more aware of the arm, the silken flow of its muscles, and also of the body to which it belongs. The jewel has made a statement which is not about itself but about relationships – the subtle interaction of nature and art. Jewels only really complete themselves when they are worn, and that is why it is such a pity that most of the great historical jewels are doomed to remain imprisoned in museum showcases.

You might expect, in a modern society, with its emphasis on freedom, simplicity of manners and social equality, that jewels would gradually be going out of fashion, that we would be starting to think of them as part of the clutter with which our ancestors burdened their lives, as props no longer required by our own forthright self-confidence. Not a bit of it. There has, instead, been a great revival in the jeweller's art. The unimaginative designs of a few decades ago have been replaced by a wealth of fantasy. Patrons have once more begun to think in terms of a jewel commissioned specially to suit a particular physique, a particular personality. They have come to realize that the jewel is one of the most direct means of making a personal statement – the wearer, by her choice, tells us a good deal about herself. What has, perhaps, changed is the notion of the jewel as part of a uniform, as a badge of status, a social indicator. There was a time when the wives of English army officers always wore the badge of their husband's regiment, fashioned in platinum and tiny diamonds, and pinned either to their bosoms, their hats or to the lapels of their coats. The moment your eye fell on this symbol, you knew where you were, both socially and sexually. I seem to see such brooches less often nowadays.

Meanwhile, there is an increasing appetite for information about jewellery – and, until now, that appetite was difficult to satisfy. This book is by far the broadest treatment of its subject that I know, and by far the most generously illustrated. The reader will find here much basic technical information, and a splendid panorama of historical styles. Looking through these pages, he will not be surprised at the amount of space given to the ancient Egyptians, to the Minoans, the Greeks, the Etruscans, because the illustrations show how much ancient jewellers could achieve, often with limited technical resources. At the same time, he or she will come to recognize the magical skill of a comparatively modern craftsman such as René Lalique. When I visited the Gulbenkian Museum in Lisbon, what I expected to be overwhelmed by was the accumulated splendour of pictures, tapestries and furniture. In fact, the high points were to be found in the first room and the last. The first room houses the small portrait head of a Middle Kingdom Egyptian pharaoh in obsidian, which is one of the great marvels of ancient sculpture. The last gallery is devoted to the collection of jewels that Gulbenkian commissioned from Lalique. The thing that a Lalique jewel and a top-class piece of Egyptian sculpture have in common is something very simple – both go so far beyond one's aesthetic expectations that they induce a sense of pure wonder.

Yet Lalique's jewels can be criticized, and are criticized in these pages, for one fault – the fact that they are often difficult or cumbersome to wear. The relationship between jewellery and practical requirements has, however, always been a subtle and paradoxical one. The function of some jewels is quite simply to assert the wearer's unfitness for demeaning physical labour – I am thinking, for example, of the elaborate fingernail cases which were once worn by Chinese mandarins. The jewel can also, especially in primitive societies, be the direct cause of physical deformity: I am now thinking of the disc-lipped women of Chad, who figure among the illustrations of this book, and I am thinking, too, of tribes whose women wear ear-rings so heavy as to pull the ear-lobes down into great loops, or chokers so high as to elongate the neck to almost twice its natural height. Even in civilized societies, people submit to small mutilations in order to adorn themselves more effectively: Indian women still pierce their noses for the sake of a nose-stud, and women all over the world – and some men – are willing to have their ears pierced. In considering such manifestations, we must not forget the psychological aspects. Can pierced ears be read in the same sense as tattooing – as the symbol of a certain, though usually unconscious, masochism?

The psychology of jewels is indeed a fascinating subject, and one which merits a far more expert and extended treatment than I can hope to give it here. Nevertheless, it is worth touching upon two points. First, that jewels are a classic area of activity for collectors, whose motivations span the whole spectrum of emotion, from the crudest to the most refined, from the lust for wealth to the rarefied appreciation of beauty which can only be fully savoured when the object is held in the hand, contemplated in solitude. Recent research seems to indicate that obsessive collectors are usually men or women in search of consolation, people who make it up to themselves for some traumatic shock – perhaps a serious illness or the loss of a parent – suffered in early life. The consolatory quality of jewels is closely linked to superstitious belief in their talismanic power, and one can easily understand, if one pursues this line of thought, why jewels (apart from their convenient size) consistently attract thieves – more so than objects which in fact are equally valuable and equally vulnerable, such as paintings.

The second point is the role played by jewels in the giving of gifts. Twentieth century anthropological research has demonstrated, in ample and fascinating detail, the fact that gift-giving is essentially aggressive. Apparently an expression of goodwill, the gift carries an overtone of hostility, because it puts the recipient into our debt, and therefore into our power. In European culture, in recent centuries, jewels have essentially been the gift of the man to the woman, the expression of a wish for physical possession. No wonder that the designs tend to be ambiguous – that we often find jewelled chokers which resemble the collars worn by dogs or slaves, and bracelets which look like manacles. Not surprisingly, painters have shown themselves to be sensitive to this kind of overtone. One instance is Lucas Cranach, whose nymphs and goddesses wear heavy chains of gold when wearing little else. As an extension of this line of thought, I also find it fascinating to note how often jewellery design is filled with an aggressive phallic symbolism: this is especially true of some examples made in the 19th century when snake rings, snake brooches and snake necklaces were so very much in vogue.

In fact, when we wear them, jewels very easily become metaphors, and the force of the metaphor is increased because instead of separating it from ourselves, putting it in a frame or on a pedestal, we actually unite it to ourselves, to our own flesh. The jeweller, the original creator of the object, thus invites the wearer to be not so much an admirer as a collaborator, a co-conspirator almost. And the partnership is not twofold but threefold, as nature too must play a part. One of the obvious, but yet striking things about jewels is the fact that the materials are important. We are far more keenly aware of the materials in a fine jewel than we are of the fact that a sculpture is made of bronze or marble and a painting of canvas and paint. And this is true even when the jeweller has made use of things which we know to be cheap, such as plastic. Nevertheless we do, I think, feel this quality the more keenly when the materials are rare and precious. Let us take the case of the Canning Jewel in the Victoria and Albert Museum – a merman whose torso is a baroque pearl. The pearl is a rarity, and nature, in creating that rarity, has so to speak already indicated what might become of it – the craftsman becomes the ventriloquist's dummy used by some power beyond himself. In this sense, the doctrine of the 'found object' entered the jeweller's philosophy much earlier than that of the fine artist; entered it, indeed, as soon as teeth and shells and the vertebrae of small animals began to be strung into necklaces.

At the same time, in jewellery the 'ready-made' cannot lead directly to conceptual art, which is what it seems to have done with painting and sculpture. Jewellery must always be material. In wearing it, we unite ourselves, not only to a metaphor, but to the substances of which the world is made – to metals, minerals, animal products such as the pearl, and fossils such as amber.

I think this is one of the reasons why contemporary jewellery has kept its sense of direction so much more successfully than contemporary sculpture. Looking through the pages of this book, I am sure almost everyone will be fascinated, not merely by the beauty and strangeness of the individual objects, but by a sense of continuity, of unity in diversity. One would not, I feel certain, get the same sensation from a comprehensive history of the visual arts. It is always supposed that the function of the visual arts is constant. I, on the other hand, have always been struck by their mutability – the fact that they have played such different roles in different societies, have spoken exclusively of religion in the high noon of the Middle Ages, of the power of the state under Louis XIV, of private pleasure under his successor, of revolutionary politics with the work of Jacques-Louis David and of anarchic individualism with that of Jackson Pollock. Jewellery, on the other hand, has always had a basic function – to adorn. The purposes for which people adorn themselves may vary, but the underlying aim is constant. And it remains a fundamental impulse even in a mobile and volatile society such as our own. So fundamental that we continue to use forms which stretch far back into prehistory. The most striking example, perhaps, is the simple bead. Beads are amongst the most eloquent as well as the most widespread of objects. I can think of no culture in which they have not been worn. Even more strikingly than potsherds, beads act as messengers from civilizations infinitely remote from us in time, in space and in attitudes. Their universality suggests that they supply an equally universal necessity.

EDWARD LUCIE-SMITH

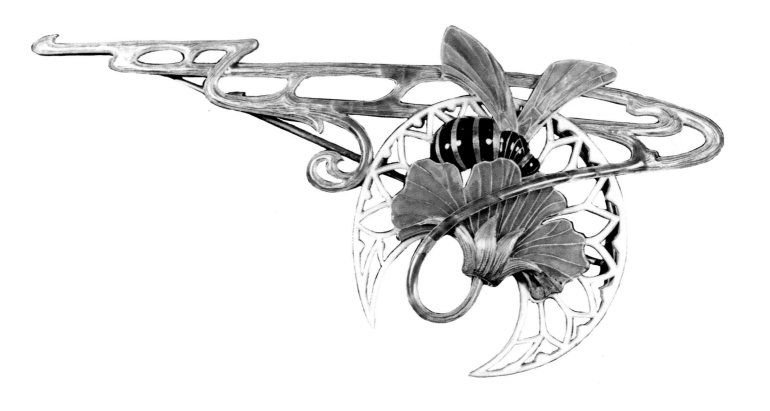

Foreword

When embarking upon this history of jewels, I was immediately struck by the enormity of the task which faced me. More than five thousand years of craftsmanship and design in the pursuit of self adornment had to be covered in a single volume. The amount of space available was indeed handsome by any standards but it was necessary to impose some restriction on the items to be included. Folk jewellery, *objets d'art*, and other products of the goldsmith's art which were not designed for wearing have, therefore, been omitted except where they represent the only surviving examples of a particular style or technique.

The sheer scope of information and its necessary compression also presented problems and I would like to take this opportunity to thank the numerous scholars whose definitive works on specific aspects of the subject I found invaluable. At the end of the volume there is a Book List which gives my sources of material but there are a few names that I should like to thank individually for their help both in editorial and pictorial research. To Mr. Graham Hughes of the Worshipful Company of Goldsmiths, to Dr. Reynold Higgins of the British Museum, to Dr. Joan Evans, scholar and author, and to all the shops, galleries and private collectors who were unstinting in their assistance – thank you.

J. ANDERSON BLACK

Contents

Prehistoric and Primitive Jewels

Objets Trouvés

Since the dawn of civilization, jewels have compensated for three of man's basic insecurities: vanity, superstition and the desire for material wealth. These three facets of the human character are as old as man himself. The motives behind the desire for jewellery may be of dubious virtue but the objects produced over the past 25,000 years are of ceaseless fascination to aesthetes and academics alike. Archaeologists use them to gauge the technical achievements of ancient civilizations; anthropologists to gain an insight into prehistoric customs and thinking; economists to assess the economic structure of whole civilizations. Because of the peculiar properties of gold, jewels have frequently survived where every other trace of a civilization has vanished. But these are secondary benefits. It is the intrinsic beauty and technical mastery of jewellery and its creation which make its study rewarding.

Where does the story begin? Science is constantly proving *homo sapiens* to be older than once believed, and there is evidence to suggest that jewels are as old as man himself. The earliest examples thus far discovered, however, date from the paleolithic period and it is interesting to note that the terms *paleolithic* and *neolithic* signify respectively: the age of primitive stone implements, and the later Stone Age when polished or ground stone weapons and implements prevailed. This could almost be taken as an assessment of the progress made in lapidary techniques from 25,000–5000 BC.

Most of the objects dating back to the paleolithic period are strictly *objets trouvés* – teeth, shells, fossils, pebbles and fish vertebrae – but the moment man drilled a hole in one of these objects, strung it and wore it round his neck, it became as much jewellery as, say, a diamond necklace from Cartier. Perhaps the earliest pieces so far discovered were three fish vertebrae necklaces found in a grave near Monaco, made between 25,000 and 18,000 BC. Now in the museum at St. Germain-en-Laye, they come from the Aurignacian culture. A second very early find was made in Eastern Europe at Předmostí; a communal grave was lined with the jaw-bones of mammoths and every body was adorned with a necklace of ivory beads.

Finds between 15,000 and 5000 BC become increasingly numerous and some technical progress is noticeable; stones are drilled, polished and graded with greater precision but, until the Bronze Age and the discovery of metalwork techniques, the jeweller was a lapidary (cutter or polisher of gemstones).

What significance this early jewellery had is, of course, uncertain, but the same *objets trouvés* survived the Bronze Age technology and were widely used by more advanced cultures for amuletic purposes. In those days, when man's needs were at their most basic, it is fair to assume that jewels were thought to offer the wearer protection against adversity. Cowrie shells, for instance, were widely favoured in neolithic times and continued to be worn by women throughout Dynastic Egypt as a protection against sterility.

Civilization has developed at a vastly different pace in various parts of the world and even today some remote tribes have developed no further than neolithic man. They furnish the academic with a living workshop, providing a deeper insight into the mind of primitive and prehistoric man. The suggestion that jewels are primarily talismanic is also confirmed. Without

exception these tribes indulge in forms of self-adornment and while the basic object is magical or sexual, it is interesting to note that the correlation between an object's rarity and its value is appreciated by the most backward tribes. The tail feather of a rare bird is more sought after than that of a common bird, regardless of its beauty.

Jewels are also used by primitive societies as a badge of office or a demonstration of some personal achievement. A string of teeth, for instance, is frequently a sign of physical prowess. This is a subsidiary function of jewellery which survives in the developed world until the present day – witness medals and mayoral chains.

More grotesque functions are also associated with primitive jewellery. Some African tribes wear enormous *labrets* (lip plugs) which distort and mutilate the mouth to such an extent that it makes talking and eating both painful and difficult. For the man, the object of this grotesque practice is to make him appear more fearsome in battle; in the case of women, it is to make them so unappealing that other tribes will have no desire to carry them off. The same function is achieved by the neck-rings of the 'giraffe women', a

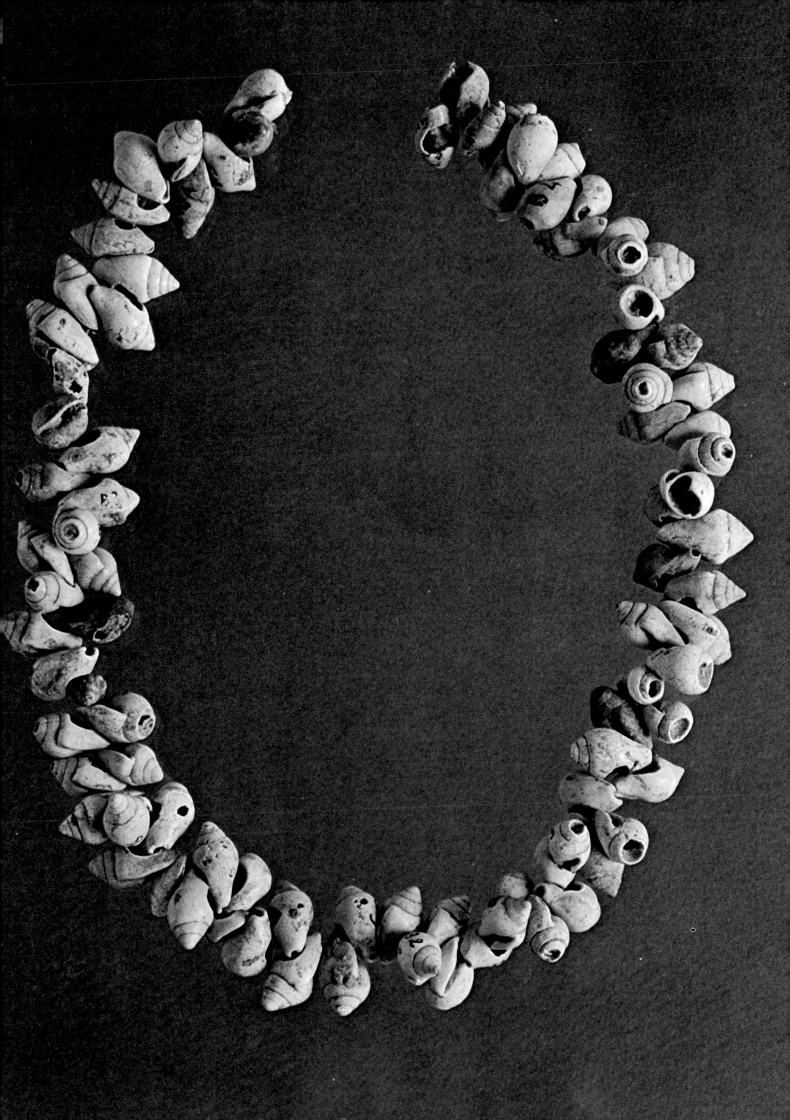

Tribal jewels both from primitive and more advanced tribes are often extremely beautiful and made with great technical virtuosity. Their design, however, is usually dictated by tradition and ritual and, as such, tribal jewels fall outside the scope of this book Right: bracelet and necklace of coloured beads from Uganda, and a Zulu pectoral from southern Africa. (Horniman Museum, London)
Far right: a jaguar's tooth necklace from the Mato Grosso, Brazil. (Private collection)

Right: amuletic jewels from the West African Ashanti tribe, perhaps the most accomplished goldsmiths working outside the developed world. (Private collection)
Far right: amuletic necklace in amber from Ecuador. (Private collection)

single ring being added each year from childhood until the neck is stretched to disproportionate length.

The history of jewellery covers a great period of time and hundreds of civilizations. It is necessary, therefore, to impose some restriction on the types of jewellery to be covered in a single volume. No further mention will be made of primitive or folk jewellery which is such an enormous subject that it would fill a volume on its own. Jewels, by definition, must be decorative, magical and precious; it is with the Bronze Age and the discovery of gold – which fulfils those three virtues – that our story really begins.

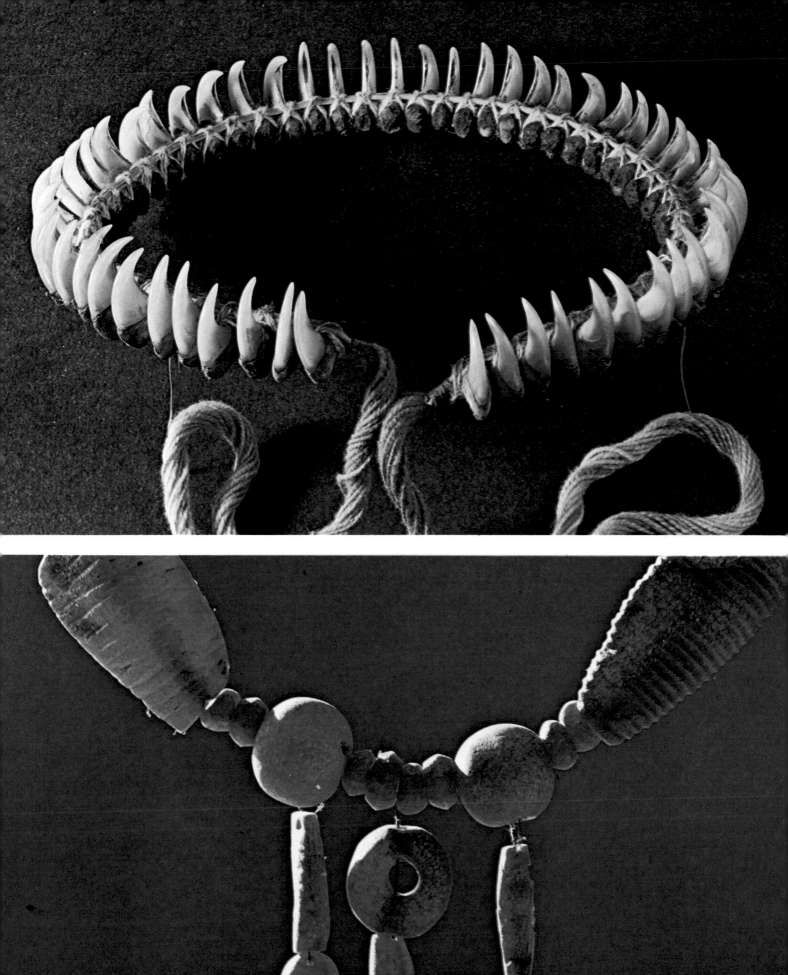

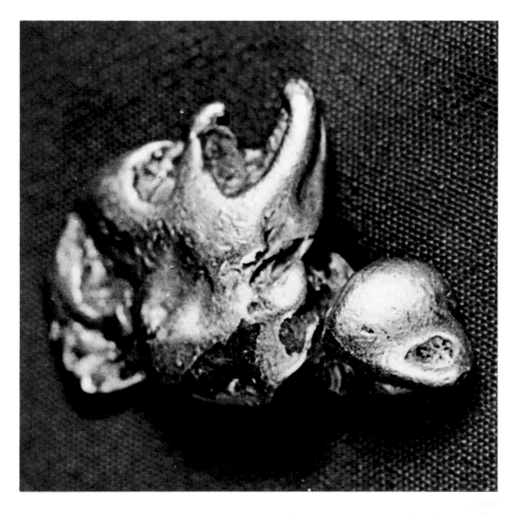

Craftsmen of the Ancient World

Gold has always held a unique fascination for man; he has worshipped it, slaved for it and died for it. For more than 6,000 years there has been a relentless search for gold in every corner of the world. Yet the total recovered in that time probably amounts to less than 120,000 tons which, if cast into a single ingot, would make no more than a 20-yard cube.

It seems extraordinary that ancient civilizations should expend their resources and manpower to extract a metal which was so soft that it was useless for the manufacture of tools, weapons or other implements essential for survival.

It could not have been its scarcity that originally made gold attractive, although this rapidly became the reason for its high commercial value. Perhaps it was its natural beauty or the belief that it held the mystical powers of the sun that first captured man's imagination. Whatever the reason, it is with the discovery of gold and the realization of its extraordinary physical properties, that the history of

jewellery really begins. For thousands of years the words 'jeweller' and 'goldsmith' have been synonymous.

Where and when gold was first worked is open to question. Discoveries by archaeologists compel us continually to change our ideas about the structure and development of the Ancient World. What is certain is that gold was being worked with extraordinary skill around 3000 BC by various communities in the Middle and Near East.

The most obvious advantage of gold for the craftsman is that it is soft, in the pure state not much harder than lead, and it can be beaten cold without fracturing. It is so malleable that it is possible to hammer an ounce into a single sheet of more than 100 square feet. It is also extremely ductile: the same quantity of metal can be drawn to 50 miles of wire. It has a comparatively low melting point, is not subject to corrosion, oxidation or attack from common acids, and does not tarnish or rust. It is the craftsman's dream come true.

Goldsmiths were always the élite of the artisans, patronized exclusively by kings, priests and the nobility. Metalwork techniques have remained virtually unchanged for 5,000 years despite the advent of modern technology, and a

jeweller's bench today must look very like that of a Sumerian goldsmith in the 4th and 3rd millenia BC. True, contemporary tools are now made of high-tensile steel instead of bronze or flint, butane or coal gas has replaced an open charcoal fire, and electric polishing machines have superseded hours of tedious work by hand. But these are merely conveniences. The basic techniques remain unchanged, and to understand the craftsmanship of the Ancient World is to understand the craftsmanship of today. The next section sets out to explain in simple terms the techniques and processes involved in the manufacture of gold jewellery.

Soldering is one of the first techniques essential to the craftsman
Right: a single sheet of metal has been bent round to form a ring held in position by binding wire; three pieces of solder (or metal of a lower melting point) are placed across the gap and heat applied until the solder melts, flows across the adjacent metal and forms a bond

Metalwork Techniques

The idea of gold nuggets is to some extent a myth. They do exist – nuggets weighing up to 160 lb have been recorded – but this is the exception rather than the rule. For the most part gold has to be extracted laboriously in tiny quantities from metal-bearing quartz or by the collection of alluvial gold washed into river beds from the mother lode by centuries of erosion. Tons of quartz have to be crushed or sand sifted to yield no more than a handful of gold specks.

The first problem facing the ancient craftsman was to convert these specks into a workable mass. To do this he had to generate a temperature of at least 1,000°F, the approximate melting point of gold. Egyptian tomb paintings give us the best idea of the techniques employed. They show goldsmiths using reed blowpipes with ceramic tips over an open fire and later with bellows-operated blast furnaces. The specks of gold would be placed on a charcoal block and the heat directed at them by blowpipe until they melted and fused together into a single lump, which could then be hammered out into sheets.

It is at this point that the goldsmith faced another serious problem. Initi-ally, the metal would be soft and yield readily but, under continual hammer-ing, it would become hard and brittle, and could only be returned to its origi-nal workable state by periodical reheat-ing. This process, annealing, must have been the first major technical discovery to be made by the goldsmiths of the Ancient World.

Soldering

The range of objects which could be made from a single sheet of metal was considerable but there came a time when two or more pieces of metal had to be joined together. At first this was achieved by riveting, pinning or liter-ally sewing the object together with gold wire. None of these techniques, however, was satisfactory. They were not only slow and unsightly but pro-vided a weak link.

The key to joining separate pieces lay in the impurity of gold. In its natural state gold is always alloyed with another metal, usually silver or copper. The proportion of impurity can vary from about 10 per cent to 50 per cent and some observant goldsmith must have noticed that when particles were fused together some pieces melted more quickly than their neighbours, thus flowing over and joining them.

It did not take goldsmiths long to isolate this lower-melting gold, which could be used specifically for joining pieces. Whether they realized that the melting point was lower as the impurity increased, and therefore produced alloys artificially, or whether they merely separated the alloys by their slight colour difference, is not known for certain.

Before soldering could be achieved satisfactorily, the problem of oxidation had to be overcome and, though there is no mention of the substance in any ancient writings, we can only presume that they used some form of flux. When gold is approaching melting point it develops a skin of oxide which inter-feres with the flow and adhesion of the solder. The surfaces to be soldered, therefore, must be coated with a flux which acts as a barrier from the air, not only preventing oxidation but also guiding the solder into the joint since this is the only area which will readily receive it. What material was used in the Ancient World is impossible to say but it must have had similar properties to borax, which is used by contemporary craftsmen.

Repoussé is a technique of metal decoration where the design is punched in relief Right: the face of the metal sheet is pressed into a bowl of warm pitch which holds it in position and gives when pressure is applied to the surface of the metal

One of the properties which makes gold so suitable for all forms of decorative metalwork is its malleability. It can be beaten extremely thin and decorated in high relief without fracturing Right: Etruscan pendant medallion decorated with repoussé head, 8th/7th century BC. *(Museo Nazionale di Villa Giulia, Rome)*

Repoussé

Decorative metalwork techniques used today were also invented and developed by craftsmen of the Ancient World. One of the oldest of these is repoussé, a relief pattern raised on sheet metal. The gold is laid face down on a bed of warm pitch, the whole design is drawn on the back with a scribe and punched out systematically with a variety of traces (blunt chisels). The pitch, being softer than the gold, gives and so allows the metal to follow the contours of the tool. The surface of the pitch is tacky

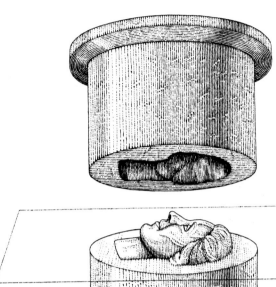

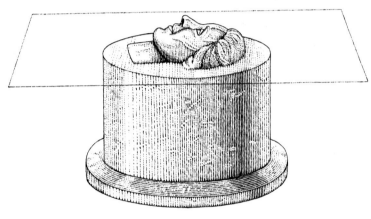

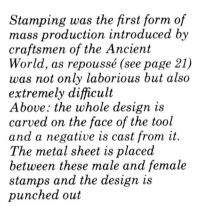

Stamping was the first form of mass production introduced by craftsmen of the Ancient World, as repoussé (see page 21) was not only laborious but also extremely difficult

Above: the whole design is carved on the face of the tool and a negative is cast from it. The metal sheet is placed between these male and female stamps and the design is punched out

Stamping

Stamping marks the introduction of the concept of mass-production to the world of jewellery. Amazingly, this technique appears to have evolved almost simultaneously with that of repoussé (see previous page) despite the considerably advanced degree of technical skill required for tool-making. Repoussé work is laborious, time-consuming and extremely difficult, so when repeating designs were required for bracelets and necklaces, goldsmiths started looking for short cuts. Rather than punching out each section of the design separately, they found that by first chasing and grinding the desired pattern on the face of a bronze tool they could produce as many copies, exact copies at that, of the same design with a few blows of the hammer (on the back of the stamp) through a thin sheet of metal onto a pitch bed.

Some craftsmen preferred to work in reverse, in which case the design would be carved in reverse on the face of a bronze tool, the gold sheet laid on top covered by a thick sheet of lead and the design hammered out. This was in fact a primitive form of the die-stamping widely used today.

Above: one of the finest examples of repoussé work ever found, a Sumerian helmet discovered at the Royal Tombs of Ur and dating from the 3rd millennium BC (see also pages 40–41). The enlargement at right shows the detail and precision achieved by these early craftsmen. (British Museum)

Right: three Greek pendants from the 7th century BC. The ones at either side are decorated with an identical pattern – a typical example of stamping, the technique illustrated in the drawing above. (British Museum)

and grips the metal sheet, keeping it flat and stopping the whole object from caving in when concentrated pressure is applied to a small area. Throughout this process the metal has to be annealed at regular intervals to prevent it from becoming brittle.

When the punching is completed, the object is removed from the pitch, cleaned and worked on the front with chasing tools to sharpen dull edges and add very fine detail. Perhaps the finest example of ancient repoussé work is the gold helmet found at Ur in Mesopotamia and dated *c*.2500 BC.

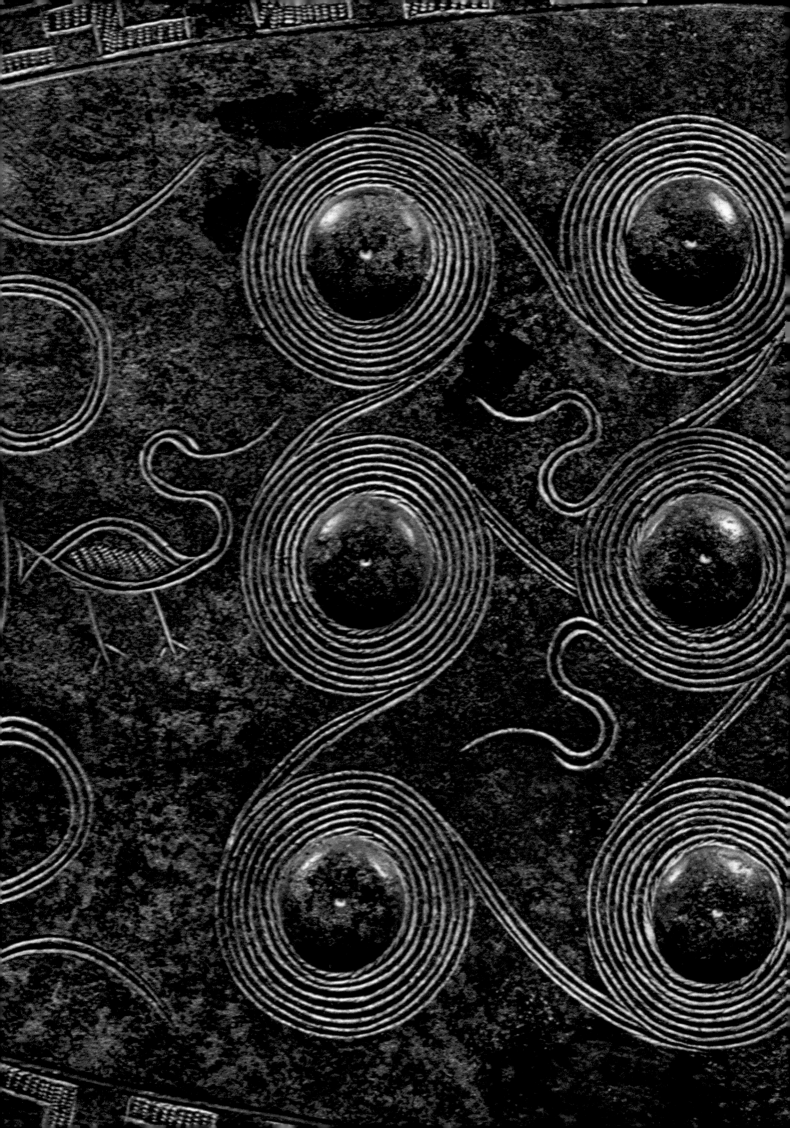

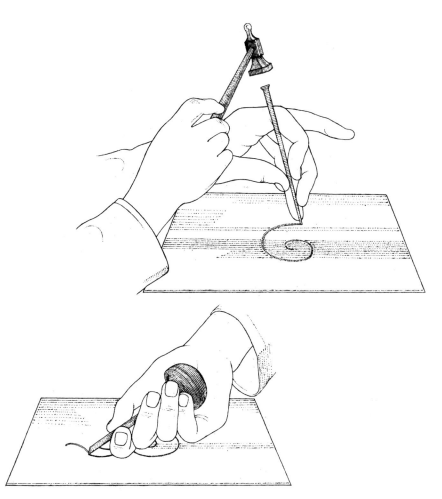

Chasing and engraving. While repoussé designs are always done from the back of the metal, chasing is a similar technique executed on the face
Top: design is punched out with a chasing tool
Above: engraving can have a similar effect to chasing; the main difference is that an engraving tool actually cuts away a section of metal rather than pushing it to one side

Left: bronze fibula from the Benacci phase (c.1050–700 BC) of Villanovan culture is a rare example of early engraving. In the detail, far left, the metal can be seen to have been cut away. (Museo Civico, Bologna, Italy)

Chasing and Engraving

Unlike the other techniques described here, ancient craftsmen found themselves severely handicapped by the inadequacy of their tools when it came to engraving. There is often confusion between chasing and engraving. A chasing tool makes an indentation in the metal by pressure; although the metal is squeezed out of the groove, no metal is lost.

Engraving, on the other hand, involves actually gouging out a section of metal with a sharp-edged tool. Recent research has shown that it is impossible to harden bronze tools sufficiently to fulfil this gouging task. None the less, examples of lunulae from the Bronze Age Irish period have been found which carry some fine engraving, presumably without the aid of steel tools.

Isolated cases of engraving have also been found in some Middle Kingdom Egyptian jewellery (c.2000 BC), possibly executed with a sharp sliver of flint, but the technique was not used on a large scale until the introduction of steel tools in 800–600 BC.

Filigree
and Granulation

Soon after they had discovered the art
of soldering, goldsmiths started to
decorate the surface of their work with
patterns of wire and granules.

The production of wire for filigree
work without machinery must have
presented ancient craftsmen with a lot
of problems. There are various theories
about the method of production but it
is generally agreed that the first step
was to cut narrow strips of gold from a
sheet with a chisel. It is how these
irregular square-section strips were
transformed into round wire that is
open to question.

Some experts claim that the wire
was hammered round and, while this
is perfectly feasible with thick wire or
rod, it would be impossible to produce
the very fine wire required for filigree
work. Another theory is that the wire
was rolled round between two smooth
stones. This would be possible but very
laborious. The most likely method,
though there are no facts to support
the theory, is that the wire was drawn
through dies, not unlike the draw-
plates employed by craftsmen today.

Bronze would be too soft for the manufacture of dies but it is possible that
the wire was drawn through drilled
hardstone beads (which had been
readily available in all the civilizations
producing gold jewellery).

However it was produced, the existence of wire offered enormous scope
for decorative patterns. With a simple
pair of bronze tweezers, the craftsman
could produce spirals, loops and wavy
lines which could be soldered onto the
face of the work. Two or more wires
could be twisted together, which in turn
became a more complex appliqué design.
To add variety to this filigree work,
designers incorporated domes or
spheres. These were originally quite
large and produced as hollow domes
punched out of thin gold sheet and
trimmed to size but, as work became
more complex and the component parts
smaller, this method proved too time-
consuming, so solid spheres were used
instead. This was the start of granulation, the most amazing of all the technical achievements of the craftsmen of
the Ancient World.

Granulation was in use in the 3rd
millenium BC but the granules used
were large and the work comparatively
crude. It was the Etruscans in the

*Above: ear-stud decorated with
filigree, New Kingdom
Egyptian period (c.1559–
1085 BC) and detailed
enlargement at right. (Royal
Scottish Museum, Edinburgh)*

Granulation, like filigree, is a method of decorating the surface of a metal object. The method was devised in the 3rd millennium BC and brought to perfection by the Etruscans in the 8th/7th centuries BC. They used granules measuring less than 1/200th of an inch Right: the tiny balls are placed individually with tweezers and soldered to the surface without the use of flux (a method called colloidal hard soldering)

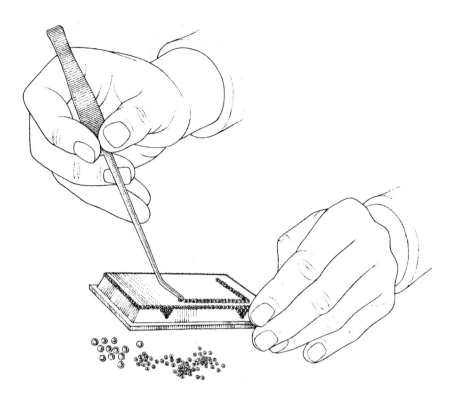

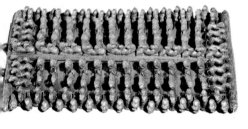

Above: the Etruscans were the unrivalled masters of the technique of granulation. The detail of this fibula (see also pages 66–7) from the 8th/7th century BC, at left, shows the precision with which the minute granules of gold were placed on the surface. (Museo Nazionale di Villa Giulia, Rome)

period 700–600 BC who perfected the technique and produced work which puzzled craftsmen and metallurgists for centuries.

So minute were the granules used, some measuring less than 1/200th of an inch, that they look more like matt bloom on the work than a collection of granules. The Etruscans used the technique to produce figurative and geometric designs of unparalleled beauty.

During the Roman Empire the art of granulation died out, and for centuries craftsmen tried to revive it but without success. Firstly, there was the problem of producing the granules. This, it has since been discovered, could have been done in one of two ways. Small pieces of gold could be laid on a bed of charcoal in a crucible, and the vessel gradually filled up with alternate layers of gold and charcoal. When heated, the gold would melt, forming minute spheres, then be cooled and the charcoal washed away. Alternatively, the granules could have been made by bombardment with molten gold dropped from a height onto a perfectly smooth surface such as a slab of marble. The granules would then have to be graded (by passing them through a series of sieves) and arranged in pat-

terns on the background before being soldered in position. It sounds straightforward enough but every attempt to reproduce the technique ended in failure. Either the granules melted, the solder flowed between the granules and clogged the design, or the flux bubbled up and shifted the minute granules.

It was not until 1933 that an English metallurgist, H. A. P. Litterdale, came up with an answer which he called 'colloidal hard soldering' and, while there is no proof that this was the method used by the Etruscans 2,500 years earlier, it is the only method so far devised which produces results even approaching their level.

Litterdale decided that flux had to be omitted entirely; the granules were glued to the background with a paste of copper hydroxide which was to become the solder as well as a temporary adhesive. When heated the copper hydroxide decomposes, turning these minute particles of copper alloy into copper oxide – then copper – to form an invisible joint with the adjoining gold. Colloidal hard soldering is still considered a highly skilful and delicate operation, so the Etruscans must have been craftsmen and metallurgists of unbelievable sophistication.

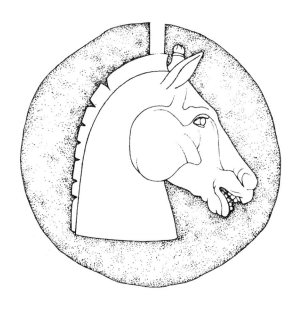

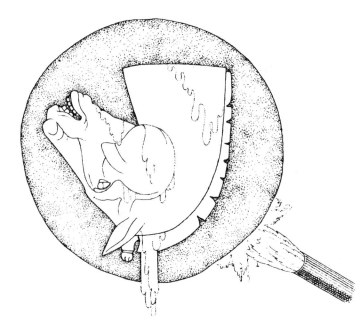

Casting

Casting is an extravagant method of producing objects in metal and for reasons of economy it was seldom used in jewellery-making until this century. None the less it was amongst the crafts which were mastered more than 5,000 years ago.

The first method employed was open casting; objects made by this method have been discovered from the Ubaid and Uruk periods in Mesopotamia (c.3500 BC). This was casting at its simplest. A shape chiselled out of stone or baked clay would be filled with molten metal which cooled and solidified into the required shape. This method was quite satisfactory for flat objects such as spearheads and axes, but when three-dimensional objects were required, craftsmen developed the piece mould which is still used today. The object was modelled in wax and coated in clay, the mould was allowed to dry, cut down the middle, and the wax removed. The mould was then assembled and filled with molten metal.

This was a simple way to achieve a perfect reproduction of an object modelled in another material, but the solid objects produced were very heavy and wasteful, so hollow casting became necessary. This involved suspending a solid object in the centre of the mould and allowing the metal to flow round this core and still assume the shape of the mould. As casters became more skilful they could increase the size of this core without it touching the mould, and produce very thin-walled metal castings.

The last and most sophisticated method of casting invented in the Ancient World was the *cire perdue* or lost wax method. Once again the object was modelled in wax and coated completely in clay except for one vent. When the clay was hard, the mould would be turned upside down and the wax melted out. The same vent which was used to remove the wax would then be used to inject the metal. The advantages of this method were that it saved time and eliminated 'casting webs' – rough lines which appeared on the piece-moulded objects where the sections of the mould joined.

When the *cire perdue* method was invented is uncertain but there is evidence to suggest that some of the objects found in the tomb of Tutankhamun (c.1350 BC) were produced by this method.

The use of casting for jewellery was comparatively limited until the 20th century when mass production required multiples to be produced from one design. Jewels being small objects can only be cast solid, which wastes precious materials. By using base metals, however, the technique ceases to be extravagant. Even today several African tribes using the most primitive methods achieve amazing results
Right: finger-ring cast in bronze, Dogon tribe from Mali in Africa, 16th century AD. (Galerie Maya, Paris)
Far right: two pendant masks cast in bronze, Benin, 17th century AD. (Coll. Mert Simpson, New York)

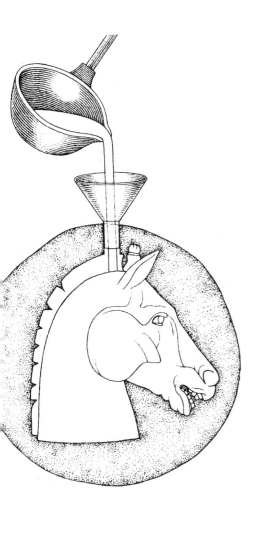

Casting was one of the very first crafts discovered by early metal-workers. At first open casting was used, then piece moulds and finally the Egyptians devised a method called cire perdue *(or lost wax)* which is still used today
Left: three simplified stages in the cire perdue *process. Firstly the model (we show a horse's head) is made in wax, then coated in plaster with the exception of one small hole. The mould is inverted and the wax melted out, leaving a cavity into which the metal is poured*

31

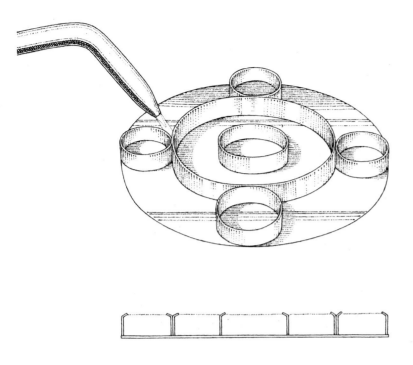

Inlay is one method of polychromatic decoration which was perfected by the Egyptians
Left: thin strips of metal are soldered to the surface and act as cells or cloisons *into which specially cut stones are fitted. The stones are then glued into position and the wall of the* cloisons *pushed over to protect the stone (as shown in the side view at left)*

The Egyptians used a wide variety of coloured stones and faience to achieve vivid polychromatic effects with inlay Below: pectoral ornament of Queen Mereret, from Dahshur c.1850 BC. The enlargement at right shows tiny gaps between the cut stone and the metal cloisons *which would not exist if the object had been enamelled. (Cairo Museum)*

With the discovery of gold, development of metalwork techniques became the chief area of concentration of ancient craftsmen. Coloured stones, pebbles and beads which had been the basis of self-adornment to their forefathers were, if not rejected, certainly forced into a subservient role by some of the early civilizations. The outstanding exception was in Ancient Egypt where the passion for colourful stones never lessened.

The art of the lapidary, as it has already been explained, is several thousand years older than that of the goldsmith. Pebbles polished and drilled have been found from the neolithic period. It was quite natural, therefore, that the two crafts should come together to produce jewellery of contrast and variety. And to this day most artist-craftsmen train as lapidaries as well as goldsmiths.

The first stones used by both the Sumerians and the Egyptians were lapis lazuli, cornelian, turquoise, agate, and jasper (mainly for the manufacture of seals). At first these stones were used in the traditional method – drilled and strung, but craftsmen were soon evolving new methods of incorporating them in their goldwork.

Inlay

One of the earliest and most popular methods used to incorporate stones was inlay, where they were set on the surface of a piece of work. The first thing required of the setting was that it should hold the stone firmly in position and the second that it should protect it from knocks and abrasion.

The Sumerians developed a setting known as *cloisonné* which has not been bettered to this day. Strips of thin gold sheets were cut, bent round until they formed a hoop of the shape and size required and soldered into position on the work, forming a cell to house the stone. A stone of approximately the right size would be selected, ground and polished until it fitted the cell exactly and then glued into position with a gum tinted the same colour as the stone. The gold walls would then be pushed against the stone, protecting it and making it more secure.

While this method was originated by the Sumerians, it was the Egyptians who were the real masters of inlay work. Some pieces found in the tomb of Tutankhamun contained no less than 5,000 different pieces of stone and faience in *cloisonné* setting.

The stones used for jewellery were readily available in the early days, but volume of production, particularly in Egypt, meant that demand started to exceed supply, and the craftsmen were forced to seek substitutes to simulate their favourite gemstones.

One method was to use transparent rock crystal backed by coloured cements. This was quite satisfactory when producing mock cornelian but it did not work as a substitute for their most precious stone, lapis lazuli, a deep blue opaque stone imported from Afghanistan. To simulate this they

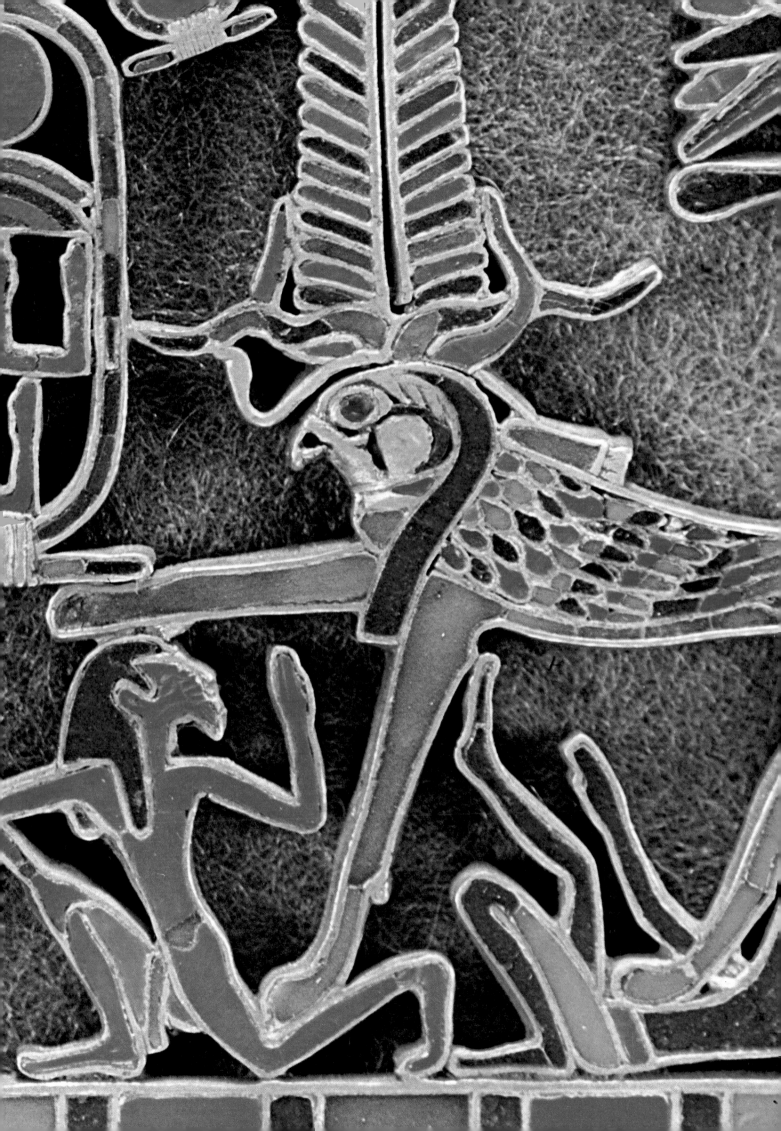

Above and opposite: the front and back of an early 17th century AD *miniature case (with details right and below) show the soft and hard edge effects of* champlevé *and painted enamels respectively. (Victoria & Albert Museum, London)*

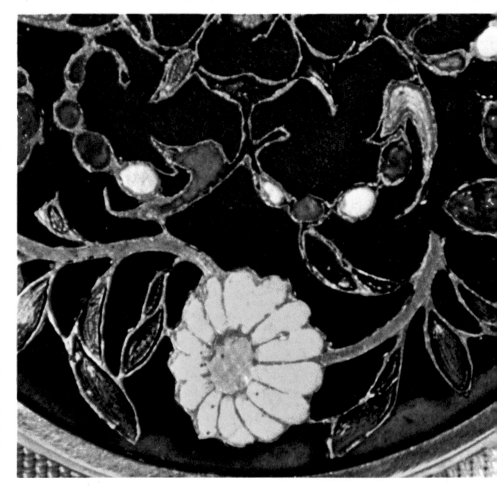

used faience, which was achieved by taking a small quantity of powdered quartz, mixing it with blue copper compounds and heating it in a blast furnace until it fused into a single lump. This could then be cut and polished for inlay work.

Another popular substitute, developed in the Egyptian Middle Kingdom, was frit – the earliest known form of glass. Frit was similar in composition to modern glass but with a slightly lower proportion of silica and lime. Much of the frit produced is opaque and would suggest that its *raison d'être* was as a gemstone substitute rather than an entity in itself. The results achieved were astonishingly convincing and many pieces of jewellery catalogued in museums as 'gold with lapis lazuli' or 'gold and turquoise' are in fact gold and glass.

It is arguable whether the Egyptians discovered the technique of enamelling. Some of the pieces discovered in the tombs have glass inlays which fit so perfectly that it would suggest that the glass was fired *in situ* and, since the melting point of frit was lower than that of gold, there would seem no reason why the enamelling techniques should not have been used.

Right: early 17th century AD pendant decorated with émail en résille sur verre, *an extremely difficult technique developed in the 17th century which involved enamelling on a glass base. (Victoria & Albert Museum, London)*

Enamelling

The earliest enamelling technique, known as *cloisonné* enamel, was identical to inlay but used molten glass rather than individually cut stones. Then the *champlevé* technique was developed, in which the design was cut into the surface of the metal and the recesses filled with molten glass.

Later, more sophisticated techniques were used, allowing continuous tone pictorial decoration, unbacked stained glass effects and polychromatic decoration in three dimensions or relief.

Another technique which is used by contemporary jewellers and owes its origins to antiquity is niello. This is a process not dissimilar to enamelling, using a combination of copper and silver sulphides. Heated together these make a black molten substance which can be placed in recesses in goldwork for outlining and highlighting. Niello was widely used for the decoration of dagger blades and spearheads by the Mycenaeans, but it was not until the 3rd century AD that there is any evidence that the technique was used in jewellery. After that the process seems to have died out entirely until the 11th century.

The Sumerian civilization
flourished in Mesopotamia
more than 5,000 years ago.
Evidence of their advanced
technology and love of self-
adornment was admirably
demonstrated by the treasure of
Ur found by British
archaeologist Sir Leonard
Woolley
Left: dummy head adorned
with circlets and necklace of
gold and gemstones found at
Ur, c.2500 BC. (British
Museum)

Jewels of the Ancient World

When discussing the history of jewellery, we are continually handicapped by the lack of specimens available. Without the discoveries of late 19th and 20th century archaeologists, such discussion could be no more than speculation. The intrinsic value of gold – and the changing fashions – have been the worst enemies of the jewellery historian; gold melts easily, cannot be identified, is conveniently transportable and an international currency.

Another problem is that gold cannot be dated by any of the methods so far devised and, during recent centuries, there has been a thriving industry in faking ancient artefacts, particularly during the 18th century when archaeology became a widely fashionable occupation for the dilettante. Even the archaeologists of the 19th century considered the profession more like a treasure hunt than the precise science it is today, and often showed little interest in dating the items they unearthed or studying the community which had produced them.

It is fortunate that neither they – nor the tomb robbers of previous centuries – were completely thorough with their investigations but left behind some tombs to be studied by responsible archaeologists such as Howard Carter, Sir Leonard Woolley and Sir Flinders Petrie. It is their work which forms the entire basis of our knowledge of the birth and development of jewellery.

In this section of the book we will look at the great ancient civilizations individually, but it is important to remember that they did not exist as watertight communities. By the 4th millennium BC it is obvious that nations were trading far afield. This is demonstrated by the existence of materials foreign to the area in which they were found. Egypt for instance had no natural supply of lapis lazuli – the nearest supply must have been in Afghanistan more than 1,000 miles away – while Mesopotamia had no natural gold supplies.

The other evidence of communication is the recurrence of design themes in different communities and the simultaneous development of metalwork techniques which go beyond the bounds of coincidence.

Most of the goldwork or jewellery available from these civilizations is tomb jewellery, some made for the living and buried with them but most of it made specifically for the adornment of the dead. This has led to the erroneous theory that some civilizations, particularly the Sumerians, created jewellery solely for this purpose. We can only hope that this tomb jewellery fully reflects the magnificence of the jewels of the living; if not, the ancient jewellers' art is lost forever.

Obviously the earliest civilizations evolved gradually rather than having a definite starting date. By the late 5th and early 4th millenia BC farming communities were starting to inhabit Mesopotamia, the Egyptians were developing their nation in the Nile Valley, Troy was being built, and communities were evolving in the Indus valley. The order in which they are discussed is, therefore, arbitrary but priority has been given to the Sumerians who produced the earliest (accurately dated) gold jewels.

Sumerian

The Sumerians inhabited Mesopotamia, which lay in the valleys between the rivers Tigris and Euphrates. Up to the 6th millenium BC Mesopotamia was under water, an extension of the Persian Gulf, but centuries of silt which came down from the Persian

37

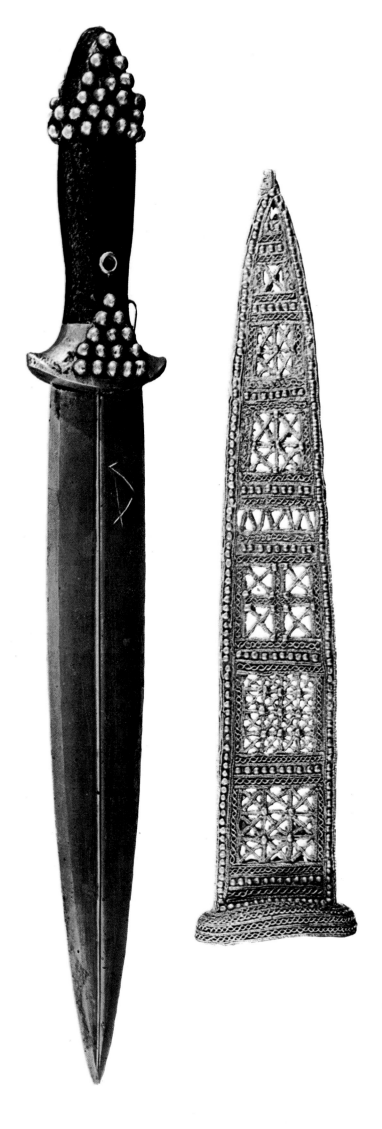

Right: elaborately decorated ceremonial dagger found in the 'Royal Tombs' at Ur. The sheath is of gold open filigree and the hilt of lapis lazuli studded with gold rivets, Sumerian, c.2500 BC. (Iraq Museum, Baghdad)

mountains built up into a natural sea wall. As the waters receded and fertile dry land was exposed, nomadic farmers from the Persian plateau, east of the Tigris, started to form small communities on the land. They discovered that it yielded better crops than they had ever before achieved but also faced them with two main obstacles. Firstly, only a small proportion of the land available was workable, the remainder being swamp land and, secondly, the rainfall was so low that drought became a major problem. The obvious answer was to drain the swampy areas and irrigate the entire valley – a task demanding vast physical resources.

So the first major communal project was put under way and the Sumerians became a civilization in the true sense of the word. Banks were built along both of the rivers to protect the plain from flooding and a complicated network of canals and dykes was constructed to allow water to be distributed how and when it was needed.

The system had been constructed before this enormous task was completed and so needed constant supervision if the canals were not to silt up and the dykes run into disrepair, so to avoid chaos some efficient form of

Right: dummy head carrying the head-dress of Queen Pu-Abi in gold, lapis lazuli and cornelian, together with gold hoop ear-rings and necklaces of gold, lapis lazuli and cornelian. Sumerian, c.2500 BC. (British Museum)

government had to be instituted.

Sumeria evolved as a series of city states each with its own ruler, unlike Egypt which at the same time was becoming a nation under one king. There was a shortage of materials for building – metals, stone and timber had to be imported from Asia Minor, Afghanistan and Oman.

The Sumerians had no currency but they became so efficient as farmers that they were soon producing a surplus and could trade by barter, which in turn led to the birth of specialized trades such as pottery, metalwork and weaving which had previously been part of the overall activity of each small family unit. The potter no longer had to sow to eat: he could swap his pots for food.

This tradition of specialist craftsmen explains why Sumerian technology advanced at a comparatively rapid pace. Bronze soon replaced copper, the potters' wheel was designed, schools were founded and writing was invented.

By 3500 BC the cities were being built along the banks of the river, cities such as Ur, Uruk, Lagash, Eridu and Nippur. During the 19th century archaeologists uncovered a number of

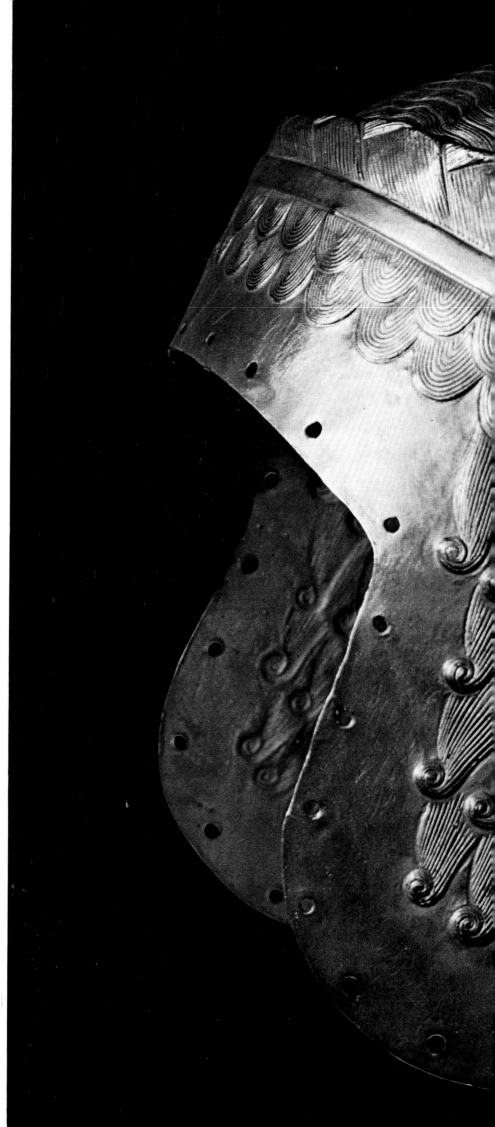

Right: perhaps the most spectacular piece of goldwork to have survived from the Ancient World – the helmet of Mesilim, King of Kish, unearthed at Ur. It demonstrates the extraordinary technical mastery of the Sumerians in the 3rd millennium BC, particularly in the techniques of repoussé and chasing. The gold is paper-thin and can be bent between finger and thumb so the helmet could only have been intended for funerary or ceremonial wear. The Sumerians employed most of the metalwork techniques that are available to this day. (Original in the Iraq Museum, Baghdad; electro-formed copy from which this photograph is taken, British Museum)

these communities, revealing some metalwork and pottery but it was not until 1922 when Sir Leonard Woolley, the famous archaeologist, travelled to Mesopotamia that the genius of the Sumerian metalworkers was realized. During the five years that he excavated the city of Ur, he unearthed jewellery and gold objects of incredible beauty and technical skill.

Ur, 12 miles west of the Euphrates, was one of the major city states of the Sumerian civilization. When Woolley first visited the site there was no more than a six-foot high mound to indicate where a city of thousands of inhabitants had stood some 5,000 years before.

During the years of slow methodical digging Woolley unearthed a mass of walls which revealed a sophisticated civilization with a complex of private houses, surrounding a huge parliament building which had once housed the temple of the moon-god Nanna. It was in the ground outside the temple walls that the cemetery was discovered, arranged not unlike a Christian graveyard. Several hundred graves were excavated (of what appeared mostly to be ordinary citizens). These were simple in construction, containing the bare essentials for the life hereafter –

Right: another example of the Sumerians' superb craftsmanship both as goldsmiths and lapidaries. The figure of a 'he-goat' (which stands 20 inches high) combines a number of different materials in the one object. The face and legs are of thin gold sheet, the fleece, shoulders, eyes and horns are of lapis lazuli and shell while the belly is electrum. Sumerian, c.2500 BC. (British Museum)

such as bowls and drinking vessels.

Some graves, however, were of an entirely different construction: long shafts lined with brick opened into large chambers which, judging by the work involved in making them, were for the kings, rulers, or distinguished citizens. They had presumably been violated at some time and gave no hint to their identity, until the grave was dug of Mesilim (King of Kish), one time ruler of the city. His skull rested in a magnificent gold repoussé helmet beaten from a single sheet of gold, so thin that it could be bent like paper. From his shoulder hung a gold ceremonial dagger with a hilt carved from a single piece of lapis lazuli studded with gold. The sheath, also of gold, had intricate patterns traced in filigree and granulation.

This was the first of many spectacular finds that were unearthed in the cemetery. The finest of these was the tomb of Queen Pu-Abi. It was apparently the custom in Sumeria for Royalty to be buried with their Court retinue – who were to serve in the after-life. A macabre sight must have greeted Woolley when he dug into the tomb. Sixty-three bodies in all were found in the outer chamber of the tomb,

or death pit as it became known. Soldiers, ladies-in-waiting and other Court attendants dressed in their finery lay in neat rows; the men with magnificent gold ceremonial weapons and the women with gold necklaces, ear-rings and head-dresses made from gold beech leaves.

In a small inner chamber the body of the Queen herself was found, dressed in a robe of gold, lapis lazuli, cornelians and agate. Beside her was a magnificent head-dress, a grander version of those worn by her attendants, made up from rows of leaves and discs made of wafer-thin gold repoussé interspersed with tubes of lapis. Her diadem was surmounted by three open flowers, she wore enormous hollow ear-rings, and round her neck was a necklace of gold, lapis and cornelian beads. Also found beside her were other objects of breathtaking beauty: talismans of gold and lapis in the shape of fish and animals, numerous rings, drinking vessels and toilet containers.

Other graves in the cemetery revealed a vast range of gold artefacts: a goat made from gold, electrum and lapis being typical of several gold talismanic objects discovered. Standing on its hind legs resting against a

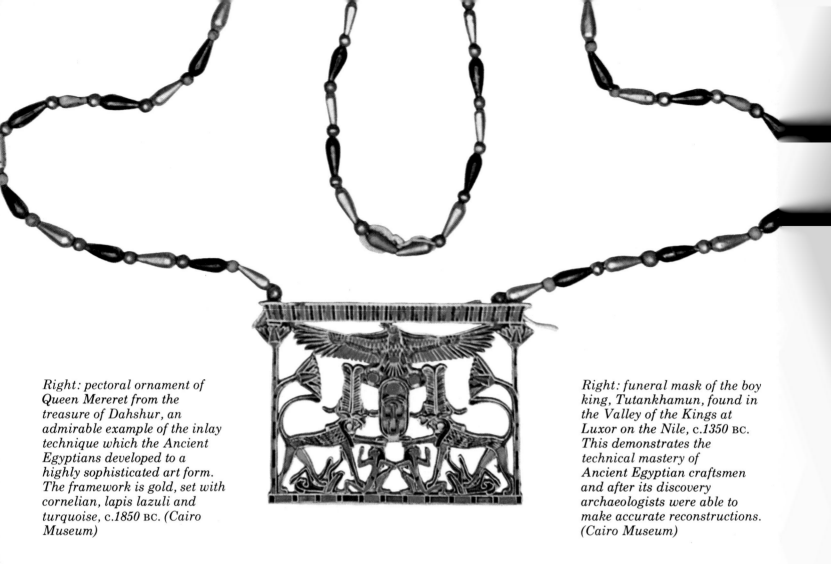

Right: pectoral ornament of Queen Mereret from the treasure of Dahshur, an admirable example of the inlay technique which the Ancient Egyptians developed to a highly sophisticated art form. The framework is gold, set with cornelian, lapis lazuli and turquoise, c.1850 BC. (Cairo Museum)

Right: funeral mask of the boy king, Tutankhamun, found in the Valley of the Kings at Luxor on the Nile, c.1350 BC. This demonstrates the technical mastery of Ancient Egyptian craftsmen and after its discovery archaeologists were able to make accurate reconstructions. (Cairo Museum)

tree, the goat measures almost 20 inches high. The face and legs are made from gold foil, with the fleece, shoulders, eyes and horns of lapis lazuli, and the belly of electrum. This one object demonstrates the Sumerians' extraordinary level of technical achievement in a wide variety of media and their ability to combine these skills in a single piece.

While the sheer number of jewels found in Egypt is far more impressive than that attributed to the Sumerians, this does not mean that they only produced a small amount. It is important to remember that of the hundreds of rulers who must have lived in Ur, only one tomb – and even that not of a king – was found intact. We can only guess at the enormous quantity of jewellery produced which has been lost forever.

It is the range of objects found at Ur which provides an invaluable contribution to our knowledge of the origins of jewels. These examples fulfilled every function of self-adornment known today. Men wore bracelets on their wrists and upper arms, also necklaces, pendants, ear-rings and pectorals. Women wore bracelets, diadems, ear-rings, necklaces and rings.

Egyptian

In 1922, as Sir Leonard Woolley was about to take his first spadeful of earth from Ur, Howard Carter was reaping the rewards of five years of painstaking investigation in the Nile Valley. He peered through a small hole and believed he saw what every archaeologist at that time must have prayed for – an unviolated royal tomb, the tomb of Tutankhamun, boy king of the New Kingdom (Dynasty XVIII) of Egypt. But because of a legal dispute with the Egyptian Government, Carter had to wait two more years before he was allowed to enter the tomb.

When examined in detail the tomb was found to be partially violated. The original robbers had obviously been disturbed, and had fled, the tomb being then resealed. Much of the jewellery the young king would have worn in his lifetime was missing and the majority of the wearable items remaining were funerary talismans. This find, however, still represents one of the greatest archaeological discoveries of all time and forms the backbone of all research into the origins and development of Egyptian jewellery.

The robbery of royal graves would

appear to have been a pursuit of unceasing popularity for more than 4,000 years and it is nothing short of a miracle that there is a single example of Ancient Egyptian jewellery left intact. When we look at the treasures of Tutankhamun and consider that he was only 18 years old when he died, we can but guess at the treasures which must have been buried with the great Pharaohs such as Ramesses II and Tuthmosis III. Ancient tomb robbers were playing for big stakes.

Robberies continued into the 20th century but by that time the jewels had a greater value intact than the the sum total of their constituents, so that many of the pieces survive, having been smuggled out and sold to private collectors and galleries throughout the world.

Other pieces of Ancient Egyptian jewellery found by scientific exploration are few and far between but add invaluable evidence, particularly to the Middle Kingdom period. In 1914 Sir Flinders Petrie and his assistant Guy Brunton were investigating the violated tomb of Sesostris II at Lahun. In the chamber where his daughter Sit-Hathor-Yunet had been buried, there was an alcove which robbers in

Three Egyptian finger-rings which show the development of the signet ring
Top: engraved seal strung on a thin piece of gold wire
Centre: the wire is replaced by a stouter rod
Bottom: the ring is cast as a single piece and becomes indistinguishable from a signet ring of today. (Royal Scottish Museum, Edinburgh)

Right: wig-ornaments and crown of Princess Sit-Hathor-Yunet. The circlet is gold inlaid with lapis lazuli and green faience and the wig-ornaments are hollow gold tubes, c.1850 BC. (Cairo Museum)
Far right: rebus pectoral of Tutankhamun with amuletic symbols – the scarab and the Wedjet eye of the sky-god Horus. In gold, silver, chalcedony, cornelian, calcite, lapis lazuli, turquoise and coloured glass, c.1350 BC. (Cairo Museum)
Traditional forms and designs survived throughout Dynastic Egypt and the Ptolemaic period, spanning 3,000 years
Below right: this falcon ornament comes from the late Ptolemaic period, Egyptian c.100 BC. The empty cloisons would once have been filled with coloured stones or faience. (British Museum)
Below, far right: gold and lapis lazuli anklet of Psusennes I from Tanis, with a winged scarab holding a sun disc, c.1050 BC, (Cairo Museum)

their haste had overlooked as it had silted up with mud. Days of painstaking excavation revealed that the alcove contained the princess's jewellery casket, wig box and toilet case. The jewellery casket contained a large number of small pieces, necklaces of faience beads and gold, anklets, bracelets, girdles of gold cowrie shells and pectoral ornaments. In the wig box were a magnificent gold and lapis crown and a dressed wig. Many of the jewels were in fragments after thousands of years' attack from the damp but Petrie and Brunton excavated the alcove, meticulously noting the position in which each piece had been found so as to allow museum experts to reassemble them accurately. This work was not only invaluable for the Lahun hoard in 1914 but also provided a guide to the original appearance of the treasure excavated by J. de Morgan twenty years previously from the tombs of Sesostris III and Ammenemes II.

Remaining examples on which our knowledge of Egyptian jewellery is based are, for the most part, odd items overlooked by pillagers, or small buried hoards in the desert stumbled on by accident. This may sound rather depressing when introducing what is

universally considered to be one of our greatest cultural heritages from the Ancient World, but it is important to realize how tiny a fragment of the Egyptian jewellers' art remains. None the less, it is more than sufficient to establish that they were superb goldsmiths and lapidaries during the 3,000 years of the Pharaohs.

All the metalwork techniques used by the Sumerians were available to them and many of these were developed to a high level of sophistication. It is for their use of colour, however, that the Egyptians must be remembered. Their inlay work of stones, faience and glass is quite dazzling, particularly in the New Kingdom where the examples look like stained glass windows, shimmering with vibrant colours.

The materials employed by the Egyptians hardly varied throughout the Dynastic period. Gold, which reflected the power of the sun, was in plentiful supply within Egypt's borders but, at the height of their jewellery production, they were prospecting further afield. Some Egyptologists maintain that their search took them down the east coast of Africa as far as the mouth of the Zambezi.

The traditional stones were blood-

red cornelian, deep-blue lapis lazuli with flecks of gold, and blue-green turquoise. Both cornelian and turquoise were found in the eastern desert but the nearest supply of lapis lazuli came from Afghanistan, and it was probably the scarcity of this material that led to the development of imitations in faience and glass. Other stones used spasmodically during Dynastic times were jasper, chalcedony (mainly for seals), amethyst and amber.

To understand Egyptian jewellery and realize the significance of its highly formalized design, it is important to know the uses to which it was put. Here we are extremely fortunate. What information cannot be derived from individual pieces of jewellery, is supplemented by tomb paintings and hieroglyphics which help ensure accurate reconstruction of damaged pieces and provide an analysis of their meaning and purpose.

Firstly, jewels were produced for the personal adornment of the living of both sexes. These served a dual purpose: to enhance their appearance and to act as talismans. This explains the recurring symbols: snakes, scorpions and other vicious animals which ward off evil spirits; scarabs, falcons and

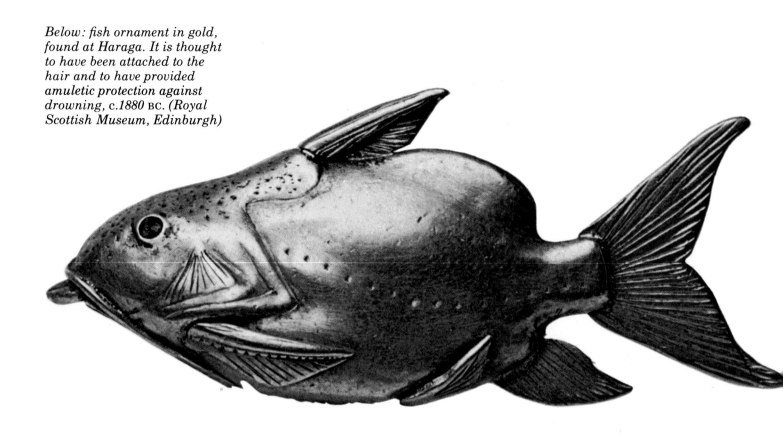

Below: fish ornament in gold, found at Haraga. It is thought to have been attached to the hair and to have provided amuletic protection against drowning, c.1880 BC. (Royal Scottish Museum, Edinburgh)

cowrie shells, all of which offered the wearer protection against various types of adversity. Other recurring themes are geometric symbols each with a specific talismanic function: the *Wedjet* eye for protection against the evil eye; the *Djed*, *Sa*, *Ankh*, and *Tyet* signs which offered the wearer health, prosperity, long life and other personal benefits. Talismanic jewellery was also produced specifically for the dead, offering protection in the after-life. In the case of the Pharaohs, judging by the quantity found in Tutankhamun's tomb, a proportion of this must have been prepared from the date of accession, thus giving constant employment to the Court jewellers.

Another source of work was producing jewellery for orders and decorations. The Pharaohs had a series of 'honours' bestowed on their subjects for gallantry and service to the State. These took the form of necklaces of gold discs or gold flies.

In life, the nobility of Egypt wore every category of jewellery known to us today. Circlets and diadems were made in gold with inlays. Some, like the crown of Princess Sit-Hathor-Yunet, had a geometric design, together with a serpent talisman. The crown of

Princess Khnumet could almost be a contemporary coronet while the floral wreath which was found in the same tomb is completely different. This last reflects, in permanent form, the tradition of plaiting fresh flowers in the hair on ceremonial occasions. Crowns and diadems were invariably worn over heavy wigs which were themselves decorated either with patterns of gold tubing, like that of Princess Sit-Hathor-Yunet, or with a complete chain mail head-cover made from inlaid gold rosettes (as the one found in the tomb of Tuthmosis III).

Ear-rings were virtually unknown until the beginning of the New Kingdom and were probably an innovation from Asia where they had been popular for more than 2,000 years. When they did arrive, however, they became very fashionable; women had their ears pierced with holes of a diameter which almost amounted to mutilation and wore enormous pendant ear-rings made from gold and inlay. At the same time ear-studs became fashionable. These were simple discs of inlaid metal or carved faience not unlike a modern collar stud, to be pressed through a pierced ear and cover the entire lobe.

Collars were popular throughout

Ancient Egypt. The most common of these, known as a 'broad collar', consisted of parallel rows of beads strung vertically to form a semicircle with gold terminals and a cord which tied behind the neck. A variation, the 'falcon collar', had the plain gold terminals replaced with falcon amulets of inlaid gold, a fine example of this being found in the treasure from Dahshur. Another type of collar was made from solid, chased gold sheet in the form of falcons and vultures. This would have been extremely uncomfortable to wear and was probably only for funerary purposes.

Chokers were fashionable in the Middle and Old Kingdoms and were almost identical to bead chokers worn today: a number of parallel strings of stone or faience beads tied at the back of the neck. But perhaps the most exciting form of neck ornament from Ancient Egypt is the pectoral – providing superb examples of *cloisonné* work, with countless inlaid pieces of stone and faience. The pectorals (chest ornaments) from Tutankhamun's tomb not only display the brilliance of the craftsmanship, but also contain almost every talismanic symbol found in Egyptian mythology.

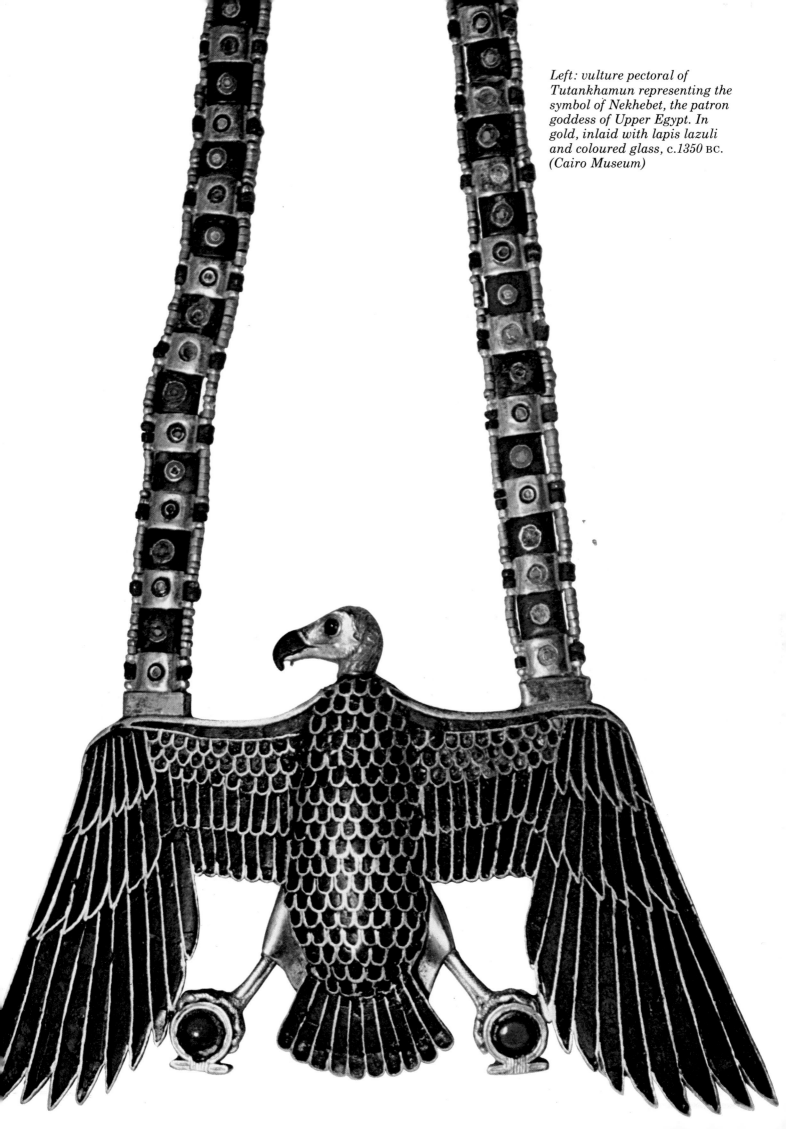

Left: vulture pectoral of Tutankhamun representing the symbol of Nekhebet, the patron goddess of Upper Egypt. In gold, inlaid with lapis lazuli and coloured glass, c.1350 BC. (Cairo Museum)

Right: floral circlet of Princess Khnumet, from Dahshur. The design in gold, cornelian, lapis lazuli and turquoise reflects the fashion in Ancient Egypt for wearing spring flowers woven in the hair on ceremonial occasions, c.1850. BC. (Cairo Museum)
Far right: gold vulture collar of King Smenkh-ka-re. This is believed to have been made purely for funerary purposes. Cut from a thin sheet of gold and chased with great skill, 2nd millennium BC. (Cairo Museum)

Bracelets appear to have been virtually obligatory. Bangles made of plain gold and gold inlay have been found from the Old Kingdom onwards, and bead bracelets constructed in the same way as the chokers. The New Kingdom, however, saw the introduction of immensely elaborate hinged bracelets for the wrist and upper arms, again decorated with talismanic symbols. Anklets follow the same pattern as bracelets and, in fact, there is often some difficulty differentiating between them.

The development of finger-rings is linked with the popularity of seals. From the end of the Old Kingdom, seals carved in stone were used as a method of identification; later the backs were carved as scarabs. These were drilled and worn on a cord round the neck, but in the Middle Kingdom it became fashionable to tie the scarab on one finger with a thread. The thread was replaced by gold wire, the wire by rod – and the world's first signet ring had been made. By the New Kingdom, shanks were being cast and the seal held by a rivet which allowed it to swivel and expose either the scarab or the signature. Later still, solid signet rings were produced from gold or carved stone.

Right: goldsmiths and joiners. This copy of a tomb painting (by Nina de Garis Davies) from the tomb of Nebamun and Ipuky, c.1380 BC, and other paintings provide us with much of our knowledge of the techniques employed by craftsmen of the Ancient World. (British Museum)

50

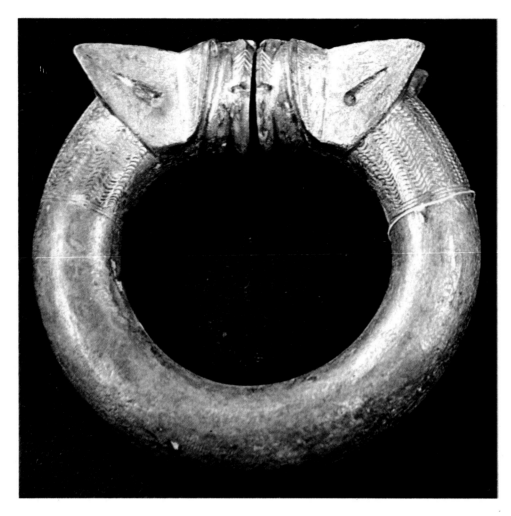

The X-Group

One of the most remarkable and dramatic archaeological discoveries made since the turn of the last century was that of the 'X-Group'. Their tombs, scattered throughout the Nubian Nile, are the only evidence of the southern neighbours of Dynastic Egypt. These finds from 4th/5th century AD should not be covered at this point, if the chronological treatment is to be strictly adhered to, but the work of the X-Group was so strongly influenced by the older civilizations under discussion in this section that their jewellery can be better appreciated at this point.

Who the X-Group were, or where they came from is uncertain. In fact the only evidence that a civilization existed in this part of the world during the first six centuries AD is derived solely from burial mounds. Once again burial rites compensate for the absence of the written word and these particular ones were perhaps the most savage and barbaric ever encountered. Ritual sacrifice was practised on a scale which would make the Sumerians appear humane.

The two biggest groups of mounds were discovered in the 1930s at Ballana

and Qostol. As usual, the majority of the tombs had been plundered and any objects of commercial value, including jewellery, removed. The very structure of the X-Group mounds, however, made unofficial excavation time-taking and hazardous. They were not the magnificent stone-built structures of the Egyptians, but mud brick and sand chambers, many of them eroded by centuries of flood water.

The first tombs excavated had already been plundered but, as always, there remained a few items overlooked or rejected by robbers. Axe-heads, lamps and other items of the highest workmanship prepared the archaeologists for the great treasures which were to come. In one of the early graves the first evidence was found of the X-Group's terrible death rituals – a horse, with its skull cleaved open, and beside it an axe which precisely matched the wound. This animal, which came to so sudden and brutal a death, had obviously been the object of considerable pride during its lifetime for it was richly adorned with decorated headstall, bit and silver discs. The ferocious style of these ornaments is reminiscent of those other great horsemen, the Scythians.

Human life was treated with no more respect. Alongside the horses were the corpses of several grooms, strangled as part of the ritual. More than 200 tombs were excavated in all, each one showing the same pattern. Most had been thoroughly ransacked, but when Tomb 14 at Qostol was dug the undisturbed chamber was found of a young girl, her throat slit. Together with her most precious possessions – her jewellery – there were two wooden flasks containing make-up. Her silver earrings, set with beryl and cornelian, four silver finger-rings and several necklaces of silver, coral and cornelian, were buried with her. The symbolistic traditions of Ancient Egypt were obvious in the style of decoration, as they had been on other less precious items found earlier. The design of the pieces was heavy and barbaric but the workmanship excellent.

Later discoveries provided even more sophisticated jewels, all of silver which, sadly, is less resistant to attack from the elements than gold. It was not, however, at Qostol but at Ballana that the most remarkable jewels were discovered. Of the 120 tombs excavated only five had escaped plunder. In these several silver, gem-set crowns were

Right: two huge silver bracelets from the X-Group treasure constructed like present day finger-rings. In the centre of each is a cabochon onyx surrounded by garnets and amethysts. (Cairo Museum)

Below: silver crown thought to have belonged to a Nubian queen of the X-Group. Many of the pieces found in the tombs at Ballana and Qostol were inscribed with the same amuletic signs as found on the jewellery of Ancient Egypt. (Cairo Museum)

discovered. While strongly Byzantine in overall feeling these pieces continued to incorporate Egyptian symbols, including the Wedjet eye, the cobra and the sun god Ra.

The most complete and remarkable personal collection was that of a Nubian queen buried in Tomb 47. On her head was a silver circlet, embossed with busts of the goddess Isis and set with cabochon cornelians, and rising above this three plumes of Isis similarly decorated. In addition to this circlet there were: 20 silver bracelets, a silver torque necklace, 14 other silver necklaces set with gem-stones, and 9 pairs of ear-rings. On her fingers she wore 11 rings; she also sported anklets of silver and coral, and toe rings decorated with flies. The most massive and magnificent items in the royal regalia were two huge bracelets formed like rings with a shank and bezel. The central stone in each was a large onyx surrounded with garnets and amethysts set in silver; the shanks were also decorated with cabochon gemstones.

Other finds in the Nubian desert are far too numerous to mention but together they amount to one of the most puzzling and exciting treasures ever unearthed.

German archaeologist Heinrich Schliemann was an incurable romantic. After years of searching for Troy, when he did unearth a massive treasure he instantly assumed it to be that of King Priam but scholars have since proved him inaccurate by almost 1,000 years. The treasure, more than 8,000 pieces, which had been taken to Germany was lost at the end of World War II Left: Schliemann's young wife, Sophia, wearing a head-dress which he attributed to Helen of Troy. It was extraordinarily intricate and made up from more than 16,000 component parts

Right: large gold pendant
ear-ring, one of the few pieces
from Troy to have survived.
(National Archaeological
Museum, Athens)

The Aegean

Our knowledge of a great Bronze Age civilization in the Aegean is due to the obsession of one man – Heinrich Schliemann. As a child in Germany he was fascinated by the epic poems of Homer, particularly the *Iliad*. He grew up convinced that these were not just adventure stories, as was the popular theory, but accurate reports of events in Ancient Greece.

Schliemann was an astute businessman. Having started as an office boy, he educated himself and by the time he was nearing fifty, in 1871, he had amassed a huge fortune and was able at last to put his theories to the test. There were various conjectures about the location of Troy in so far as experts would admit to its existence at all, but Schliemann had his own ideas. He followed Homer's description to the letter and decided that a mound at Hissarlik, near the Dardanelles in northern Turkey, concealed the Troy of King Priam. His obstinate faith in the Homeric tales was vindicated: he found not one city but several, built one on top of the other, and in the three years he worked there he removed more than 2,500,000 cubic feet of soil which yielded pottery,

weapons and various types of tools.

On 15 June 1873, the day before Schliemann was due to cease his operations in Troy, he noticed a piece of metal at the base of a wall which was being dug. He wisely dismissed his Turkish labourers and, together with his young Greek wife Sophia, he scraped away the soil with his hands. The treasures revealed staggered even Schliemann. There were more than 8,000 gold finger-rings, 60 gold earrings, six gold bracelets, buttons and various vessels of gold and silver, but the prize of the collection proved to be two diadems of incredibly intricate design and workmanship. The larger one was made from more than 16,000 individual pieces of gold; a long, fine gold chain was designed to encircle the wearer's head and from this numerous short chains hung over the brow in a fringe, longer chains being attached to the side of the head-dress which in turn hung over the shoulders.

As there were signs of burning on the wall Schliemann, who had no method of dating his finds, quite naturally assumed this was the treasure of King Priam hidden when Troy was under siege, and that the diadem had belonged to the beautiful Helen. It is still called

The Minoan civilization
flourished in Crete throughout
the 3rd and 2nd millennia BC,
when it became absorbed by the
Mycenaean civilization of
mainland Greece
Below: gold daisy pin of the
Early Minoan period, 2500–
2000 BC. (Metropolitan Museum
Museum of Art, New York)

Right: Middle Minoan gold
pendant depicting two hornets
feeding at a honeycomb,
in repoussé and coarse
granulation, c.1600 BC.
(Heraklion Museum, Crete)
Below: gold repoussé pendant
from the Middle Minoan period
depicting a wild goat, c.1600
BC. (British Museum)

Priam's treasure but further investigation has proved that Schliemann's finds originated about 1,000 years before Troy is said to have fallen to the Greeks.

Ecstatic with his success at Troy, Schliemann set out to find another great capital mentioned by Homer – Mycenae – the Golden City of King Agamemnon. The experts scoffed when he started digging in southern Greece in ruins which were the legendary remains of Mycenae, but again his obsessional faith paid off. He found a series of shaft graves, carved out of the rock beneath the city, which contained bodies richly adorned with gold and precious stones. The men wore golden burial masks and breastplates; the women dresses decorated with gold discs; while the bodies of several small children were completely encased in gold foil. There were diadems beaten out of sheet gold with repoussé designs both floral and geometric and pins with animal motifs. Relief beads stamped from gold sheet were found in numbers almost amounting to mass production.

Again Schliemann's imagination ran riot; one figure with a gold mask was, he proclaimed confidently, Agamemnon who was murdered by his treacherous

wife after his return from Troy. As before, he was several hundred years out but his finds supplied later – and more methodical – archaeologists with a clue to the development of civilization in the Aegean.

The bull figured among the designs found in Mycenaean metalwork – a sign of contact with Crete, the scene of a much older culture which flourished from 3000 BC. Schliemann had, in fact, realized this and shortly before his death negotiated for a plot of land in Crete which he firmly believed to be the site of Knossos, palace of the legendary King Minos. The owner of the land tried to cheat the German archaeologist and the deal fell through, but once again his instinct was proved sound, although he did not live to see the evidence. It was left to another great British archaeologist, Sir Arthur Evans, to excavate the site nine years later. Evans, unlike Schliemann, was an academic born and bred but was none the less a romantic. He named the civilization he found in Crete 'Minoan', after King Minos, which makes about as much sense as calling the entire history of Germany since the birth of Christ 'Hitlerian'.

Crete was inhabited more than

5,000 years BC but it was not until 2800 BC that civilization reached the island from Mesopotamia (via Syria).

Minoan

The Minoan civilization is split into three periods, Early Minoan (c.2500–2000), Middle Minoan (c.2000–1600) and Late Minoan (c.1600–1100). Throughout these three periods, the Minoans were gradually colonizing and developing a civilization on the mainland of Greece, a civilization which Schliemann had named Mycenaean. The earliest examples of goldwork and jewellery were found in the eastern part of Crete, notably Mochlos. The workmanship was simple and rather crude compared with that found in the royal tombs at Ur but none the less the Sumerian influence is unmistakable.

Diadems were fashioned from thin gold sheets, while others had simple designs beaten out in dot repoussé. The nature of these designs, eyes, animals and geometric patterns, suggests that jewellery might already have assumed a talismanic function on the island.

Many hair-pins were found with heads like daisies, pendants with gold repoussé leaves, and bracelets of gold

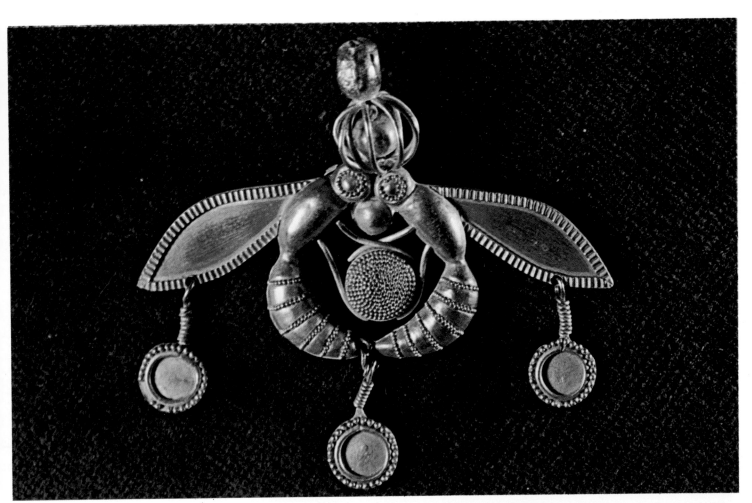

wire or gold foil over another material. This technique of beating very thin gold foil round other materials, particularly in the manufacture of beads, illustrates the rarity of gold in Crete, which has no natural resources. Cornelian, amethyst and faience were also used to eke out supplies.

Finger-rings and ear-rings were unknown in this period, or at least none have been recovered.

By 2000 BC the centre of Minoan civilization had shifted from the east of Crete to the centre and south where were the great palaces such as Knossos, Phaistos and Mallia. Crete is an island prone to earthquakes and all the great palaces were destroyed in about 1700 BC and rebuilt in an even grander style; consequently very little jewellery from the early Middle Minoan period survived, but the pieces found from later in the period show enormous strides forward both in workmanship and design.

Filigree and granulation appear for the first time, new materials are introduced including lapis lazuli, and a variety of stones and faience are found in *cloisonné* settings. Egyptian influence in design is strong both figuratively and geometrically.

Fashions changed between jewellery

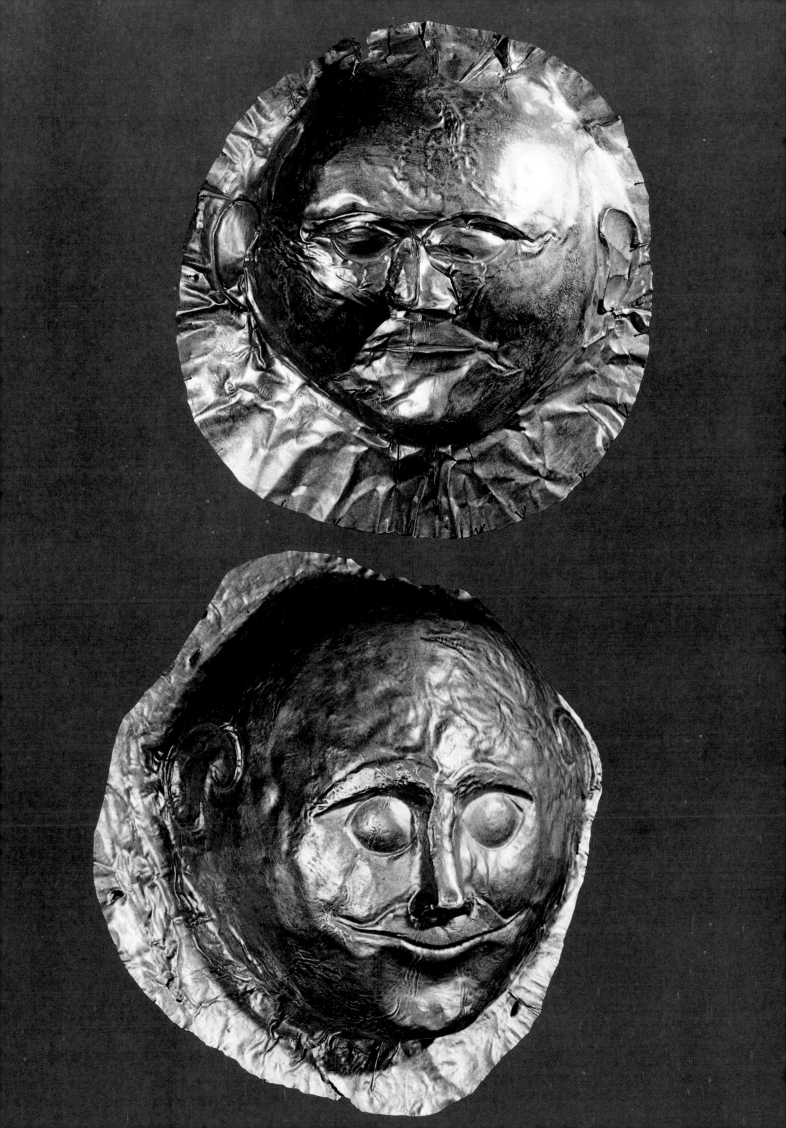

discovered from the early period at Mochlos and that made after 1700 BC. Diadems lost their popularity while hair-pins became more elaborate with a shepherd's crook design supplementing the traditional floral pattern. Earrings make their first appearance – simple hollow hoops of gold for pierced ears, not unlike those found by Sir Leonard Woolley in Mesopotamia.

Beads were being stamped from gold sheet in large numbers for use in bracelets, necklaces, pendants and ear-rings. Many of these were decorated with geometric designs of dot repoussé, filigree and granulation. Pendants continued to be fashionable with the traditional leaf designs together with heart shapes and stylized animals. They were generally larger and two examples could be described as pectorals: one shows a pair of hornets feeding at a honeycomb, in repoussé, filigree and granulation; the other is of a man holding two birds, showing a particularly strong Egyptian influence.

Finger-rings also became popular at this time. Again these were not unlike the Egyptian, with the scarab making a brief appearance. Rings fulfilled the same triple function; decorative, talismanic and signatory. Some bezels were

round but for the most part they were oval, with designs chased from gold sheet or inlaid. Seal-cutting had been a traditional Minoan craft and, like the Egyptian style, these seals were generally worn round the neck during the Early period but with the Middle period they were incorporated into ring-making. Initially soft materials such as steatite, which could be cut with a copper chisel, were used, but during the Middle period Cretan craftsmen were cutting hard stones such as rock crystal, cornelian and agate with incredible skill, depicting animals, magical symbols and hieroglyphics.

Mycenaean

Crete suffered more earthquakes at the beginning of the Late period but the natural resilience of the islanders soon led them to become more prosperous than ever before. Their influence over the inhabitants of mainland Greece was increasingly pronounced until 1400 BC when the position was reversed: the Mycenaeans conquered Knossos and assumed overall power of the Aegean Empire.

The craftsmanship, however, in both civilizations during this period must be considered Minoan. Whether jewellery was exported to the mainland from Crete, produced by Minoan craftsmen living in Mycenae or produced by the Greeks under instruction from Minoan masters, will never be known but work from the two civilizations during this period is virtually indistinguishable. Some of the finest examples of Minoan art of this period are therefore those found by Schliemann in the shaft graves at Mycenae. The story comes full circle.

Technically the jewels mark a logical progression from the Middle period with granulation and filigree becoming increasingly intricate and the introduction of *cloisonné* enamelling. Diadems, which were becoming unfashionable, disappeared altogether and by 1400 BC the use of hair-pins appears also to have been abandoned.

There were two areas of significant development: beads and seal-cutting. Beads of carved stone, faience and gold were being produced in large numbers. Because of the scarcity of gold, relief beads were made in two sections and filled with sand to give them bulk and strength. Dozens of identical designs were stamped out for use as necklaces and pendants. Initially these were comparatively simple but later they were decorated with filigree granulation and enamelling. The motifs were generally plant or marine life including cockles, lilies, rosettes, beetles, papyrus, palm leaves etc. Non-figurative beads constructed from wire in geometric spirals were also found.

The art of seal-cutting reached unprecedented heights; single figures were replaced with complex human situations involving several figures, religious ceremonies, animals fighting or mating and Minoan bull-baiting. One unusual thing about the seal-rings produced was that (in some cases) the shanks were so small that they could not possibly be worn, even by a child. This would suggest that the practice of wearing them on a cord round the neck had come back into fashion.

Talismanic pectoral ornaments also enjoyed an increasing popularity, with remarkably realistic animals depicted in repoussé and granulation with the traditional flat gold discs suspended below. The bull was once again the favourite animal but goats, lions, ducks and toads were also produced.

Chains were used as neck ornaments, fine ones being found in the shaft graves. Rings became increasingly popular and sophisticated. They were

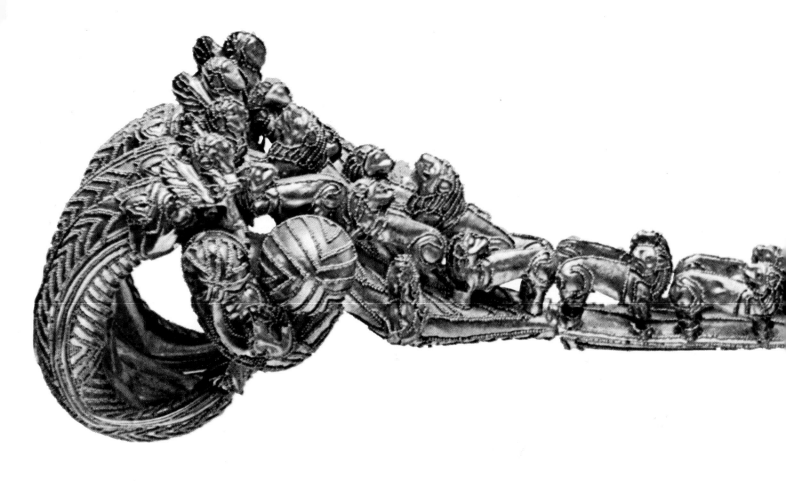

still being produced in gold, or in gold set with carved gemstones, but a new arrival was the use of *cloisonné*-set stones and enamelling. Two particularly fine examples were found by Schlieman in 'Agamemnon's' tomb in Mycenae.

With the fall of Knossos the Aegean Empire came into the hands of the Mycenaeans and spread both east and west. The Egyptian influence became increasingly strong but the type of jewellery remained virtually unaltered until about 1100 BC, when the entire Empire was destroyed, and impoverished, by the Dorians (the new Greek invaders) and so produced little or no jewellery.

The return of civilization and the revival of the crafts in Greece is dealt with in the following section.

Etruscan

At the beginning of the 7th century BC a new nation of jewellers and goldsmiths emerged in northern Italy. The Etruscan civilization lay in an area between the rivers Arno and Tiber, known as Etruria, and in the 400 years that it flourished produced jewellery of unparalleled beauty. Where the Etruscans came from is open to question, but most leading anthropologists consider that they were migrants from Asia Minor who became minority rulers of the Villanovan natives, a more backward civilization already established in the area.

The Etruscans used the only non-Indo-European language ever found in Italy and their writings, with the exception of a few words, have never been satisfactorily deciphered. Our knowledge of the culture, therefore, depends on observation of the artefacts uncovered by archaeologists and the writings about them of other nations through the years.

Both the Greeks and Romans were unanimous in their opinion: one of condescending jealousy; Etruscans, they claimed, were not only decadent pirates but also too keen on luxury.

Right: Etruscan ear-ring, decorated with an enormous plaque, in gold with repoussé and granulation. 7th century BC. (British Museum)

The Etruscans were the finest craftsmen of all ancient civilizations Above: serpentine fibula in gold with granulation is decorated with a parade of animals. It is hollow despite its size (over 7 inches long) and weighs little more than an ounce, 7th century BC. (British Museum)

They had to admit, however, that the Etruscans were great musicians and athletes and above all great *craftsmen*.

The earliest evidence of the civilization was found in a series of great tombs constructed in the middle of the 7th century BC. The very design of these tombs – a great earth mound covering a stone drum and inside a chamber entered by a long corridor – is another reason to believe that the nation originated in Asia Minor. Inside the tombs was found a great mixture of treasures in ivory, bronze and faience, from different civilizations in the Aegean and Asia Minor. These treasures might in themselves justify the claim that the Etruscans were pirates, or perhaps they were just traded for copper and iron which were abundant in the area. With these foreign objects, the first Etruscan jewellery was discovered. The workmanship of these early pieces is quite amazing, fine repoussé, filigree work and granulation executed with a skill and precision that has never been equalled to this day.

It is doubtful whether the Etruscans ever made diadems in the 7th century. The examples which have been found are so similar to those found in Mycenae

that they must be considered as imports. Hair-adornment at this stage took the form of hair-spirals made in decorated gold wire. Ear-rings were fashionable in the later part of the century; hoop ear-rings were common, a design which could have been borrowed from several different civilizations where they were already traditional. The two shapes which were peculiarly Etruscan were the horn-shaped ear-ring and the satchel-shaped *baule*, both being elaborately decorated with granulation.

Bracelets were produced from single sheets of gold with intricate figurative and geometric designs depicted in repoussé and/or granulation. Necklaces from this period are rare, but the few that were found consist of a chain or chains strung with beads and pendants. The design of the pendants varies considerably but the overall design is virtually standard.

One form at which the Etruscans excelled was the fibula. This started out as a simple safety-pin for fastening a cloak and was used by the old Villanovan civilization. The Etruscans saw it as a perfect example for demonstrating their considerable technical and decorative skills.

At first these fibulae were decorated with patterns of granulation along the sides and terminals but later they were encrusted with three-dimensional figures of lions, horses, sphinxes – themselves decorated with finest granulation. The workmanship in these early fibulae is quite breathtaking, incorporating all available techniques.

During the 6th century BC the Greek influence on Etruscan jewellery became increasingly strong. This affected the design, workmanship and the type of objects produced. Granulation was to some extent replaced by filigree which was quicker and easier. The art of inlay was introduced and employed with considerable effect.

Despite tremendous Greek influence, however, the Etruscans never lost their sense of identity and the jewellery produced during this period could not be confused with contemporary Greek examples.

The most significant area of development in the 6th and 5th centuries was the necklace, which became increasingly complicated as gold chains encircled the neck, from which hung dozens of beads. Three or four different kinds of beads, symmetrically arranged, were combined in the same necklace.

63

Human heads, satyrs, lions' heads, acorns and other representational themes were widely used, presumably with a talismanic as well as a decorative function.

Finger-rings made their first appearance. Again these were of an early Greek design – gold shanks with an oval bezel engraved with figurative designs. Bracelets in the form of wide bands executed in repoussé or open filigree continued their popularity. One new style, however, was the spiral of open filigree, almost serpentine in appearance.

Other objects of self-adornment already established in Etruria continued through the period of Greek influence although their styles changed; these included pendants, hair ornaments, ear-rings, pins and fibulae.

About the turn of the 5th century BC, there was an inexplicable resurgence of Etruscan independence in both design and craftsmanship which was retained until the Etruscans were finally absorbed by the Roman Empire in the mid-3rd century.

In many ways the jewellery made in the period between these two dates was similar to the earliest Etruscan jewellery, showing a return to their bold design style. Filigree disappeared almost entirely, granulation was used once again but with more discipline and precision, while repoussé work reached a new peak of perfection.

One new item which joined the Etruscan jewellers' repertoire during this period was the wreath. Composed of arrangements of leaves, some wreaths were so flimsy that they could only have been made for funerary purposes or possibly to be sewn onto a cloth band. Others were stronger and three-dimensional, the leaves and berries sprouting from a solid stalk. The terminals of these stouter wreaths depicted various characters retained from the days of Greek influence.

Some of the traditional ear-ring designs survived during this period, but there were also exciting developments. Hoop ear-rings were decorated with enormous panels of thin gold sheet (some measuring more than four inches in depth) beaten into repoussé designs and decorated with granulation. Two of the finest examples of these can be seen in London at the British Museum. One is of a woman on an ornamental panel, herself wearing ear-rings; the other depicts flowers, fruit and berries.

Ear-rings were one of the Etruscan's favourite form of jewellery. They were highly stylized and fell into several categories
Left: boat-type ear-ring with decorated pendant in gold with granulation, 7th/6th century BC
Far left, top: boat-type ear-ring in gold decorated with granulation, 7th/6th century BC
Below: baule *(satchel-shaped) ear-ring in gold decorated with granulation, 6th century* BC.
(All at British Museum)

Beads, pendants and necklaces continued very much in the fashion of the previous period, whereas bracelets virtually died out. Finger-rings also remained unaltered, apart from the increasing popularity of the scarab.

In about 250 BC, the Etruscan civilization was absorbed into the expanding Roman Empire but the Romans, always quick to appreciate talent, employed Etruscan goldsmiths for their own purposes.

The work executed by them after this date must therefore be considered Hellenistic, and subsequently Roman.

Pages 66–7: detail of an Etruscan fibula magnified more than 50 times. From this you can gauge the incredible precision of Etruscan craftsmen as some of the granules measure less than 1/200th of an inch in diameter. 7th century BC. *(*Museo Nazionale di Villa Giulia, *Rome)*

Right: Greek fibula in gold with chased design. Here the modern safety-pin design can be seen to have been pre-empted by several thousand years. 8th century BC. *(British Museum)*

Seal-cutting both in gemstones and metal was one of the oldest crafts of ancient civilizations
Below: superb example of a Greek seal ring in gold depicting a chariot drawn by four horses, c.400 BC. *(British Museum)*

Archaic and Classical Greece

After several hundred years of near artistic stagnation, the Greeks once again emerged as masters of both the major and the minor arts. Sculpture and decorated pots from the Archaic period (600–475 BC) are plentiful but examples of jewellery are pitifully few. There is a very simple explanation for this – lack of materials. Greece had virtually no access to supplies of gold except in their far-flung colony in southern Italy and southern Russia. Greek craftsmen spent this period, therefore, working for foreign powers such as the Etruscans, the Scythians and the Sarmatians; the jewellery produced by these various nations during the Archaic period is described in this chapter under different headings. It is important to realize that despite comparative domestic poverty in this field the craftsmen worked and developed new techniques and designs.

In 475, after the Persian Wars, the Classical period begins. The domestic supplies of gold still appeared to be very limited, and with the exception of one tomb at Eretria you must look to

*Below: three different styles of
Classical Greek ear-rings
Left: boat-type ear-ring with
pendants decorated with
granulation, c.400 BC
Bottom: spiral-type ear-ring
with floral decoration, possibly
Cretan, c.400 BC
Right: spiral-type ear-ring with
pyramid terminals decorated
with granulation, c.450 BC
(All at British Museum)*

such islands as Cyprus and the Peloponnese for examples of Classical jewellery. In the 4th century, examples of pure Greek jewellery were also to be found in south Russia, presumably manufactured for domestic consumption by craftsmen working primarily for nomad chiefs. The techniques used at this time were for the most part filigree and repoussé; granulation appears to have lost favour, as it did in Etruria, and inlay was hardly used.

Diadems were made out of tissue-thin gold leaves which must either have been sewn onto a band of material or used solely for funerary purposes. Rather thicker strips of gold were also used, decorated with repoussé rosettes, or figurative scenes.

Wreaths were common at this period as they were with the Etruscans but, unlike some of the earlier Greek-inspired work, the two are easily distinguishable. Wreaths produced by Greeks for Greeks were much less stylized and attempted to represent accurately wreaths made from leaves.

Ear-rings came in four basic designs. The boat-shape had a fine wire terminal which ran through the pierced ear; this design was elaborated with the addition of plates (plaques) or pendants and

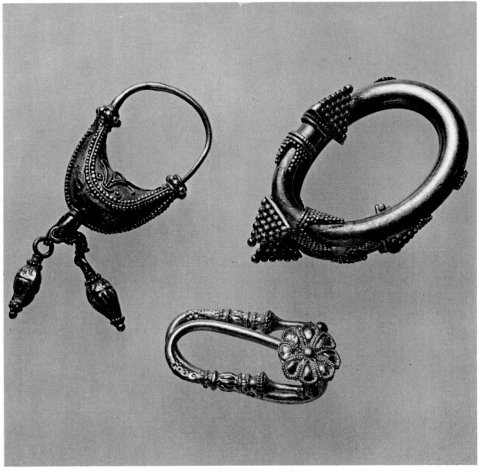

Above: simple spiral bracelet in gold, Greek, 5th century BC. *(Private collection)*
Left: a superb example of Greek craftsmanship from Tarentum. Necklace with hollow pendant beads portraying heads and buds, in gold decorated with filigree and granulation. 4th century BC. *(British Museum)*

decorated with filigree granulation and appliqué. Spirals were very popular, with the terminals heavily decorated with either geometric patterns or animal heads. Then, towards the end of the Classical period, pendant ear-rings came into fashion but the best examples were developed during the Hellenistic period. The last variety, ear-studs, were constructed like a shirt-stud, in the way used by the Egyptians. The face of these was decorated with geometric patterns, animals and human faces.

Throughout these periods, women wore necklaces, mainly constructed from beads. Several examples have been found with a neckband of repoussé rosettes, and gold acorns suspended below. One particularly elaborate version of this design has a main necklace of flowers with, hanging from it, repoussé heads, hollow spherical beads and half-open buds. Pendants were also used, one example found being a repoussé medallion depicting a man wearing an elaborate helmet; below the medallion hangs a network of chains, spirals and buds.

Simple bangles of plain or decorated metal were widely used but some more complicated bracelets were also found. One very beautiful example is an

absolutely plain, hollow hoop of gold with ram's head finials; another is a decorated hoop with two superbly-sculptured sphinxes as terminal whose paws intertwine to form a catch. Finger-rings changed very little in appearance or function from the late Minoan/Mycenaean civilization. Stone seals swivelled on rivets or were fixed in a *cloisonné* setting. Other rings made out of gold were found with designs cut both in intaglio and relief. The shape of the bezel in both categories varies and the shank is sometimes left plain, sometimes twisted or decorated.

Two particularly fine examples of goldwork from the Late Classical period are decorated pins – the 'Sphinx' pin and the 'Capital' pin found in a tomb on the Peloponnese. The head of one pin, which measures less than two inches, is a bud decorated with four rampant lions, four hornets and four sphinxes picked out in repoussé, filigree and granulation.

Fibulae which proved so popular with the Etruscans were never much used by the Greeks. Some were found of the boat-type, richly decorated with appliqué rosettes and linear granulation, but these must be considered Etruscan both in design and execution.

71

Hellenistic

During the Classical and Archaic periods Greece consisted of a number of self-governing city states but by the early 4th century BC they were united under Philip, King of Macedonia. After Philip's untimely death in 336 BC the situation was consolidated under his son Alexander the Great. Alexander was ambitious for territory and the spread of Greek ideas, and in a series of brilliant campaigns he established an empire which covered Asia Minor, Syria, Egypt, Mesopotamia, Persia, Afghanistan and on to the Indus Valley. The spread of Greek culture brought about a style of jewellery which is common to all these territories – Hellenistic. Rather than imposing their old designs on the newly-conquered territories, the Greeks absorbed what was best from the art of each nation and evolved a hybrid. This was undoubtedly the richest period for jewellery and goldwork in the history of the Aegean world. For one thing gold was more readily available both from deposits in Asia and Egypt, and from looted treasures which could be broken up and the metal re-used.

Jewellery in the Hellenistic era was no longer the preserve of royalty and nobility. A new class of rich merchants emerged and they, influenced by the luxury-loving Persians, became great patrons of the goldsmith's art. This new and broader market accounts for the vast quantity and variety of jewels attributed to Hellenistic Greece. New motifs and techniques were evolved. The 'Heracles knot' (a reef knot) was common in necklaces, diadems, rings and bracelets. The symbol existed in Ancient Egyptian and old Minoan jewellery but in comparatively small quantities. Both ancient and new civilizations believed it to have talismanic value, particularly for healing.

The most important innovation, however, was the introduction of colour; inlay and the use of stones was rare in Ancient Greece but the jewels of the Hellenistic period are a riot of colour. The stones they favoured were cornelians, garnets, emeralds, amethysts, pearls, together with faience and enamels. In general, the designs were more complex, sometimes even fussy, but they have a unique charm. Technically the pieces are superb, with their fine filigree and granulation used with the discretion of the late Etruscan period. The forms were virtually

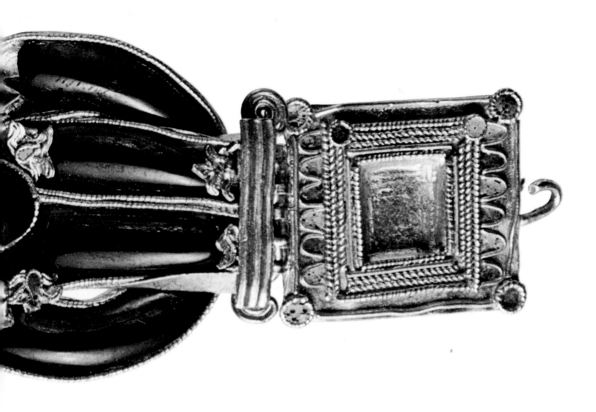

Left: gold pendant ear-ring with elaborate repoussé and filigree decoration reminiscent of Etruscan jewellery. 3rd century BC. *(Museo Nazionale di Villa Giulia, Rome)*
Right: gold hoop ear-ring with goat's head terminal inlaid with garnet, 3rd century BC. *(British Museum)*
Far right: gold hoop ear-ring decorated with a winged figure, 3rd century BC. *(British Museum)*

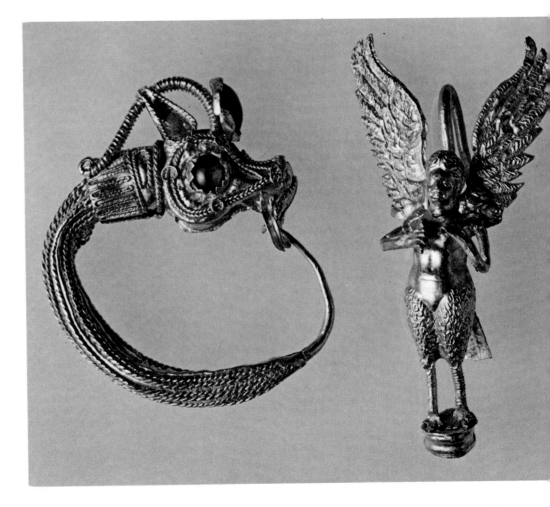

Towards the end of the Hellenistic period ear-rings became increasingly complex and new materials were introduced
Far left: pendant ear-ring in gold, garnets and pearls with a cock in white enamel, 1st century BC
Left: complex non-figurative pendant ear-ring in gold and garnets with repoussé and granulation, 2nd century BC
Right: disc and pendant ear-ring, gold with filigree and granulation, 3rd century BC.
(All at British Museum)

unchanged; diadems made of embossed strips were popular in the early stages but, by the 2nd century BC, were superseded by a much more elaborate style with a strong Persian influence. The most impressive of these was found in Kerch in southern Russia. The central point is a huge knot of Heracles in gold filigree and garnet, surmounted by two sea-serpents and a winged victory. The main headband is tubular gold, heavily decorated and hinged; from this hang complex pendants of garnets and gold.

The knot of Heracles was also used in another piece of headwear, found at Tarentum which is generally described as a hair-net. When fastened it resembles a skull-cap, made from flexible gold netting studded with cabochon garnets at every link point. At the crown of the cap there is a repoussé medallion depicting the head of Medusa, while the headband is decorated sheet metal with a Heracles knot of gold filigree and garnets.

Fashion in ear-rings changed radically. The boat-shape, so popular in Classical times, lost favour and had vanished entirely by the 2nd century BC. This was replaced by the hoop variety, similar to those found in Etruria, made from twisted gold wires

or hollow gold tubes, tapered to a point at one end with a decorated finial at the other. Many different themes were used for these finials, including lions, bulls, goats, dogs and human faces. This basic hoop became even more elaborate and, by the beginning of the 1st century BC, stones and glass were incorporated either as beads threaded on the hoop, or as inlay to decorate the finial. An addition to the animal theme was the dolphin.

Ear-studs made a brief appearance but had vanished entirely by the end of the 3rd century BC. Pendant ear-rings on the other hand became increasingly popular and elaborate. Once again the main area of development was the introduction of colour but the overall design became more complex, the animal themes being supplemented with figures from Greek mythology. Wreaths continued to be totally representational but here again the use of colour to depict flowers and berries adds to their overall magnificence.

Several new types of necklaces were introduced, the most common being the strap, not unlike the design widely favoured by the Etruscans, the main difference being that the pendants were geometric rather than figurative and

stones were widely used. Heavy, simple chains were also worn round the neck with elaborate finials with animal heads. Finally, beads became popular made from a mixture of decorated hollow gold, glass and stone with similar finials to the chain necklaces. An unusual type of bracelet looked like a miniature Celtic torque, made from wires twisted round a solid core with terminals decorated with human or animal faces. This style survived until the end of the 2nd century BC together with circular bracelets made from open filigree and tubular gold, some solid, some hinged. Spiral serpentine bracelets continued from the Classical period. In some cases the snake heads are replaced with Triton demi-gods (mythological sea-creatures) and the tails of the two creatures intertwine to form a knot of Heracles.

A miniature version of the serpentine was adopted as a finger-ring. Signet rings continued to be made in both solid gold, and gold and carved stone, while many complex rings with uncut stones were worn purely for decoration.

Other items of jewellery such as pins and fibulae, borrowed from Greek colonies and adapted to the Hellenistic style, were used throughout the period.

Roman jewellery has been much maligned. Its simplicity has been confused with a lack of imagination and technical virtuosity. The Romans did, however, produce many jewels of great beauty
Left: encaustic painting on wood of a Romano-Egyptian woman wearing a necklace of coloured stones. Mid-late 2nd century AD. (British Museum)

Left: a simple bracelet of half spherical, hollow gold beads joined by links. From Pompeii, 1st century AD. (British Museum)

Roman

The concern with which the 20th century economists view their nations' gold reserves is far from a new phenomenon. Shortage of gold was a problem which worried the Romans perpetually during their struggle for expansion. By the 5th century BC gold was considered throughout the civilized world as the acceptable currency for international trade and a country which had a good supply was rich; Rome, a small insignificant city state, which had no domestic supply was therefore by definition poor. According to Pliny, writing of the Rome of 390 BC, the total stocks of gold were no more than 1,000 lb (a Roman lb being five-sixths of a modern lb), which, he added sadly, was rather less than one-seventh the weight of Croesus' offering to the Delphic Oracle 150 years earlier.

By the middle of the 4th century, despite this handicap, Rome gained control of central Italy, absorbing the Etruscan civilization. This improved the situation but only marginally. As the embryonic empire continued to expand, other gold-producing territories in North Africa, Spain, France and the East produced a regular and reliable flow, but there was still no metal to spare for the luxury of self-adornment. Rome had a huge standing army stationed in their foreign territories and the Senate needed every ounce of gold they could lay their hands on to maintain it.

Two laws were passed to control the use of gold, one in the 5th century BC and the other in the 3rd century BC. The first, the Law of Twelve Tables, limited the amount of gold which could be buried with the dead. The other, *lex oppia*, dictated that no woman should be allowed to wear more than half an ounce of gold. The Romans were a more methodical, less romantic people than the Greeks and they kept their priorities straight. The result, however, was that for more than three centuries jewellery in the western Mediterranean suffered a period of almost total stagnation. What few pieces have been found which could be attributed to this period are of Etruscan or Hellenistic design, if not of origin. It was not until the beginning of the Imperial period (c.27 BC) when Roman internal politics underwent a complete shake-up, that the situation changed dramatically and the first true Roman jewellery was produced.

The jewellery made in the first two centuries owes its origins to Hellenistic Greece both in form and execution but, as time passed, the Roman love of bulk and simplicity overcame the tradition for delicacy and intimacy.

By the 2nd century AD, the Roman jewellers seem to have broken completely free from their Greek heritage. They introduced two new techniques to their repertoire. One was *opus interrasile* which is a fretwork design in gold sheet, executed with a chisel. At first the work produced by this technique was comparatively simple, sometimes even crude, but as the Romans perfected the technique their work became increasingly sophisticated, laying the foundation for the beautiful open-work produced during the Byzantine Empire. The other technique was niello, an inlay technique not unlike enamelling and although this had been used in Greece for decorating weapons, the Romans were the first to use it for jewellery.

The other major development arose out of the Romans' love of colour; they used virtually all the precious stones and semi-precious stones available to us today. Emeralds were brought from mines in Egypt, garnets from Eastern Europe, sapphires, topaz, pearls, agate and even uncut diamonds were all widely employed; the softer ones were cut *en cabochon* (polished, but not shaped or faceted), the harder polished in their natural crystalline state.

The rejection of the policy of austerity, together with an increase in the availability of gold lifted all restrictions on ownership of jewels and they rapidly became a status symbol. Petronius, in a passage from the *Satyricon*, describes the vulgar attitude of the *nouveaux riches* to their possessions, the first recorded case of 'keeping up with the Joneses': '... Soon Fortuna took bracelets from her great fat arms and showed them to the admiring Scintilla. Then she even undid her anklets and her gold hair-net which she said was of pure gold.' Trimalchio looked at it and said: 'A woman's chains you see. This is the way us poor fools get robbed. She must have six and a half pounds on her'. He went on to describe a bracelet, made up from 'one-tenth per cent offered to Mercury – and it weighs not less than ten pounds.' He then proved this with scales, testing the weight.

Accounts like this not only give us a clue to the uses to which jewellery

was put but, together with paintings and sculpture, give us a picture of the range and appearance of the objects produced since once again we are faced with the problem of insufficient examples. The first two centuries AD are represented by finds from Pompeii and Herculaneum. Head-ornaments continued in this period but were doomed to go out of favour. Examples of wreaths found are more akin to the Etruscans, than Hellenistic, stylized rather than realistic, whereas the few diadems which have been recovered are of the repoussé-strip type common in Greece.

Two new types of ear-rings would appear to be of mixed parentage. One, the ball, is a semi-spherical disc of undecorated gold with a simple ear-wire. The other, the chandelier type, is constructed with one large stone set in gold with three other stones suspended below, fully articulated so that they rattle when the wearer moves her head. Other ear-ring designs include the hoop which was so popular with the Etruscans and Hellenistic Greeks.

The most common necklace design also derived from the Greeks; a simple chain of stones arranged symmetrically in bezel settings. The two Roman contributions to this necklace design were the use of a more varied selection of stones and the incorporation of panels of *opus interrasile*. The use of simple and complex chains continued to be popular but with much less heavily decorated finials; the favourite form of elaboration of chain necklaces was the addition of a medallion or coin as a pendant.

The coin theme was also used in the design of finger-rings; they were, judging by the enormous number recovered, the most popular form of jewellery throughout the Imperial period. One contemporary report, which should be taken with a pinch of salt, speaks of a man who wore six rings on every finger. What is certain is that the habit of wearing two or more rings was widely accepted, as was the pursuit of establishing collections. For the first time rings were used as tokens of betrothal and marriage by the Romans; they were also awarded for acts of distinction, and used as a signature in the fashion established by the Egyptians more than 2,000 years earlier. Solitaire rings were popular, as were bands of *opus interrasile* and rings similar to today's eternity ring with stones set all round a simple band.

Rings also incorporated some of the most exciting carved gems and cameos ever produced.

The Hellenistic influence is again apparent in the design of bracelets – typified by the frequent incorporation of the knot of Heracles and the representational serpent – but one notable exception to this is the ball bracelet. This consists of two rows of simple gold balls, the same type as used in the ear-rings mentioned above, linked together to make a flexible chain. Bracelets of *opus interrasile* were either left plain, or set with stones in simple bezels or *plique-à-jour*.

Roman jewellery has, for the most part, received rather harsh criticism from experts, notably in the 20th century, but while some of the workmanship is comparatively shoddy the Romans made two major contributions to the development of jewellery which were both adopted and improved by the Byzantines.

Firstly, they switched the emphasis from gold towards precious stones; secondly, they stopped the move towards increasing complexity of design and encouraged a simplicity which had been the strength of the Sumerian goldsmiths some 3,000 years earlier.

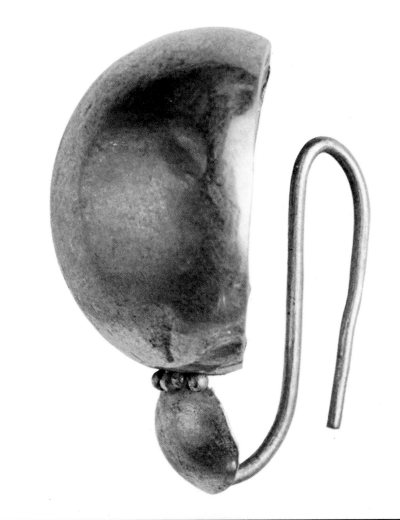

Right: three Roman finger-rings housing coins and medallions. These were particularly fashionable in the 2nd and 3rd centuries AD *when they were used very much in the manner of badges of livery in the Middle Ages. (British Museum)*

Scythian and Sarmatian

In the 7th century BC, Scythian horsemen swept across the Eurasian steppes, defeated the Cimmerians, and became the newest of many nomadic tribes to control the steppes. Like their predecessors, they were savage barbarians who lived by the sword, a constant threat to the civilizations on their borders.

To call the Scythians a civilization would be a contradiction in terms but, none the less, they were a cultured and intelligent people in some areas of their life. They were, for instance, the most original and exciting jewellery designers of the Ancient World.

It was traditional for these nomadic tribes to bury their dead in barrows (grave mounds) with all their finery. The earliest tomb excavated at Kaikop (c.2300 BC) contained beads of gold, turquoise and cornelian; gold wire earrings; finger-rings; and two gold diadems decorated with appliqué rosettes. This was the first of many finds dating throughout the 3rd and 2nd millenia, but the jewellery itself was almost undoubtedly imported, or stolen from neighbouring civilizations in the Aegean and Asia Minor.

It was not until the 5th century BC that the Scythians developed their own powerful style. Their theme was animal life and the ferocity and energy with which the animals are depicted reflects the character of the people themselves. The animals were almost all wild: boars, wolves, birds of prey, together with mythical beasts, fighting to the death or crouching ready to pounce.

Early Scythian jewellery was very simple in form and included repoussé plaques which were worn on clothing, together with ornaments for horses which were buried with their masters. It was not until considerably later that jewellery was made for women.

It is generally considered that the Scythians learned their techniques from Greek goldsmiths. It is even possible that all the jewellery was made by Greeks to Scythian design. The craftsmanship, whose-ever it might have been, was superb.

There have been many mounds dug which have revealed Scythian royal tombs. Needless to say, most had been robbed but some were found at least partially intact. The Chertomlyk burial was one of the best examples. This was

an enormous tomb. The main chamber had been plundered but several of the side chambers were left virtually undisturbed. In these were found a bronze torque (neck-ornament), rings and earrings of gold, and 400 gold strips depicting animals and monsters; in one chamber there was a gold torque decorated with the figures of lions. In another chamber there were two skeletons: one of a woman was wearing gold ear-rings and her clothes had obviously been decorated with gold plates; the other, a man, had gold bracelets. The decoration of these objects was, for the most part, repoussé and the figures show an obvious Greek influence. The true Scythian 'animal style' had not yet been developed.

The most impressive collection of pure Scythian jewellery was found, not in a tomb, but in a casket exposed after a landslide in Kurdistan. This became known as the Ziwije treasure. By this time, women's jewellery was obviously fashionable. The treasure included necklaces, ear-rings, finger-rings, bracelets, buckles and brooches, a glove made from gold netting, a solid gold breast-plate and a gold belt; small gold griffins; horse brasses and an abundance of vessels in both gold and silver. Here the animal style was portrayed with enormous energy, both two-dimensional and in the round.

No Scythian writing has ever been found but a detailed account of the tribe, its origins and customs, was left by Herodotus, a contemporary Greek historian, who lived for some time in a Greek colony on the south Russian coast. He tells us that another nomadic nation, the Sarmatians, who had lived to the east of the Scythians, gained rapidly in strength and, by the 4th century, defeated the Scythians who moved south into the Crimea.

The Sarmatians remained dominant in the Eurasian steppes until the 3rd century BC. At first Sarmatian burials were comparatively simple. Isolated examples of women's jewellery were found but they might well have been late Scythian. Gradually, however, the Sarmatians took over from the Scythians as customers of the Greeks and inherited some of the designs. They introduced *cloisonné* work to their jewellery. Some particularly fine examples of this were found in the Oxus treasure, uncovered on the border of Russia and Afghanistan, and thought to have been made about the 4th century BC. This treasure, to be seen at

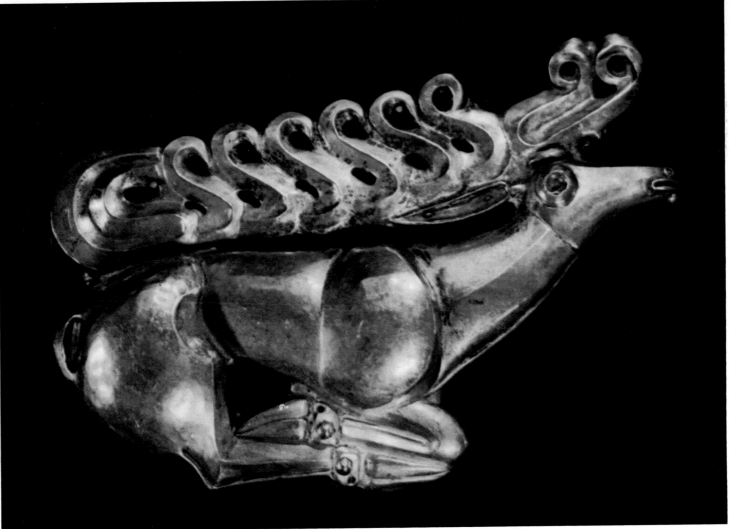

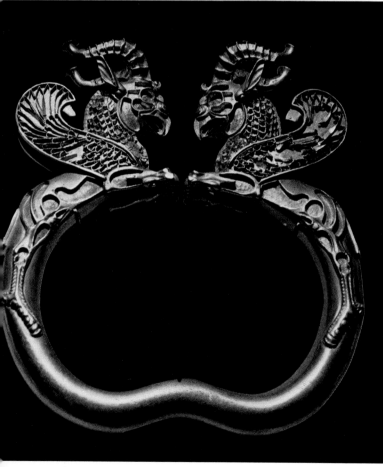

the British Museum in London, included bracelets of twisted gold rod with animal head terminals and a magnificent gold penannular (almost ring-like) bracelet with winged griffins.

Other goldwork was found in various sites in Siberia and collected by Peter the Great (1672–1725) who was a great connoisseur of the jewellers' art.

The best examples were plaques, presumably worn on the belt, made in open repoussé work. They have all the energy of the Scythian design, depicting savage fights between all kinds of ferocious animals. Others depict human situations, horsemen, wrestlers, and hunting scenes. Once again the stress is on action.

From the 2nd century onwards, burials were rather grander and two groups of burial mounds excavated from this period housed some very elaborate jewellery. One of the finest single items was an open-work diadem encrusted with amethysts, garnets and chalcedony, depicting stags walking through woods, and two geese. An open-work gold collar with necklace band showing parading griffins was found in the same grave. Other finds from the 2nd or 3rd century AD continue to be attributed to Sarmatians.

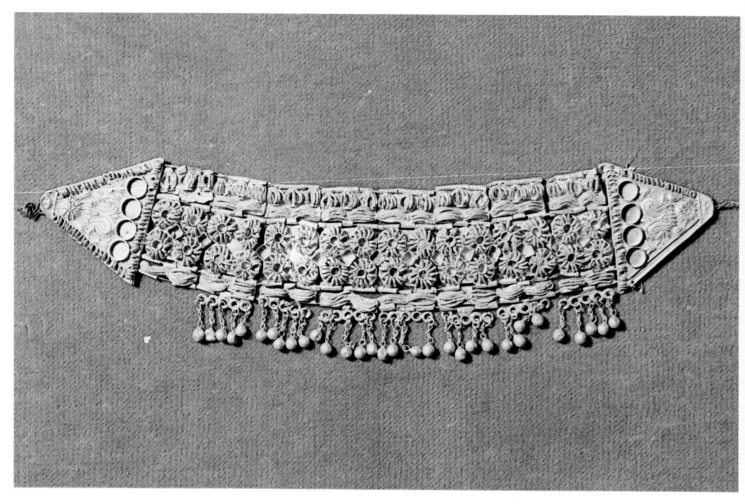

Phoenician

The Phoenicians played a vital role in the development of jewellery in the late 2nd and early 1st millenia BC. Originally nomadic desert dwellers, they settled in an area of the eastern Mediterranean which is now Lebanon. The Mediterranean was for centuries controlled by the Minoans and the Mycenaeans but, with the destruction of the Aegean civilization, the Phoenicians rapidly took over and, by about 1000 BC, they had become skilful sailors trading throughout the western Mediterranean, through the Straits of Gibraltar and on into the Atlantic. There is evidence to suggest they were trading with the pre-Celtic Irish. Certainly they were buying tin from parts of western Europe.

As their trade routes became more predictable and regular, they set up cities at strategic points, in Cyprus, Crete, Sardinia, Egypt, Sicily, southern Spain and throughout North Africa. Some of these were no more than small trading posts but others, notably Carthage, outgrew anything they had built in their homeland.

In their travels they came in contact with many civilizations and cultures at different stages of development or decline and were thus a channel of communication between remote parts of the ancient world, encouraging the interchange of ideas and techniques.

It would be a mistake, however, to speak of the Phoenicians purely as merchant profiteers; they were accomplished craftsmen and designers if somewhat plagiaristic. It is generally considered that they learned their metalwork techniques from the Mycenaeans and passed them on to craftsmen in their colonies. Evidence suggests that they took the technique of granulation from the Aegean to the Etruscans and, if this was their only contribution to the art of jewellery, they are worthy of admiration. It is uncertain whether 'Phoenician' jewellery was made by themselves or by Greeks working for them but the design is hybrid with influences from Greece, Egypt and Asia Minor. The finest single collection, the Aliseda treasure, was found in southern Spain.

The Egyptian influence is obvious in several of the objects. An open-work bracelet, for instance, has palm finials decorated with delicate granulation, and a pair of pendant ear-rings consists of plain gold hoops with a frieze of bells

One of the few collections of Phoenician jewels is the Aliseda treasure found in southern Spain
Above: gold diadem, and (right) two gold bracelets decorated with filigree and granulation
Pages 94–5: section of a gold sword belt decorated with figures in granulation. All from the Aliseda treasure, Phoenician, 6th century BC. (Museo Arqueológico Nacional, Madrid)

and palm leaves. Another fine hoard of Phoenician goldwork was uncovered in Tharros in Sardinia. The star of this collection certainly has a strong Egyptian feel about it: a hinged bracelet made from gold sheet, beaten in repoussé and decorated with line granulation, the centre panel depicting a winged scarab and the other four panels having a stylized palm motif.

The Phoenician civilization flourished for six centuries but was finally broken up by Republican Rome in the Punic Wars.

Of all the goldworking civilizations of the Ancient World, none is more mysterious than Bronze Age Ireland. In apparent isolation a highly sophisticated level of craftsmanship was developed here in the early 2nd millenium BC. Examples of this work have been found throughout Ireland and on the west coast of England
Left: the Rillaton gold cup was found in Cornwall but is generally considered to have been made by Irish craftsmen, c.1500 BC. (British Museum)

Bronze Age Ireland

Of all the ancient civilizations, none is more mysterious than Ireland. Finds of goldwork attributed to Irish craftsmen date back to the late 3rd millenium BC yet virtually nothing is known of the people who produced this jewellery of dazzling beauty. Perhaps they were nomadic tribes of the neolithic period who reached Ireland via England from Central Europe.

Though initially limited, Irish goldwork is unique, in both form and design. The earliest objects discovered were *lunulae*, crescent-shaped ornaments cut from thin sheet gold and chased or engraved with geometric designs. What function these served is uncertain. Theories that they were a neck-ornament are unconvincing (a fall would probably end in decapitation) but it is possible that they were hair-ornaments worn like a diadem. While about half a dozen have been found elsewhere in Western Europe, it is almost certain that they were of Irish origin and that this form of ornament was developed in Ireland by Irish goldsmiths.

Other objects of the early 2nd millennium were ear-rings of the basket form (not unlike those found in the shaft graves at Mycenae, but to suggest that there is any connection would be sheer speculation), and decorated gold discs which were probably dress-ornaments.

Whatever influences reached Irish craftsmen at this early stage, there is no doubt that new forms were introduced to their repertoire from Eastern Europe by the 14th or 13th century BC. The most significant of these was the torque. The introduction of this form of neck-ornament also marked a basic change in metalwork techniques. Previously all objects had been made from sheet metal or wire, whereas the torques were generally made from rod. Soldering, casting and the repoussé techniques were also introduced. The two most common designs for torques at this time were the twisted rod or twisted ribbon which fastened behind the neck with a simple clasp.

Bracelets also made their first appearance about 1200 BC, some like miniature versions of the torque, others as broad bangles with repoussé designs beaten in sheet metal.

Beads of amber, and faience of about the same date indicate the establishment of trade routes, either direct or

Above right: group of penannular gold items, thought to be clothes-fasteners. Bronze Age Irish, c.1000 BC. (National Museum of Ireland, Dublin)
Right: a lunula, the oldest known form of self-adornment from Bronze Age Ireland. Cut from thin gold sheet, and chased, the original use of lunulae is unknown. Theories that they were neck-ornaments are impractical. Irish, c.1700 BC. (National Museum of Ireland, Dublin)

indirect, with the Mediterranean and the Balkans.

Whether or not the Irish had their own source of gold is unknown. It is quite possible that there were surface deposits which have long since been exhausted or that they imported their gold from known sources in Germany. By the beginning of the Dowris Phase (c.800 BC), however, supplies would appear to have become more readily available. Jewellery of this period has been found in large quantities.

The forms employed at this time

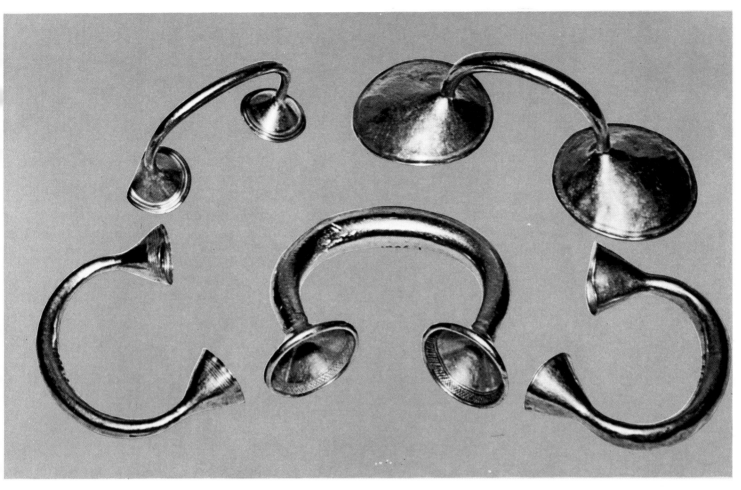

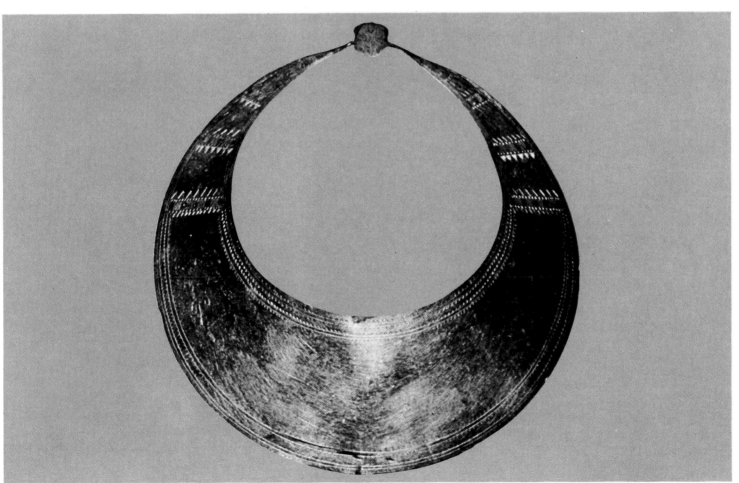

Left: gold gorget with cupped terminals and decorated with repoussé. Irish, 7th century BC. *(National Museum of Ireland, Dublin)*

Torques were the typical ornament of the Celts in Central Europe and the appearance in Ireland of such items is an indication of the contact between the two cultures
Right: two torque bracelets and a necklace in gold, found in Ireland. (National Museum of Ireland, Dublin)
Below: ribbon torque in gold, found in Ireland in the Bog of Curry, County Sligo. (British Museum)

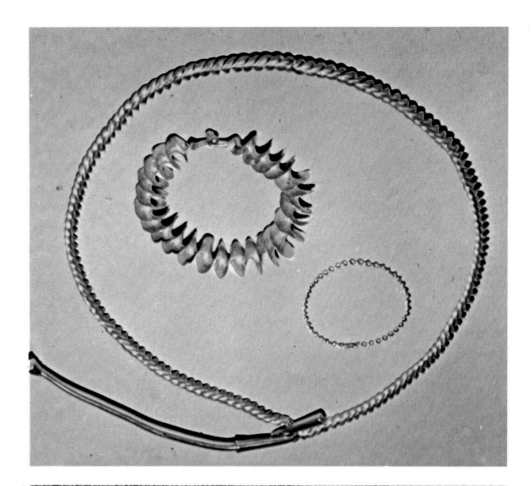

remain virtually unaltered – bracelets, torques, hair-rings, and gold discs. But there were two new arrivals: the clothes-fasteners, which were made from a semicircle of tubular gold with conical terminals and measuring about three inches across; and the gorget, a unique form of neck-ornament peculiar to Ireland. These are perhaps the most beautiful gold objects ever produced by the Irish. The finest example was found at Shannongrove, a broad crescent of sheet metal with an intricate geometric repoussé pattern in the form of concentric ribs; at the top terminals two decorated dish-shaped discs are soldered.

Almost all the Irish jewellery so far uncovered is housed at the National Museum in Dublin. Unlike the artefacts of any of the other civilizations described, the most breathtaking aspect of Irish goldwork is its size: some of the pieces are huge. The designs, of complex geometric and zoomorphic patterns, are never fussy and the workmanship is astonishing. It is sad that our knowledge of the civilization which produced them is so sketchy and we can only guess at the amount of goldwork which has been lost for ever.

Left: three Celtic gold
torques. The one in the
foreground is hollow and the
workmanship is quite superb.
(National Museum of Ireland,
Dublin)

The Dark Ages

The Celts

The 7th century BC saw the emergence of Classical Greece, and the Etruscan civilization. It also saw the first signs of a new culture in central Europe – that of the Celts. The first phase of the Celtic world is known as 'Hallstatt', named after a cemetery complex found at Hallstatt near Salzburg in Austria. Here more than 2,500 graves were dug, and objects recovered from these, together with finds in nearby salt mines (the source of Celtic wealth), are the foundation upon which our knowledge of the civilization is based.

The graves revealed very little jewellery but the few items that did survive – fibulae, bracelets, finger rings and torques, together with jewelled weapons, show a highly-developed sense of design and workmanship.

By the 5th century, the Hallstatt culture had given way to the 'La Tène' based further west in Switzerland and this was the start of the Celtic period of expansion, a factor which shows in their design. In 390 the Gauls travelled through northern Italy and sacked Rome; to the east they travelled down the Danube valley into the Balkans and were gaining territory in Asia Minor

when they were finally halted by Attalus I of Pergamum, but not before they had established a kingdom in Galatia (the Galatians of the Old Testament). To the west they inhabited France and Belgium (Gaul) and made tentative inroads to the British Isles; in Spain they mixed with the local population to become the Iberian Celts.

Their goldwork was influenced by local designs wherever they went yet, despite the distance between the colonies, their work retained a remarkable unity. The forms were those of the Hallstatt culture but the influence of the Etruscans, Hellenistic Greeks and the Nomad tribes of the steppes is increasingly apparent.

Torques retain their popularity, but are more complex. Some solid, some with two hinged sections, they range from a twisted rod with plain spherical terminals to complex rope patterns with tyre-shaped terminals decorated in repoussé. Bracelets of this period are for the most part miniature versions of the torques. Celtic rings are of a totally new style. The bezel, traditional in other civilizations, is eliminated and the ring made as a simple band decorated with repoussé or pearls. The design motifs used to embellish all

forms of Celtic jewellery were generally non-figurative and highly stylized, a feature which is peculiar to their work for many centuries. As the Roman Empire became a reality, the Celts went into a decline. Their strongest territory, Gaul, fell in the 1st century BC and the Celts dispersed or were absorbed.

One of the most popular territories for the migrant Celts was Britain but their foothold in England was short-lived. The Roman invasion of Britain drove them further west into Scotland, Ireland, Wales and Cornwall. Finds of Celtic jewellery of this immediately pre- and early-Christian period are too isolated to build a complete picture but their love of self-adornment is reported by contemporary historians. Diodorus, for instance, wrote '. . . They wear bracelets on their wrists and arms, round their necks thick bands of solid gold and they wear finger-rings and even gold tunics'.

The last item mentioned – gold tunics – might explain one of the most remarkable gold artefacts ever uncovered in Britain, an enormous, decorated sheet of gold found wrapped round a skeleton. The object was found in 1833 at Mold in North Wales and weighed more than 18 ounces. It was

101

decorated with intricate repoussé geometric designs. When it was discovered it was in several pieces and attempts to reconstruct it have produced various theories as to its function, one possibility being that it was worn over the shoulders as a short cloak.

The Celtic influence in Scotland, Ireland, Wales and Cornwall remained undisturbed throughout the Roman period, where the traditional Celtic system of tribal kingdoms was adopted and Gaelic became the working language. Their influence remained virtually undisturbed until the 10th century, and in Ireland until the 16th. During the ensuing centuries, they made many significant contributions to the world of jewellery, not least the circular ring-brooches.

The Vikings

Of all ancient civilizations the Vikings must have the most inaccurate and romanticized reputation. Hysterical writers of the 8th and 9th centuries, elaborated on by popular 20th century literature, portray tribes of bearded thugs in horned helmets piling into ships and raiding everyone in sight. Even the beards and the helmets are inaccurate and arose from a mistranslation. While it is true that at one stage the Vikings did carry out extensive raids throughout Western Europe this was for a comparatively brief period in their history. They were for the most part a more settled and civilized nation than the people they raided. Great traders, their routes reached as far as Byzantium, Persia and India; they discovered and colonized Iceland and Greenland; and reached North America at least 500 years before Columbus. The Scandinavian lands were first considered to have been inhabited on a large scale (about the time of the birth of Christ) by tribes of pastoral farmers. From this beginning they built up a sophisticated culture which lasted until about AD 1100 and even then it was not violence but Christianity which ended their independence.

Once again our only real clue to the Vikings' attitude to self-adornment comes from discoveries in graves and it is a happy coincidence that, for reasons unknown, they abandoned the rite of cremation during the 2nd century AD and adopted inhumation.

The earliest Scandinavian burials found yielded a certain amount of jewellery and other objects made from

precious metal but none of these was of Scandinavian origin. For the most part the items were Greek, Roman or Celtic, with whose nations they were trading freely – exporting skins, furs, dairy produce and slaves. These finds were in themselves exciting and included a spectacular torque of South Russian origin and several particularly fine fibulae. It was during the great period of migration that the Scandinavians came into their own, and for them this was a period of prosperity.

Large quantities of jewellery, particularly dating from the 5th and 6th centuries, have been unearthed; much of this was disappointing, consisting of plain bands and rings which were presumably designed to enable easy transportation of personal wealth rather than specifically for self-adornment. Other finds, however, prove that the Scandinavians had evolved a highly individual art style with its roots in classical lands. They appear to have been obsessed with animal themes and, while some of the earliest work is purely representational, by the 9th century their patterns became highly stylized, reflecting only the rhythm of animal movements.

Technically, the Viking goldsmiths

were astonishing. They developed a new technique – chip cutting – which involved cutting the surface of a flat sheet of metal with a chisel and so creating a number of facets which caught the light and glimmered. Other favourite techniques were filigree and repoussé but they used stones sparingly, unlike their Barbarian contemporaries. The intricacy and precision of some of their pieces is almost reminiscent of the craftsmen of Etruria.

An interesting illustration of the Scandinavian move towards abstraction is found in four medallions (a favourite form of self-adornment) spread over three centuries. The first is the head of a Roman Emperor surrounded with a floral repoussé design, the second has a much simplified head; the third a grotesque one, and the fourth a geometric pattern. The overall design of each of these medallions, or bracteates, is virtually identical apart from the gradual dissolution of the representational element.

Perhaps the finest jewels ever discovered in Scandinavia are two gold collars found in Sweden, at Färjestaden and Alleberg, which are now in the Museum of National Antiquities in Stockholm. They were both probably

made in the 6th century and certainly before the animal theme had become totally abstract.

The Alleberg necklace is constructed in two sections and hinged. One section is made from three hollow gold tubes, the other from three solid ones. On each side the tubes are joined together to make a band and, when the necklace is closed, the solid tubes fit neatly into the hollow ones, making a complete circle. The tubes are decorated with complex rings at regular intervals and the whole piece is embellished with an incredibly fine filigree of beaded wire. On top of all this, the gaps between the tubes are filled with tiny animals and faces.

The Färjestaden necklace is of almost identical construction but it is deeper and constructed out of eight tubes instead of three.

These necklaces, together with other finds of the 6th century, represent the peak in Scandinavian mastery of goldwork. Later finds are increasingly simple; in fact, from their simple, uncluttered geometric designs, some of the penannular bracelets found in an enormous hoard on the island of Gotland could well have been produced in this century by modern Scandinavian designers.

The Barbarians

Throughout the dissolution of the Roman Empire and the establishment of the Byzantine, hordes of semi-nomadic barbarian tribes occupied the majority of south-western Europe. They were in control from the Danube in the east (the effective border between them and the Byzantine Empire) to Spain in the west. From the 4th century to the early 8th, the Barbarian tribes chopped and changed, forming settlements which were destined to become the outline for the Europe of the Middle Ages.

The five major groups were the Visigoths in Spain, the Ostrogoths in eastern Germany and Austria, the Franks in western Germany, the Anglo-Saxons in England and the Lombards in northern Italy. All were closely related in their origins and for this reason, together with the fact that all their goldwork was very similar, they are generally lumped together under the collective title of the 'Barbarians'. The choice of word is somewhat unfortunate since it implies everything that is uncivilized and, while this might be true of their behaviour towards their neighbours, it certainly does not apply

Above: Barbarian brooch in gold with coloured stones and central cameo, c.7th century AD. (Saint-Germain-en-Laye Museum, Paris)
Right: two Barbarian finger-rings set with coloured stones, c.6th century AD. (Museo Civico, Reggio Emilia, Emilia-Romagna, Italy)

The finest collection of Barbarian jewellery was found in the ship burial at Sutton Hoo in Suffolk, England, presumed to be the personal possessions of a local ruler in the 7th century AD. (See also pages 112–13)
Left: Sutton Hoo helmet, c.7th century AD. (British Museum)

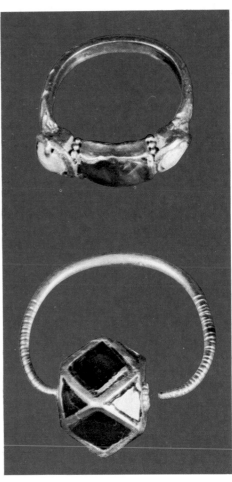

when you consider their art.

The Barbarians produced some of the most exciting and technically brilliant jewellery ever seen. Fortunately the practice of burying treasure with their dead survived through this period or, with the total lack of written material, we would probably never know they ever produced jewellery, let alone be allowed to appreciate its beauty. Barbarian jewellery can best be visualized by describing individual discoveries, but there are a few overall observations about the forms and techniques which were common to virtually all the items found. The most usual form found was a clasp. This came in various types: fibulae, shoulder-clasps, belt-buckles and cloak-pins. It is quite understandable, when you consider that all these peoples were in a state of continual unrest, that the jewellery they produced should be of a practical nature; and goldsmiths also worked as armourers.

Other forms found are necklaces, pendants and tubular neck-ornaments similar to a Celtic torque. Less common are pendant ear-rings, reminiscent of late Roman or early Byzantine styles. Other items which were undoubtedly produced purely for Royal burials, such

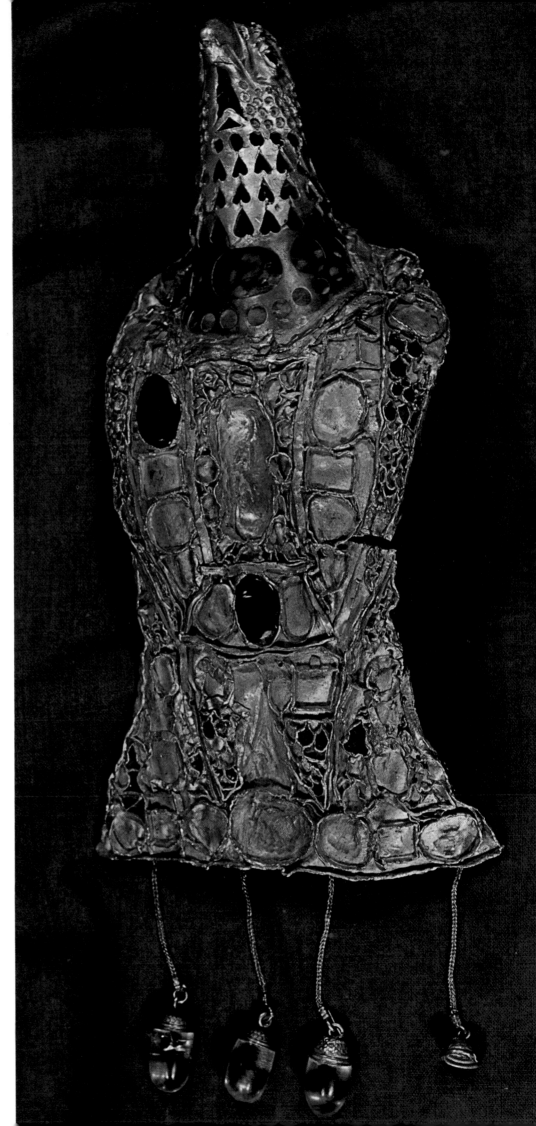

as crowns, cannot be considered part of the general pattern of jewellery-making, although there are indications that Royal patronage of the goldsmiths' art reached a new degree of exclusivity in Barbarian times only matched by certain periods of Ancient Egypt.

Barbarian craftsmen had complete command of all the techniques developed by earlier civilizations. Repoussé, filigree, granulation, enamelling and open-work are all found but it is for inlay that they will remain famous. All the Barbarian tribes had a passion for colour and, unlike the Byzantine designers, they would cover the entire surface of an object with tiny geometric shapes of precious stones or enamel which were then polished flat until they were flush with the *cloisonné* settings, giving the appearance of a tiny stained glass window. Never since the Middle Kingdom Egypt had lapidary been executed with such incredible patience and skill.

The designs used were a mixture of intricate geometric patterns, birds and abstracted designs from nature; seldom if ever did the human figure appear in their jewellery.

The materials are the variable by which you can distinguish jewellery

made by tribes in different locations.

In the North, gold was used sparingly and we can assume that it was in short supply; the stone most commonly found was garnet. In Spain, however, gold was used much more liberally, together with pearls and sapphires, which indicates that the Visigoths had established trade routes with the eastern Mediterranean and Asia Minor. Since there is no contemporary documentation, it is difficult to guess at the talismanic significance of the jewels produced by the Barbarians but the complexity of some of the geometric designs, repeated over and over again, would indicate that they had some such value.

One of the earliest treasures attributable to the Barbarians was accidentally uncovered in 1653 by a labourer near Tournai in France. What he had found was the treasure and remains of Childéric I, founder of the Merovingian Dynasty and effectively the first ruler of France, who had been buried without record in AD 481. Childéric was still in all his regalia – magnificent robes decorated with 300 golden bees, buckles, swords and bracelets – all of gold inlaid with *cloisonné* garnets. Louis XIV, who was then on the throne of France, used the dis-

covery as proof of the ancient and distinguished history of France and put the jewels in the *Bibliothèque nationale* in Paris where they rest to this day. Napoleon Bonaparte, when he became Emperor, was anxious to emulate the great rulers of Ancient France and had his entire regalia designed on the basis of the objects found with Childéric.

Another even earlier hoard of Barbarian art was stumbled on, again by labourers, in Romania during the early 19th century. By the time the authorities heard of this Petrossa treasure, only 12 pieces remained intact. These are now in the National Museum of History in Bucharest. Of the pieces that survived most are fibulae, one of which is undoubtedly the most magnificent single jewel produced by Barbarian craftsmen. It is huge, more than 13 inches in length, fashioned as a bird of prey; the head and neck are fully-sculptured with feathers cut out in *opus interrasile*; the body and chest are sculptured in relief and studded with precious stones in *cloisonné* settings; and below this magnificent beast are suspended four pieces of highly-polished quartz on gold chains. The power and understanding with which the craftsman has portrayed the bird

Left and right: two of the Visigothic votive crowns found at Toledo in Spain which make up part of the Guarrazar treasure. Gold and precious stones, mid-7th century AD. *(Cluny Museum, Paris)*

Above: shoulder-clasp from the Sutton Hoo treasure. In gold inlaid with stones and glass, c.7th century AD. *(British Museum)*
Left: Merovingian belt buckle in gold, c.7th century AD. *(Archaeological Museum, Bucharest)*

has never been seen since the Scythian 'animal style' a thousand years earlier.

One of the oddest examples of Barbarian goldwork was discovered near Toledo in Spain during the 19th century and is generally called the 'Guarrazar treasure'. Among the pieces found there were 11 gold crowns, all of considerable weight. Various techniques had been used to make them – repoussé, *opus interrasile*, and chasing; several were encrusted with precious stones or semi-precious stones and without exception they had pendants of stones or cut-out letters in gold sheet. They have been identified as having belonged to Swinthila and Recceswinth, two Visigothic kings who ruled during the mid-7th century. What is odd about the crowns is that they were all attached with chains, enabling them to be suspended from a ceiling, which had led to the theory that they might not have been for wearing at all but purely for ceremonial use.

The finest and most complete collection of pagan jewellery – at Sutton Hoo – was not unearthed until as late as 1939, for which we can be grateful since it meant that it was recovered intact under professional guidance. This Sutton Hoo burial contained

the regalia of a 7th century local Anglo-Saxon ruler. The ship burial, not unlike those employed by the Vikings, was uncovered in a sandy barrow near Woodbridge in Suffolk, England. The contents were both of amazing beauty and immense archaeological significance. Again the emphasis was on brooches of various kinds, of simple overall design but with dazzling decoration. The finest piece is a two-part hinged shoulder-clasp with complex geometric designs picked out in red and blue *cloisonné* enamel. So fine is the workmanship that in the space of a quarter-inch square there are 20 separate squares in different enamels, making up a chequer-board design. Another particularly fine piece is a chased gold belt-buckle inlaid with niello and decorated with three gold rivets. The complexity of the interwoven patterns defies description.

The discovery of the Sutton Hoo treasure (together with similar finds such as the Celtic torques at Snettisham in Norfolk, and the Kingston brooch found in 1771 in a grave on Kingston Downs in Kent), give great encouragement to those who long to know more about the jewellery of the Dark Ages.

The Byzantine Empire and the Middle Ages

Byzantium

In 330 AD, as wave after wave of barbaric invaders assaulted the western territories of the Roman Empire, Emperor Constantine founded a new city in the comparative safety of the East. With the establishment of Byzantium (Constantinople – or Istanbul as we now know it) the emphasis of the Empire transferred to the East and Rome's importance gradually diminished. As successive generations went by, the western territories declined but the Byzantine Empire flourished and became increasingly wealthy. At its height, in the mid-6th century, it controlled the Balkan lands as far as the Danube, Syria, Asia Minor, Egypt, Libya and theoretically all Italy. This empire, with fluctuating fortunes, survived until the 15th century.

To understand the Byzantine concept of jewellery it is important to understand the complex and unsettled religious situation which troubled the Empire throughout its thousand years' existence. Constantine was the first Christian Emperor, which confused an already difficult situation in the eastern sector – an uneasy combination of western philosophy and oriental tradition.

The arrival of Christianity had a profound effect on all branches of the arts but the goldsmith, who was about to have his first taste of church patronage, was affected more than most. It also meant the ending of the tradition of burying the dead with their jewellery. This factor alone presents the historian with a new problem: the disappearance of the source of information which had been his life-blood for more than 3,000 years. However, isolated finds throughout the Byzantine Empire, together with frescoes, mosaics, and contemporary reports are just about sufficient to give some idea of the splendour of their goldwork.

With the decline of the West, Constantinople became the logical home for the itinerant goldsmiths of the world. There was a considerable demand for their work for Court purposes, religious establishments and individual personal adornment. Together with this outlet for work, Byzantium was enormously rich in gold. In the year 518 Emperor Anastasius is reported to have handed down a personal fortune of more than 320,000 lb of gold which, when you consider that the entire supply in Rome at one time was less than 1,000 lb, is an astonishing volume.

As is true of every branch of the arts, early Byzantine jewellery is dominated by the deep religious feeling of the times and the figures depicted are not of this life but of the life hereafter. The jewellery was extremely ornate in both construction and design, a complete reversal of the bold clean simplicity of the pieces produced at the end of the Roman Empire. The Byzantines did, however, learn a considerable amount from their Roman predecessors, particularly the technique of *opus interrasile* which they developed to new heights. The other technical process at which they excelled was enamelling, which they executed with a delicacy and precision never before seen. This, as with their mosaics, was used to portray figurative and abstract designs. Both granulation and filigree were widely used to put the finishing touches to a design.

Materials employed were much the same as those in Rome: gold, precious stones, semi-precious stones, and glass.

An idea of the sheer volume and complexity of Byzantine jewellery can be got from the mosaic on the wall of the Church of San Vitale in Ravenna. Here Emperor Justinian, Empress Theodora and their retinue are depicted in all

Early Christianity had a profound effect on Byzantine jewellery and many religious symbols and themes were adopted
Left: Early Byzantine gold pendant cross, showing Christ and four apostles. (Benaki Museum, Athens)

Opus interrasile (chiselled open-work) was a technique started by the Romans and developed by Byzantine craftsmen
Right: 4th century AD gold plaque, presumably worn as a brooch, the background patterned with opus interrasile and chased with a picture of a horseman and his dog on a lion hunt. (British Museum)

Enamel was one of several techniques at which the Byzantine craftsmen excelled
Right: gold and enamel pendant, 12th century, depicting St. George. (British Museum)

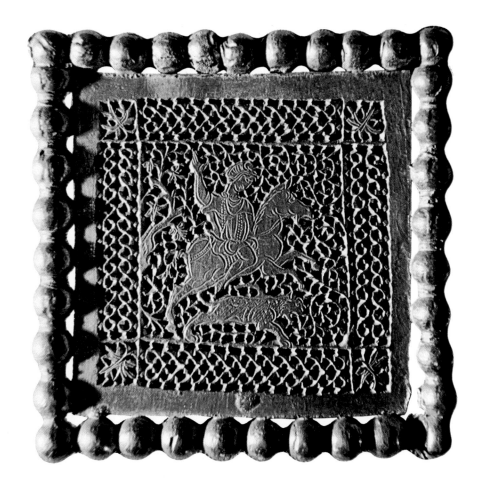

their finery. Theodora is wearing a huge crown of gold with precious stones, pendant ear-rings which appear to be made from gold, garnets and sapphires, and hanging hair-ornaments of pearls; round her neck she has a complex series of necklaces and her cloak is fastened with one large rectangular brooch at the throat and two oval clasps on each shoulder, both of gold inlaid with precious stones. The Emperor also wears a crown, ear-rings and a huge floral clasp at one shoulder. The servants, while not so extreme, are also admirably bejewelled.

Pieces actually recovered lie in several museums, in Istanbul and Athens, the British Museum, and the *Museo dell'Alto Medio Evo* in Rome. Individually they are of immense beauty but they can no more than hint at the volume and complexity of the Court jewels of the Byzantine Emperors (which were lost forever in the name of religion – during the 4th Crusade in 1204).

The forms of jewellery favoured are much the same as those of the Romans. Ear-rings take two basic forms, the crescent and the pendant. The former is not unlike the boat design popular with the Classical Greeks and Etruscans. Some have been found cut from

sheet gold and decorated with geometric designs in *opus interrasile*, others
in filigree in *cloisonné* enamel.

The pendant ear-rings remind one of
the elaborate pendants produced at the
height of Hellenistic Greece, simplified
by the Romans and now elaborated
again by the Byzantines. One particularly fine example is in the Archaeological Museum in Istanbul. At the top
it has a circle of gold wire, half filled
with a pattern of filigree and granulation; below that, suspended by three
chains, is a larger piece of filigree
shaped like a capital 'B' which has
fallen on its side; below that again there
are seven pendants of chain, precious
stones, and baroque pearls. The whole
ear-ring is encrusted with smaller
pearls, and granulation used for spacers
and decoration.

A later pair of pendant ear-rings now
in Athens shows a move away from
open-work. Once again the design is
surmounted with a simple gold ring but
below the stones are *cloisonné*-set in
solid sheet in rigid geometric patterns
and decorated with fine granulation.

Pendants were extremely popular:
many of these were executed in *opus
interrasile* round or hexagonal shapes
cut into incredibly intricate geometric

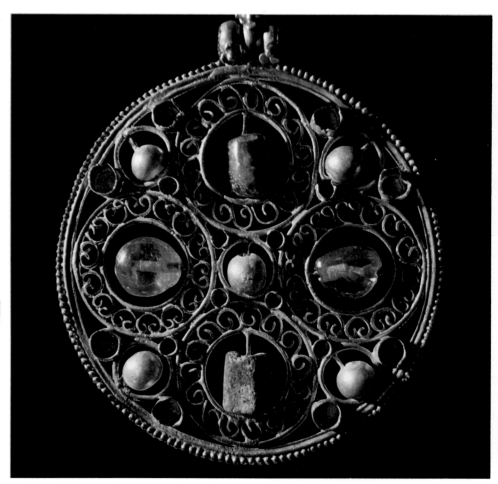

Left: 7th century Byzantine gold opus interrasile *ear-ring chased with birds. (British Museum)*
Right: Late Byzantine plaited gold chain with circular pendant set with an engraved gem. (Victoria & Albert Museum, London)
Below: 10th/11th century Byzantine boat-shaped ear-ring in gold filigree. (British Museum)

patterns. A necklace of these open-work discs attributed to the 9th century can be found in the British Museum. It consists of two rows of small discs, 92 in all, terminating with two much larger ones. The workmanship in this piece is truly astonishing and compares with anything we could produce today with the help of machinery. The other form of pendant used was the medallion which was also incorporated into necklaces, along with faience beads, pearls and other stones.

A few bracelets have been found; these are mostly simple, broad bands of gold with enamel inlay. The best surviving example is in Salonika. This, again 9th century, has 20 small panels of enamel, predominantly blue, depicting scenes from nature with great delicacy and precision. These panels are bordered by filigree and granulation.

Finger-rings were apparently common and continued to have their Roman significance of betrothal. The designs, however, remain essentially Roman, some produced in *opus interrasile* and others incorporating Byzantine coins. As to the other forms of jewellery, so vividly depicted in the mosaics at Ravenna, we can only guess, as no examples remain.

121

*Right: 6th century Byzantine
signet ring
Below: Late Byzantine (10th/
11th century) pendant in gold
inlaid with enamel.
(Both Coll. Robin Symes)*

Carolingian

The crowning of Charlemagne as Emperor of Europe in the year 800 had a profound effect on the jewellery of Western Europe. He consolidated the influence of the Christian Church throughout Europe and one of his decrees was that the practice of burying jewels with the dead should cease. The only pieces to survive from the 9th and 10th centuries are those which were preserved in cathedrals and other religious establishments.

He also established that amongst the laity jewels should be the sole prerogative of royalty and the nobility. Consequently, the goldsmith's art was applied mainly to religious objects during this period; crosses, sceptres, gospel covers and other religious regalia reflecting both the skill and fashion of contemporary jewellers.

The Barbarian love of colour survived but the techniques employed represented a close link with the Byzantine Empire. *Cloisonné* inlay lost favour and was replaced with enamel, niello and cabochon stones set in relief in claw-settings. The flat appearance the Barbarians achieved by polishing the inlaid stones flush with *cloisonné*

settings disappeared forever. Towards the end of the period antique cameos and gems which had survived from the Roman era were used and highly prized.

Reflecting the increased strength and consistency of the Christian faith throughout Europe, the goldsmith's art became primarily a monastic affair and, because of their comparative stability and excellent communications, the goldsmith monks were responsible for evolving an eclectic style of jewellery apparent from the mid-11th century. The fact that the monks were also literate means that for the first time the work of individual craftsmen, such as Mannius of Evesham and Leo of Ely, can be identified.

As for the isolated pieces of jewellery either preserved or found, they are so tied up with legend and superstition that it is often extremely difficult to discern their true origin. A typical example is the crown traditionally belonging to Pope Gregory the Great, which would put it somewhere in the late 6th or early 7th century. It is a circlet of six panels, each decorated with repoussé rosettes with a large cabochon stone set in the middle and bordered with enamel in a floral design. The techniques employed are so typical of the Carolingian period that it must be considered 9th or 10th century.

Another object surrounded by legend is the talisman which is reputed to have belonged to Charlemagne himself, a gold pendant now preserved in the cathedral at Rheims. Each side has a huge cabochon sapphire in a border of filigree set with garnets, emeralds and pearls. Between the two sapphires are relics of the Virgin's hair and a fragment of the True Cross. The talisman was buried with Charlemagne in 814 (presumably contrary to his own decree) and recovered by Otto III in the year 1000 when the tomb was opened. It was then preserved as a cathedral treasure until 1804 when it was presented to Empress Josephine to wear at her coronation. The talisman remained in the family's possession until 1914 when it was donated to Rheims Cathedral.

Perhaps the most impressive single object attributed to this period is the crown (known as the crown of Charlemagne) now in the *Kunsthistorisches Museum* in Vienna. It carries the insignia of the Holy Roman Emperor and could possibly have been made for the coronation of Otto the Great in 962. It has also most certainly been altered over the centuries but it still remains the one outstanding piece of jewellery which evokes the spirit of the period to the full. It is constructed from eight hinged, arcade-shaped panels forming a circlet. Four of the panels are decorated with a flat metal panel with religious subjects depicted in enamel, surrounded by a border of filigree encrusted with pearls and precious stones. The intermediary panels are of open filigree raised from the back panels and decorated with precious stones in claw-settings. A jewelled cross surmounting the front panel and a bridge connecting the front and back (shaped to follow the dome of the head) are generally considered to have been added at a later date. It is an example of superb, uninhibited design and craftsmanship reflecting the devotional enthusiasm and love of display which is common to all the religious objects of the time.

In England three objects with royal connections have been found from this period. The best known of these is the Alfred jewel discovered at Atherney in Somerset in 1693. This small object, less than two and a half inches in length, consists of a tear-shaped panel of enamel, protected by a layer of rock crystals, depicting the head and shoulders of a man carrying two

sceptres – the whole bordered by a collar of gold filigree. It also bears an inscription which was responsible for its name 'Aelfred me heht gewyrcan' (Alfred had me made). Its location suggests that the jewel might have been lost by King Alfred in about 878 while he was hiding from the Danes.

The purpose of the piece is unknown; it might have been made to decorate a staff or be the centre jewel of a crown; then again it could once have had a loop or pin for use as a pendant or brooch.

The other two pieces were also easy to identify since they carry their owners' names. They are the finger-rings of King Ethelwulf of Wessex and Queen Ethelswith of Mercia, sister of Alfred the Great. Both are gold with niello inlay and though not particularly fine examples of the goldsmith's art, are of considerable historical interest. Ethelwulf's ring is fashioned like a Bishop's mitre and decorated with two swans separated by rosettes, while the Queen's ring has a simple, circular bezel with a griffin chased and inlaid in niello.

The patterns of this period set the foundation for the jewellery of the entire Middle Ages, the styles being ruled by love of display and reliance on patronage of the church and nobility.

Right: late 10th century brooch found at Canterbury, Kent. Alternating rows of beaded and twisted silver wire with an engraved central portrait. (Ashmolean Museum, Oxford) Below: another legendary piece, the Alfred jewel. It is thought to be 9th century and to have been lost by Alfred the Great while he was in hiding from the Danes. The inscription on the side reads: 'Aelfred me heht gewyrcan' (Alfred had me made). In gold filigree, enamel and rock crystal. (Ashmolean Museum, Oxford)

Ottonian

The Christian influence and the return of Classical themes affected jewellery from Northern Europe rather later than in the Carolingian Empire. The marriage between Emperor Conrad of Germany and Empress Gisela reinforced ever-increasing links between Byzantium and Europe. German goldsmiths of the 10th and 11th centuries produced jewels of great delicacy and technical virtuosity; two 11th century shield brooches of German origin (now in the British Museum and Victoria and Albert Museum in London) illustrate this admirably. One, a dazzling example of repoussé and engraving, is circular with a raised boss and decorated with griffins and lions; at two points around the circumference of the brooch there are rows of tiny stones inlaid as a frieze. The other, the Towneley brooch, is of similar overall construction but the boss and outer circle are inlaid with enamel.

The use of Classical cameos as pendants in Ottonian Germany is also evidence of the influences affecting them at the time. The finest collection of jewellery was found in a cellar at Mainz and is believed to have belonged

to Gisela and have been worn at her wedding. The treasure includes necklaces, lunette ear-rings and a number of brooches. Two of these, strikingly similar to the Carolingian jewels, are in the form of a Maltese cross of filigree, heavily decorated with sapphires, amethysts and pearls. The third, however, has a strong Oriental feeling about it; in the centre of a circle of open-work is an eagle of gold and enamel, so stylized that it could almost be Egyptian.

Much of the Mainz collection was lost in World War II, but what survived shows us that an eclectic attitude had spread throughout Europe, culminating in the magnificent jewels of the Gothic era.

It seems fair to assume that virtually no personal jewellery was made in England and France during the 11th and 12th centuries. This is not a negative argument based on the fact that no examples have been found, but is deduced from the records of the goldsmiths' workshops in the abbeys which, while elaborating on the manufacture of *vessels* and *religious objects*, make no mention of *jewellery*. One important development in this time, however, was the training of lay craftsmen by the abbey goldsmiths. At first they worked on a freelance basis, employed when monks found themselves overworked or incapable of carrying out a specific task. By the end of the 12th century, however, there were enough craftsmen to justify forming a trade guild – the forerunner of the present-day Worshipful Company of Goldsmiths.

Two possible reasons why jewellery went out of favour during this period are due to economics and changing fashion: firstly, the Norman invasion impoverished the French and disrupted Britain; and secondly, the fashion for the two-layered form of tunic with long sleeves and a high neck, worn with a belt and fastened at the neck with a brooch, did not leave much scope for jewellery.

Again functional jewellery reflects unsettled times. Belts themselves were seldom decorated beyond simple studding although the buckles offered some scope to the 12th century goldsmith. One particularly fine example, thought to have belonged to Nicholas of Verdun, is in gilt bronze, and depicts a king on one side of the clasp and a queen on the other. It is executed in bas-relief and reflects the sculptural style of his era.

Brooches at this stage varied considerably but were generally round and

set with cabochon stones; some were thick clusters on a solid background, others were a narrow ring of gold set with smaller stones. The latter design was the forerunner of the ring-brooch which became the most popular form of jewellery in the 13th century. These have been found in large quantities and, judging by the romantic and talismanic descriptions common to most of them, it can be presumed that they were given as tokens of betrothal or gifts between close friends.

The 13th Century

Throughout the early Middle Ages royal and religious patronage became increasingly exclusive and this was a situation which was consolidated towards the end of the 13th century when a law was passed in France forbidding commoners to wear precious stones, pearls and belts or circlets of gold and silver. For the first time in Western Europe, jewellery became an official privilege of the privileged.

The 13th and early 14th centuries were the years of great 'Royal' jewels and, in particular, great crowns and coronets. Fashion had hardly altered and, while brooches were sewn onto the clothes later in the century and cruciforms were worn round the neck, all forms of jewellery were reserved for ceremonial occasions and not designed for everyday use.

Royal inventories form one of the best sources of information as to the forms of jewellery worn throughout the Middle Ages. A list of jewels belonging to Blanche of Castille in the early 13th century included several crowns set with rubies, emeralds, sapphires and pearls; brooches set with rubies, sapphires, emeralds and other precious

stones. In 1272 it is reported that Henry III lodged jewellery with his sister in Paris, including many rings, 67 jewelled belts, 45 ring brooches and other assorted ornaments. Other similar lists tell us of large royal hoards of the nobility of Europe. The quantities are impressive but the items mentioned confirm the limited number of forms used.

One of the most beautiful crowns of the 13th century was that worn by Richard, Earl of Cornwall, at his coronation as King of the Romans. It is a simple uncluttered circlet of gold, surmounted by four fleurs-de-lis and four crockets. Stones and cameos are set symmetrically and are used with great restraint and taste, unlike the extravagant abandon of two centuries earlier. A simple gold cross and a bridge between two of the fleurs-de-lis are thought to have been added later for a coronation or some other ceremonial occasion. The crown, which is now in the Cathedral treasure at Aachen, displays a subtlety and awareness of design which is more typical of the Gothic era.

The cameos used in this crown reflect an increase in popularity of ancient carved gemstones with pictorial themes, valued above the traditional precious stones. They were widely used in brooches and the value attributed to them, both commercial and talismanic, is shown by the intricacy of the settings provided for their safety.

One superb example of this is the Schaffhausen onyx: an antique cameo of 'Peace' is housed in a very deep filigree setting encrusted with rubies and pearls; the side of the setting, which is about half an inch deep, is decorated with tiny gold lions, so tiny that they could be mistaken at a glance for texture; the back of the brooch is engraved with a falconer. The workmanship of this piece reflects the zenith of early Middle Ages craftsmanship.

Gothic Vogue

The division of history into sections is, for the most part, a convenience. Changes in fashion and attitudes are of course gradual but, for the purpose of this study, the 'Gothic' era can be said to begin at the outset of the 14th century and end in the mid-15th century.

The Gothic style, with its roots in Romanesque, developed in northwestern France and spread throughout Europe until its influences reached from Portugal in the south to Finland in the north. The word 'gothic' is tainted in the same way as 'barbarian', but once again the art of the Gothic era was anything but crude. It is with architecture that the style is most commonly associated – those richly decorated columns soaring to great pointed arches, encrusted with gargoyles and elaborate foliage – but it spread to every branch of the arts, not least jewellery.

The Gothic era saw an increasing appreciation of the artist as a creative individual instead of being just another artisan, respected well enough but in the same class as an armourer, tailor or any other skilled tradesman. It is for this reason that works of art, previously anonymous, start to be attributed to one man. Guilds established in the previous two centuries were strengthened and received official recognition. Strict regulations were laid down for members to ensure that patrons were not cheated and insisted that specifications, laid down when an order was placed, were adhered to. Witness a commission for an altarpiece from the Bishop of Arezzo which stated that '. . . the best gold leaf to a quality of 100 leaves to the florin, and

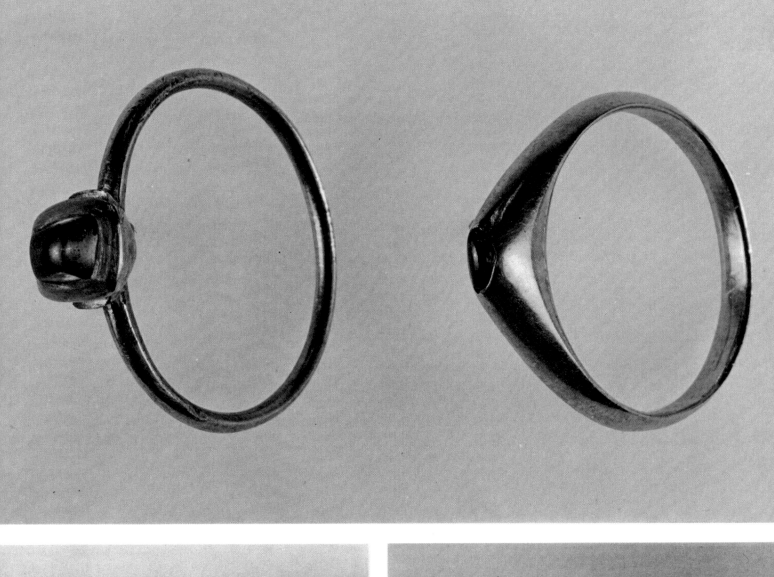

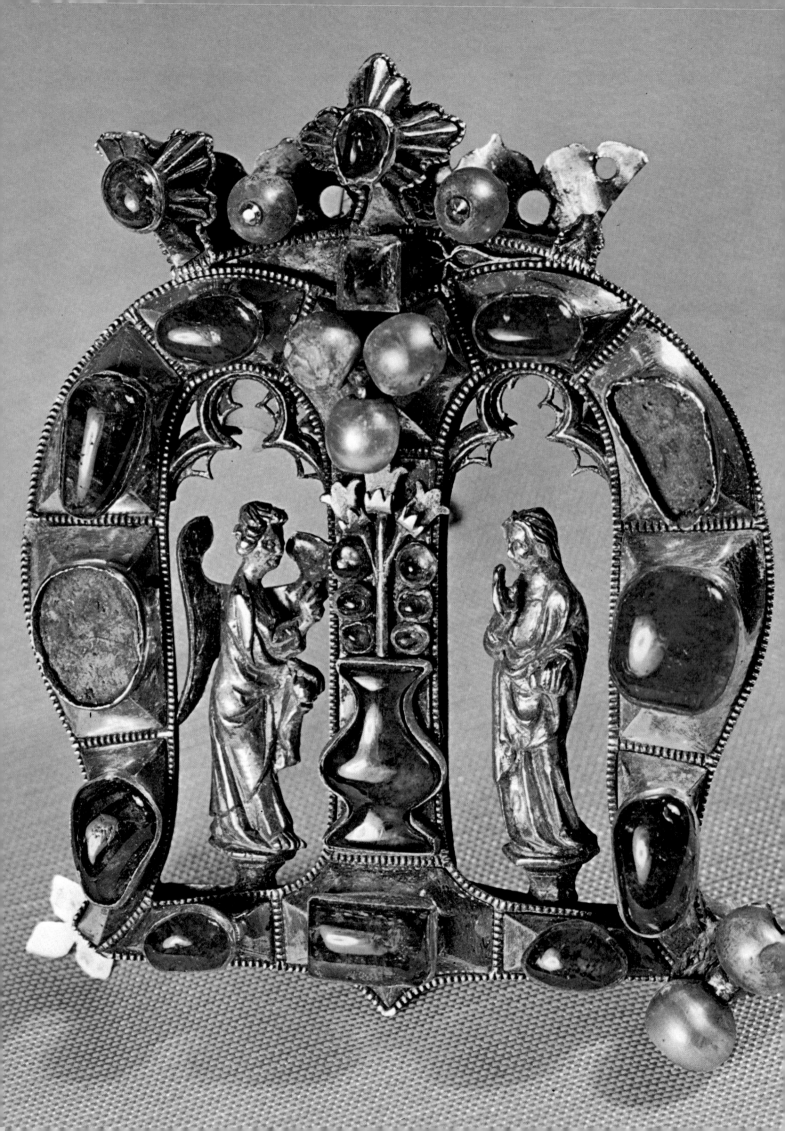

Architecture and the fine arts have always had a profound effect on jewellery design. During the 14th century the Gothic vogue can be clearly seen in various jewels which have survived
Left: one of the most famous Gothic pieces, the Founder's Jewel, bequeathed to New College, Oxford by its founder, William of Wykeham, in 1404. In gold, pearls and precious stones. The Lombardic 'M' shape is derived from early medieval calligraphy. (New College, Oxford)
Right: late 13th/early 14th century cameo ring. (British Museum)
Below: early 14th century Spanish ring-brooch with central cameo depicting lions, surrounded by foliated gold and set with rubies. (Victoria & Albert Museum, London)

genuine azure ultramarine (lapis) should be used.' These rules, imposed by the Guilds to protect their Members' reputations, were reinforced by laws passed in France between 1331 and 1355 which abolished the use of paste gems, limited the use of river and Oriental pearls and even forbade the practice of placing coloured foil behind stones to improve their colour.

The austerity of the French court, which had for more than a century precluded elaborate self-adornment, gradually came to an end by the beginning of the 14th century. It was replaced by a love of luxury and objects of beauty. This, together with a radical change in the mode of dress, had a profound effect on the jewellery made in the Gothic era. This did not mean that jewels were any more available to the bourgeoisie – if anything the laws confirming them as the prerogative of royalty and the nobility were strengthened rather than weakened.

In 1363 Edward III passed a law, not unlike that passed in France a century earlier, forbidding commoners to wear any form of self-adornment which contained gold, silver or precious stones. Even knights could not wear rings or brooches of precious materials. It is

interesting to note a mercenary element in the law, however, which allowed jewels to be worn by squires with land rentable at more than 200 ducats per annum and merchants with capital assets of more than £500. In Spain the laws were even more restricting; only the reigning monarchs and the infantas (princesses) were permitted to own gold, silver or precious stones.

Once again, therefore, we enter a stage of the history of jewellery where patronage by royalty and the church becomes virtually exclusive. An increase in the volume of both stones and metals reaching Western Europe, together with the above legislation, meant more and richer jewels for the royal houses. Never before have jewels received so much attention in written documents; they seem to have become an area of one-upmanship between monarchs. This, in fact, is the first time that they receive a collective title: in France the old word *jouel* was adopted to embody all forms of jewellery.

The same luxurious attitude that developed in France reached England later in the same century and personal collections are enumerated in royal inventories which provide a picture of jewellery fashions. Edward II, for instance, was reported to have had ten crowns in 1324, while Edward III's mistress boasted of a collection of more than 20,000 pearls.

The basic forms used in the 14th century changed very little but the styles and methods of decoration have a renewed elegance, reflecting the architecture of the times. One important technical development which marked the first stage in a new era in jewellery was stone-cutting. Diamonds had previously been set in their natural crystalline form but, during the 14th century, lapidaries discovered that they could cut a single crystal through the middle, leaving two pyramids. Later, the top of the pyramid was cut or polished flat and produced a crude form of 'table cut,' the simplest form of facet-cutting.

Brooches retain their popularity from the previous century but there are many developments from the simple ring brooch which by this stage was produced only in base metals and sold to commoners. Brooches produced in precious materials make a very definite move away from the functional towards the purely decorative. At first the overall circle was rigidly adhered to and the decoration was achieved within its limitations; a popular form of decoration in the early part of the century was the wreath of delicate leaves in fine gold sheet, set with small precious stones; the Kames brooch from Scotland shows a similar desire for elaboration but instead of leaves an animal theme has been used; in some cases the outer circle is twisted much in the style of Celtic ribbon torques.

Eventually there was a break away from the rigidity of the outer circle. An early example of this can be found in the British Museum in a gold brooch set with pearls, sapphires and emeralds with the outer circle elaborated with a floral pattern. Later on, brooches of the same basic construction were being produced in a number of different shapes. The heart-shaped brooch, enamelled or set with precious stones, is a more emotive version of the 'love token' ring-brooches of the previous century. In Scotland the circle was often bridged with a decorated rib and later with several ribs resembling the spokes of a wheel.

One of the most exciting specimens to come out of this development from the ring-brooch is the Founder's jewel

which was bequeathed to New College, Oxford by its founder William of Wykeham in 1404. The overall shape of the brooch is a Lombardic 'M', the spaces between the two outer strokes of the letter and the centre stroke being shaped like Gothic windows. In the left 'window' stands the Angel of the Annunciation, and in the right the figure of the Virgin Mary, both superbly modelled in the Gothic style. The centre stroke of the 'M' is decorated with a ruby vase containing three lilies, above which are three large pearls, while the remainder of the letter is decorated with a variety of precious stones set in collets. The entire brooch is surmounted by a lavish crown. Despite the complex design, the Founder's jewel has a delicacy and symmetry typical of the best jewellery of the 14th century.

Later in the century cluster-brooches make a reappearance and, although few of these have survived, they are vividly described in a number of royal inventories. A tendency in the second half of the century was to fill the centre of a ring-brooch with figurative designs; the best examples of these are in the Cathedral treasure at Essen. In each case the outer circle is made from tubular gold and the centre features scenes from nature depicted in a combination of enamel and precious stones. Quite complex scenes are portrayed in the small space available: a huntsman slaying an animal, a lady in a garden, deers and floral arrangements.

Some brooches produced were definite demonstrations of rank. In France, for instance, the fleur-de-lis brooch could only be worn by the Royal family on ceremonial occasions. The one surviving example is in the Royal regalia of France. It is diamond-shaped with a panel of tiny fleurs-de-lis in enamel which forms a patterned background for a much larger fleur-de-lis of gold set with sapphires and amethysts. The outer rim of the brooch is a thick border of gold set with a large number of smaller stones.

In England, France and Germany, eagle brooches were adopted by Royal families for state occasions. The two examples (illustrated on pages 166–7) are typical of the immediate forerunners of heraldic brooches, some of which start to appear at the very end of the century, such as the 'bear and ragged staff' of Warwick and the 'crowned plumes' of Norfolk.

The complex and rigid social barriers of the Middle Ages were responsible

A new technique to emerge in the 15th century was enamelling en ronde bosse, *a method of decorating figurative objects modelled in the round or in relief*
Above: 15th century Italian rosary which was worn as a necklace. Hollow agate beads contain scenes from the life of Christ enamelled en ronde bosse. (Louvre, Paris)
Right: mid-15th century Swan brooch found at Dunstable, Bedfordshire. In gold and white enamel, probably French. (British Museum)

for the foundation of hundreds of societies, orders, guilds and associations relevant to a man's trade, social standing, religion or distinction. The heraldic badges mentioned above are examples of a sycophantic display by followers of a particular camp, announcing their allegiance in the hope that it would improve their position. The most distinguished of these orders was undoubtedly the Order of

Right: early 15th century French pendant jewel depicting the Virgin and Child in gold and white enamel. (Victoria & Albert Museum, London)

the Garter which, so legend has it, was founded by Edward III who, when a certain lady (the Countess of Salisbury) dropped her garter in his company, fastened it to his own leg and said to the assembled company: '*Honi soit qui mal y pense*' (the shame be his who thinks ill of it).

In France Philip the Good, Duke of Burgundy (1419–1467), founded his own Order of Chivalry – the Order of the Golden Fleece – which became the principal Order in Spain and Austria, its membership limited to 31 knights.

The Danish Order of the Elephant was instituted on the same lines and again was limited to 31 members – including the heir to the throne. Each of these Orders, operated on true Arthurian lines, had its badge of membership, the design of which has remained unaltered to this day.

Decorated collars were also widely used in both England and France. The earliest-known English collar carries a double 'S', which is considered to be a badge of livery instituted by John of Gaunt for his retainers.

Successive monarchs and noblemen elaborated on the symbol with jewelled pendants carrying the family coat of arms. Later still, Edward IV established

In the mid-15th century women's crowns were incorporated into elaborate head-dresses
Below left: Margaret of Denmark, Queen of Scotland. Her head-dress has golden network side-pieces and is hung with pearls. Detail of a painting, 1476, by Van der Goes. (Reproduced by gracious permission of H.M. the Queen, Holyrood House collection, on loan to National Gallery of Scotland, Edinburgh)
Right: Anne de Beaujeu. Detail from the famous triptych by 'Maître de Moulins,' c.1498. (Moulins Cathedral, Bourbonnais, France)

his own pendant of 'suns and roses with a lion'; Richard III replaced the lion with a 'silver boar'; and other alterations and adaptations were effected over the centuries. In France collars of livery started about the same time.

In 1389 Philip, Duke of Burgundy, had two collars of white enamel, one depicted five fleurs-de-lis and the other 25 doves. By the end of the century dozens of different emblems had been incorporated into various orders of livery to represent different factions.

Towards the end of the century, there was increasing interest in jewels for women, particularly in the field of head-ornaments. Sadly, none of these have survived but it is a trend which continued into the next century and can be examined from both reports and portraits in which they are depicted in perfect detail.

Examples of men's headwear are also absent from present-day collections, apart from two votive crowns. These by their religious connotation are rather more restrained than those mentioned in royal inventories and reflect the sombreness of the previous century.

About 1340 the short doublet came into fashion and belts assumed a new

importance. Unlike earlier examples, the actual belt as well as the buckle was heavily decorated with enamel or goldwork. The fashion was extended to women and some delicate buckles have been attributed to the late 14th century, once again sculptural in form and richly decorated.

Around the same time, finger-rings came back into fashion but with one important difference: they appear to have lost both their functional and talismanic roles and become purely decorative. A number of styles have been found – solitaires, stone-clusters and sculptured settings were all common, many engraved with the owner's name picked out in niello.

Other forms of jewellery such as necklaces are occasionally mentioned but they are neither described nor have any examples survived and, judging by the paintings of the next century, they must have been the exception rather than the rule. There is, however, evidence to suggest that rosaries and cruciforms were worn round the neck and, while these must be considered devotional in origin, their decorative function seems to have rivalled their religious significance and they can be considered as jewellery.

The 15th Century

By the first decade of the 15th century, the Dukedom of Burgundy had become enormously wealthy and Philip the Good was to emerge as the greatest patron of the jeweller's art in the Middle Ages.

Stones and precious metals were imported in even greater quantities and the workshops of the Rhine experienced a new freedom which had a profound effect on the jewels produced until the end of the Middle Ages. The Gothic architectural style continued to influence all branches of the arts and the effect on the form of jewels is even more obvious than it had been in the previous century.

Important technical innovations had their effect also: stone-cutting became more complex and 'diamantslypers' were recognized as craftsmen in their own right. A technique known as enamelling *en ronde bosse* was developed which involved enamelling figurative goldwork made in relief or in the round and was later extended to decorating the background of cameos. Again, surviving examples of jewellery are depressingly few but we can, as before, refer to royal inventories and

141

portraits. Painters of the 15th century were frequently trained as goldsmiths and not unnaturally they portrayed jewels with great accuracy.

The finest single piece from this period is the crown of Princess Blanche (daughter of Henry IV) which was worn by her at the age of ten when she was formally married to the Elector Ludwig III in 1402. It is a piece of great beauty which demonstrates the Gothic influence to the full. It is constructed in 11 hinged sections to form a circle, and pieces can be removed or added to alter the size. Each of these brooch-like sections is a long-stemmed fleur-de-lis springing up from a narrow circlet of gold and precious stones. The pinnacles are set with emeralds, sapphires, diamonds, pearls and balas rubies, some facet-cut, others 'en cabochon'. Women had been wearing smaller versions of male crowns for several centuries but Princess Blanche's crown has a delicacy which suggests that it was designed specifically with a young girl in mind.

Jewels were becoming part of fashion rather than being symbolic of rank. Two portraits painted towards the end of the century show how women's crowns were adapted to become part of everyday hair-ornamentation. One by Van der Goes in 1476 shows Margaret of Denmark (wife of King James III of Scotland) with an elaborate head-dress of gold netting which holds her hair tightly against her head. Above these side pieces there is a circlet of gold and precious stones and the whole piece is encrusted with hanging pearls. A similar, if rather more austere, head-dress is seen worn by Anne of Beaujeu in the triptych of the Maître de Moulins, painted about 1498.

By this stage, relatively low-cut dresses were in fashion, making necklaces virtually *de rigeur*. The same portrait of Margaret of Denmark shows her wearing two strings of pearls separated by large cabochon stones and decorated with a triangular pendant. Other very elaborate necklaces are described in contemporary reports.

Margaret of Austria, for instance, was reported to have been given by Ferdinand II (the Catholic), King of Aragon: '... a heavy gold collar formed of 27 pieces and 27 points, with a network overall enamelled in black, white and red; and another of 43 roses with diamond centres joined by little snakes and all enamelled ...'

The most popular form of neck-ornament, however, appears to have been the pendant. Some pendants were purely decorative and took the form of clusters of pearls, a logical progression from the brooch designs of the previous century, but many were devotional.

Several reliquary pendants have survived and they are masterpieces of miniature. The centre is generally a scene from the Nativity or the Crucifixion, executed in enamel or cameo and protected by two small doors, much in the fashion of a present-day locket. In some cases the objects were further decorated with precious stones. Other forms of religious pendants were elaborately decorated cruciforms.

Rosaries, which were worn as necklaces in the 14th century, became even more popular and ornate. The most intricate ones follow the pattern of the devotional pendants, being constructed from strings of hollow beads which, when opened, show religious scenes enamelled *en ronde bosse*.

The pinched sleeves of the 14th century lost favour and with the introduction of wide loose cuffs, bracelets came back into fashion. None of these has survived but there are reports of bracelets belonging to the Duke of Burgundy: '... one enamelled with bands in the colours of his livery and

Right: mid-15th century gold brooch set with ruby, diamond and pearls, with enamel decoration en ronde bosse. (Kunsthistorisches Museum, Vienna)
Below right: 15th century German cross-shaped brooch in silver gilt, set with precious stones and four pearls. (Victoria & Albert Museum, London)

set with 12 "good pearls", fastening with a hanging lock of beryl set with two diamonds; another made like a towel, enamelled white, set with diamonds and rubies, with a hanging ring; and a third made as a circlet with an enamelled inscription round.' Other reports say bracelets were fashionable in England and Italy by about 1430.

Jewelled belts continued to be worn but towards the end of the century fashion dictated that they should be worn diagonally across the chest from shoulder to waist. Some belts were formed from linked gold plaques decorated with enamel while others were fabric studded with plaques.

Buckles continued to be the main area for ornamentation and one example of Italian origin, now at the Victoria and Albert Museum in London is in two sections of delicate gold tracery, depicting branches and foliage, and inlaid with enamel.

Towards the end of the century, in the transitional period between the Gothic and the Renaissance, fashionable clothes became tighter and items of jewellery were supplemented with precious stones sewn onto the fabric – a fashion which we will see taken to extreme lengths in the 16th century.

The 16th Century

'Renaissance' is a word frequently used without any real knowledge of the period it covers. In recent years it has become fashionable to play down the prestige of this particular 'rebirth' (the literal translation) and write it off as the culmination of the artistic traditions of the Middle Ages combined with foretaste of the 'baroque' magnificence to come of the 17th century.

There is, however, no doubt that the late 16th century was a period of dramatic reassessment in all branches of the arts and sciences. More than a thousand years had elapsed since the collapse of the Roman Empire and it is not surprising that the Italians looked back with longing at the magnificence of their past, surrounded as they were with tangible evidence – great architecture, engineering, philosophy and art. They must have seen in the order and discipline of a humanist, rather than religious, society a formula to make their own culture great once more, and in a reversion to Classical styles and methods the first logical step towards creating this revitalized civilization.

It was not, however, a sudden realization with immediate results; the signs were all there from the mid-14th century but it was not until the early 16th that the full impact can be appreciated. Like all blanket expressions created to describe periods in art history, the 'Renaissance' is used to cover the peak of a much longer period of evolution.

The early Italian Renaissance was not a true revitalization of Roman culture; it was an eclectic style which drew from all the Classical lands. The general style of the major arts of the Renaissance was derived from Classical sculpture with its great sense of order and symmetry. This influence also affected jewellery, which did not in fact derive anything from jewellery of the Graeco-Roman period, examples of which must have been virtually unknown. The only real link between Classical and early Renaissance jewellery is the use of cameos and engraved gems, but even this is not a new phenomenon since they were consistently popular throughout Western Europe from the 13th century. Now they were used with even more enthusiasm, and this great increase in demand led to the opening of dozens of lapidary workshops in Florence, Rome, Venice and Milan.

These cameos and engraved gems show a marked difference from their

The painting known as the Montefeltro altarpiece (Madonna with angels and Federico, Duke of Montefeltro) by Piero della Francesca (below). This painting demonstrates the major artists' interest in and knowledge of jewellery. Many leading Renaissance painters and sculptors, including Ghiberti, Donatello and Botticelli started their training at the goldsmith's bench. One of the charming anachronisms to arise from this background was the artist's use of contemporary 16th century jewellery on figures portraying Classical and religious scenes. Note the hair-brooch and choker necklace worn by the angels in the detail shown to the left. (Brera, Milan)

Left: typical devotional hat-badge (enseigne) of the early 16th century, in gold and enamel depicting Christ and the Woman of Samaria. (British Museum)

Classical forerunners. A new awareness of perspective was achieved by undercutting and throwing the figures forward in three dimensions. Despite the developments in technique, however, subjects from Classical mythology retained their popularity.

The early jewellery of the Renaissance, therefore, was influenced more by the new sculpture and painting than by its Classical origins. This influence is understandable as the jeweller's workshop was considered to be the finest training ground for those wishing to progress to the major arts. As early as 1400, Lorenzo Ghiberti was trained as a goldsmith before he became one of the most distinguished of Florentine sculptors, as well as painter and art historian of the early 15th century. His art history, unfortunately, cannot be taken too seriously since it was so devoted to explaining how superior Ghiberti was to his contemporaries.

Later, however, many other great artists followed this training pattern, such as Donatello, Botticelli, Domenico Ghirlandaio, and Antonio Pollaiolo. Albrecht Dürer was the son of a goldsmith and was apprenticed to his father for many years before achieving fame as a painter.

The influence and benefits were two-fold. Sculptors and painters entered their trades armed with the delicacy and precision already learned at the jeweller's bench, and they in turn produced work which inspired younger goldsmiths who tried to emulate the great masters in miniature. An interesting result of their early training is evident in the work of Renaissance painters: both religious and mytho-logical figures are shown wearing 16th century jewellery, a charming ana-chronism which supplements our know-ledge of the fashions of the day, not only from the point of view of design but also of the choice of jewels.

An angel from the Montefeltro altar-piece by Piero della Francesca, for instance, shows an angel with a choker-necklace of coral beads incorporating a floral motif of other precious stones, a V-shaped pendant-necklace and a cluster-brooch – all of which are typical of those worn in contemporary por-traits. Botticelli was also given to adorning his figures with pendants and clasps which, no doubt, he would have been making as jewellery had he not reached more exalted heights in the field of painting.

The most famous of these craftsmen-turned-artists must have been the legendary Benvenuto Cellini, whose life was a more tumultuous version of Ghiberti's a hundred years earlier. He wrote grossly self-opinionated auto-biographies which laid as much empha-sis on his scurrilous adventures as they did on his work as an artist-craftsman.

Despite his enormous fame there is only one piece of goldwork in existence now which can be attributed to him with any certainty and even this was produced in his transitional period between goldsmith and sculptor. It is a ceremonial salt cellar commissioned by François I of France (his patron after the Medici family whom he aban-doned when forced to flee Italy). It is a piece of magnificent extravagance and superb technical mastery which has caused a number of great jewels of the period to be attributed to him but without foundation.

Owing to Cellini's tendency towards self-aggrandizement, the documents he left behind are invaluable, giving de-tailed accounts of the jewels he pro-duced, techniques employed and types of patrons available. These provide, after the adventure story aspect has been discarded, one of the most im-portant historical documents of the early Renaissance. The most common forms of jewellery described, reflected in portraits and inventories as well as surviving examples, are devotional *en-seignes* (hat badges/brooches), pen-dants, belt-buckles and necklaces. He also explained that jewellery would be made up to a customer's own design.

The sculptural genius of the early Renaissance jewellery is best reflected in medallions produced for *enseignes* and pendants. At the beginning of the century they were mainly enamelled gold but later carved stones and cameos were added. The best early examples, from Italy, can be found in the British Museum, one depicting the Judgment of Paris and the other the Conversion of Saint Paul. These illustrate the two most popular areas of subject matter: religious, much favoured in England, and mythological, in France.

The inventory of Mary Tudor in-cluded brooches of Abraham, Solomon, David, Noah and many others. A French royal inventory a few years later, on the other hand, included *enseignes* of Hercules, Atlas and the Judgment of Paris. The technical vir-tuosity of these medallions is quite extraordinary. Complex scenes involv-ing up to a dozen figures, horses and

Right: hat-badge with an enamelled portrait of Charles V (Charles I of Spain), who had recently been elected Emperor of Germany, dated 1520. (Kunsthistorisches Museum, Vienna)

From the 1520s onwards hat-badges (or brooches) were firmly established as the most fashionable form of jewellery for men and offered an ideal medium for self-expression for metalworker, lapidary and enameller
Left: hat-badge with cameo portrait of Emperor Charles V in an enamelled gold mount, probably Italian, mid-16th century. *(Kunsthistorisches Museum, Vienna)*
Right: hat-badge in enamelled gold depicting St. George and the Dragon, mid-16th century. *(Kunsthistorisches Museum, Vienna)*

Left: enseigne *with the head of John the Baptist, enamelled white on a red background, carrying the biblical inscription* Inter Natos Mulierum Non Surexsit *(Among those born of women none surpasses him). French, early 16th century. (Victoria & Albert Museum, London)*

Below: hat-badge with agate cameo in enamelled gold mount, mid-16th century. (Kunsthistorisches Museum, Vienna)

buildings, are depicted in incredible detail in an area of about one and a half inches, reflecting either the embryonic talents of a great sculptor or jealousy by the goldsmith for the status of exponents of the major arts.

The origin of jewels from the early Renaissance is extremely difficult to determine particularly after the first 20 years of the period. Goldsmiths, traditionally itinerant, were given even greater opportunity to travel. Cellini worked in France; the German painter, Hans Holbein, worked for many years in Switzerland and died in London. Though not himself a practising craftsman, he designed jewels for Henry VIII (as well as being appointed painter to the King in 1536); and innumerable other goldsmiths received their training in one capital and practised it in another.

More confusing still was the publication of pattern books. These books produced by jewellers and engravers, containing page after page of designs for all types of jewellery, were widely circulated and adopted by lesser craftsmen throughout Western Europe. The greatest of these was produced by Virgil Solis, an engraver from Nuremberg, and included designs for belt-

Pattern books produced by designers and engravers during the 16th century had a profound effect on jewellery design. They circulated throughout Europe, offering design ideas to workshops who employed metalworkers rather than designers. One of the effects of this innovation is to make it difficult to tell the origin of individual jewels
Right: design for a pendant jewel by Etienne Delaune, c.1560
Below: pendant jewel in gold and enamel set with topaz, early 16th century. (British Museum)

Right: portrait of Henry VIII by Hans Holbein, showing him wearing the huge 'balas ruby' chain or collar designed by Holbein himself (Galleria Nazionale, Rome)

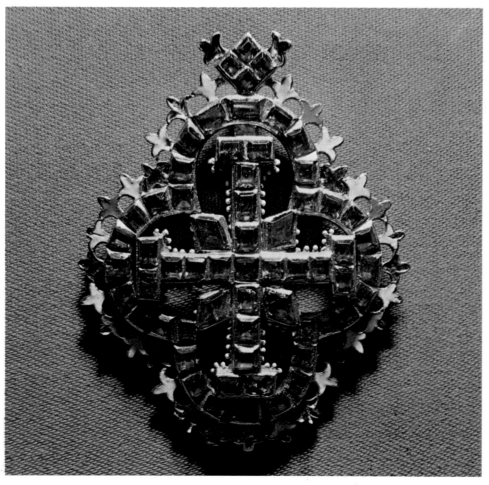

buckles, chains and pendants. One of these pendants is a prototype for a design which became widely popular throughout the High Renaissance. It is pear-shaped with two large cabochon stones set in raised claw-settings, with two figures sitting on the lower stone and supporting the upper; below the pendant are suspended three baroque pearls, a feature which is common to many late 16th century pendants. Other pendants designed by Solis have a religious overtone, being formed as crosses set with cabochon stones, with foliage and tiny cherubs.

Solis was the first of many master craftsmen to sell their designs wholesale. Another great example is Etienne Delaune, a Frenchman working in Strasbourg, who produced a pattern book, including a more elaborate version of Solis' pear-shaped pendant. Most of his designs are preserved in the Ashmolean Museum, Oxford. Others such as Erasmus Hornick, Matthias Zündt, Dürer and indeed Hans Holbein also produced engraved designs for publication. Much of this material, though conceived before 1560, took time to circulate and the designs are more relevant to the jewellery of the late Renaissance than the period under

ÆTATIS · · SVÆ · XLIX ·

Near right: chalcedony cameo in enamelled gold setting, depicting Leda and the Swan with Cupid, late 16th century
Centre right: chalcedony cameo in enamelled gold setting, depicting Europa and the Bull
Far right: enamelled gold medallion of St. John the Evangelist, late 16th century. (All at Kunsthistorisches Museum, *Vienna)*

Chain necklaces became popular for both men and women during the 16th century. The two mid-16th century portraits here show different styles of chain necklace adopted by women
Right: Cranach's Portrait of a Young Lady. (National Gallery, London)
Far right: a Medici princess by Bronzino (Uffizi, Florence)

review in this particular section.

The fashion for portrait cameos for use in both *enseignes* and pendants is thought to have originated in Italy very early in the century. Certainly by 1530 the fashion had spread to France and England and both François I and Henry VIII retained their own cameo-cutters.

Cameos and gold were combined in a number of ways: traditional cameos protected by a framework of enamelled gold, and cameo heads against a background of enamel. The first of these two methods tended to reduce the work of the goldsmith to that of a stone-setter. The competitive attitude of the time would not allow this and so the goldsmiths took to producing portrait medallions solely from gold and enamel; while some of these are rather crude, pieces such as the head and shoulders of Charles V (King of Spain and Emperor of Germany – illustrated on page 150) demonstrate a new degree of skill in the enamellers' art.

In other medallions goldsmiths tried to prove their superiority over lapidaries by setting enamel portraits against flat areas of polished stone, thereby confining the lapidaries' skills to that of stone-polishers.

155

Right: enamel, gold and pearl pendant designed and possibly made by Etienne Delaune, depicting Joseph at the Well. English, c.1550. (British Museum)

In the 16th century, as in many previous centuries, jewellers relied largely on royal patronage. Many goldsmiths were therefore attracted to England from the Continent to take advantage of the extravagant love of jewels shown by Henry VIII and Elizabeth I of England Right: portrait of Elizabeth I (attributed to Nicholas Hilliard), c. 1575, demonstrating this exaggerated love of display indulged by the English monarchy. (National Portrait Gallery, London)

Another popular form used for both brooches and pendants, possibly inspired by illuminated manuscripts, was the monogram. Intertwined initials of a husband and wife were used as a sign of betrothal, usually in gold set with precious stones. Judging by contemporary reports, Henry VIII appears to have had a penchant for these and commissioned Holbein to design them for him and, with that monarch's marital upsets, this must have amounted to a standing order.

A votive version of this monogram brooch was the IHS (*In Hac [Cruce] Salus* – In this [Cross] is Salvation). Here again the letters are made of gold, decorated with precious stones and surmounted by a small cruciform.

Heart-shaped brooches and pendants continued to be fashionable, particularly at the English Court. Henry VIII is reported to have had 39 of them but it is impossible to judge how many of these were produced in the 16th Century and how many were inherited from ancestors. Cruciforms were a standard form of self-adornment by this time, and indeed continue to be so to this day.

Women's fashions changed radically and more quickly than before. Hair styles were no longer constricted to

the extremes of the 15th century and cluster-brooches were widely used on top of the head or at the ear, to hold the arrangement in place. Ear-rings which lost favour in the 15th century start to make a re-appearance but are still the exception rather than the rule. The only examples portrayed are pearl drops of indifferent design.

The fashion for gold chain necklaces is again thought to have originated in Italy. Some of these were massive. Henry VIII was invoiced in 1511 for £199 for a single chain weighing 98 ounces (about the weight of 500 wedding ring bands). These chains served a dual purpose: firstly, the obvious function of self-adornment; secondly, the links were each weighed and represented a unit of currency so that in an emergency they could be removed and used as payment for goods received.

In France and England these massive chains were worn solely by men but in Germany and Flanders women also wore them. This is illustrated in Beham's portrait of Ursual Rudolph Stüpf wearing two chains so massive that you cannot imagine her frail neck standing the weight for more than a few minutes at a time.

Lighter chains were worn by women

everywhere, either plain or with a pendant. When on their own, these chains were allowed to fall inside the low-cut square neckline, but with the pendants attached they were worn outside the dress. A portrait of a Medici princess shows her wearing an elegant chain of moderate weight with a portrait medallion and, at the base of her throat, a simple row of pearls – which was another popular line in neckwear.

Chokers, similar to the one worn by the angel in the Montefeltro altarpiece, are quite common in early 16th century portraits. One such, a portrait by Baldassare Estense, shows the same basic design of two rows of small stones separated by larger ones, but worn at the base of the throat rather than round the neck itself. Other paintings show double rows of beads worn in the same position and decorated with pendants.

Heavy jewelled chains were also worn by both sexes. The most famous of these is undoubtedly that of Henry VIII, designed for him by Holbein and displayed in the same artist's portrait of the King. Alternate round and square, facet-cut balas rubies (red spinels) are set in medallions of gold foliage, and between each ruby there

About half-way through the century large, pear-shaped pendants came into fashion. Designers like Hans Collaert included them in their pattern books
Left: detail from the portrait (right) by the 16th century artist Antoine Caron shows a typical pendant. (Alte Pinakothek, Munich)
Above right: engraving from a pattern book by Hans Collaert. (Victoria & Albert Museum, London)

are two massive pearls similarly set; and the entire piece is hinged to make a flexible chain. A duplicate of this magnificent piece, made later to Holbein's design, can be seen in the British Museum. Henry, together with François I and the Medici family, was one of the great patrons of this period and records show that he possessed several necklaces of similar design but set with different stones.

A portrait of Eleanor of Austria (wife of François I) shows her wearing a similar chain, again worn over the shoulders rather than round the neck, forming a yoke. Alternate pearls and rubies are set in oval scrollwork medallions of gold and niello, interspersed with smaller circular gold beads also decorated with niello. Another interesting feature in the same painting is her string of pearls. This extremely long set of matched pearls (which would reach to her waist if worn in the traditional fashion) is fastened at the top of her cleavage with a brooch, thus forming a 'W' encircling the breasts.

Carved gems were widely used in finger-rings. There is nothing particularly original about the overall design of rings for men or women incorporating heraldic devices and mythological

Renaissance jewels are typified by the use of baroque pearls. They were incorporated into figurative designs with considerable inventiveness. Nowhere was this achieved with greater success than in the famous Canning jewel Left: the Canning jewel is set with pearls, rubies and diamonds, the entire torso of a merman being formed from a single pearl, c.1580. It was said to have been given to one of the Mogul emperors by a Medici prince, and was later named after Lord Canning, the first viceroy of India, who acquired the jewel there in the mid-19th century and brought it back to England. (Victoria & Albert Museum, London)

Many jewels of similar design to the Canning have been found originating from workshops in different parts of Europe, which emphasizes the impact of pattern books
*Right and below: two baroque pearl pendant jewels in gold, enamel and precious stones, probably Italian, late 16th century. (*Museo degli Argenti, Florence)

scenes, but a new design of reliquary-ring appears towards the end of this period. These rings have high box-bezels which open to hold reliquaries and are particularly interesting examples of enamelling. The shoulders and the shank are usually enamelled with geometric patterns both inside and out and, in some cases, the bezel is set with pearls or precious stones.

More elaborate jewellery appears towards the end of this period and is so typical of the late Renaissance when extravagance was seen on a scale never before contemplated.

About half-way through the 16th century there was a definite change towards 'mannerism' in major arts, a change which was reflected in jewellery about ten years later. Not that forms themselves changed radically, or materials, or techniques; it was a change of personality, a change of emphasis from classic simplicity to an elaborate showiness which was utterly contrary to the basic philosophy of the prime movers of the early Renaissance.

Excess was the essence of late 16th century taste. Everything was exaggerated to the point of becoming comical or grotesque. Dress, under the influence of the newly-wealthy Spain,

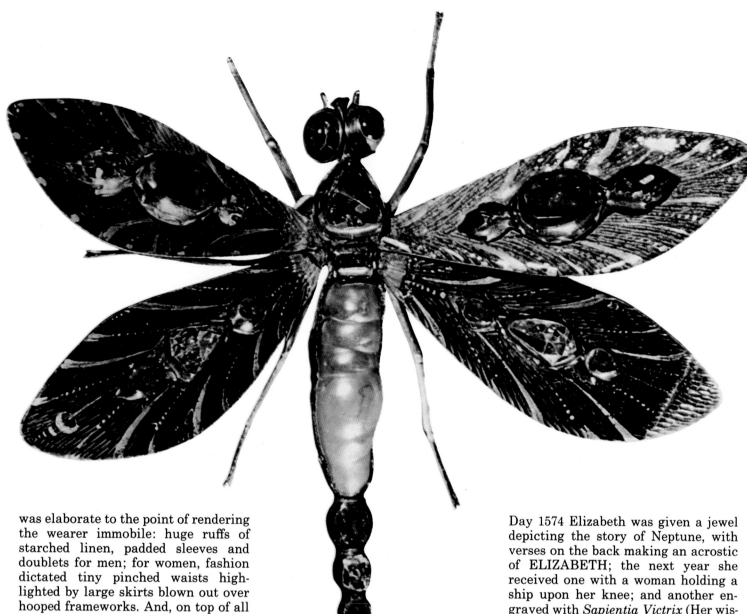

was elaborate to the point of rendering the wearer immobile: huge ruffs of starched linen, padded sleeves and doublets for men; for women, fashion dictated tiny pinched waists highlighted by large skirts blown out over hooped frameworks. And, on top of all this, jewellery was worn in profusion. Precious stones were sewn onto clothing, necklaces, head-dresses, jewelled collars; rings were worn on every finger, fans were jewelled – nothing was left undecorated.

Perhaps the most important development that this profusion brought about was the trend towards the *parure*. Until this time jewels had been made as individual items, but now the idea of matching sets was introduced, often consisting of a short pendant-necklace, a long necklace and a head-dress. But *parures* could be composed of any number of pieces. Henry VIII was reported to have had three *parures* but he was rather ahead of his time.

His daughter, Elizabeth I, was even more enthusiastic about jewellery and it became a tradition amongst her courtiers to present her with *parures* or single pieces of jewellery on New Year's Day. Dr. Joan Evans, the art historian, tells us that on New Year's

Above and right: brooches in gold, enamel, precious stones and baroque pearl. Dragon-fly, late 16th century; cockerel, Italian, late 16th century from the collection of the Grand Duke of Tuscany. (Museo degli Argenti, *Florence*)

Day 1574 Elizabeth was given a jewel depicting the story of Neptune, with verses on the back making an acrostic of ELIZABETH; the next year she received one with a woman holding a ship upon her knee; and another engraved with *Sapientia Victrix* (Her wisdom rules).

In 1584, Sir Christopher Hatton gave her an attire for the head of seven pieces, three formed as crowns Imperial, four as victories, all set with diamonds, rubies, pearls and opals. On New Year's Day the following year he gave her a head-dress and collar, the former of links formed as crowns Imperial and hearts.

Apart from these gifts, Elizabeth retained a number of Court goldsmiths to satisfy her insatiable demand for jewels. The two most distinguished of these were Master Spilman, a German and the only foreigner in the team, and Nicholas Hilliard, the painter, miniaturist and jeweller who was the third generation of a family of London goldsmiths.

There may be a connection between Elizabeth's importance and power, both at home and abroad, and the fact that at this time there was a definite change of emphasis away from jewels for men

Opposite page: pendant jewel depicting St. George and the Dragon in gold, enamel and precious stones with pendant pearls, late 16th century. (Grünes Gewölbe, Dresden)
Left: pendant jewel in the form of a figure on a cornucopia, in gold, enamel and precious stones, late 16th century. (Museo degli Argenti, Florence)
Below: devotional Agnus Dei pendant in enamelled gold with diamonds, garnets and pearls. Central European, late 16th century. (Victoria & Albert Museum, London)

and towards jewels for women. (Henry VIII, for instance, certainly owned more jewels than all his wives put together.) No matter who was the guiding light it was a fashion keenly adopted throughout the Royal families of Europe where women found themselves, partly by circumstance and partly by design, in a much more powerful position in the second half of the century. Men opted for rich clothing embroidered with precious stones sewn onto the material rather than a profusion of loose jewellery.

The three major patrons of the late Renaissance were Elizabeth, her arch rival Philip II of Spain (whose father, Emperor Charles V, had been a great patron earlier in the century) and once again the Medici family. The Spanish Court was richer than ever before, thanks to the gold and precious stones which were being shipped back from the New World, an action which helped the jewellers of Europe but destroyed several magnificent gold working civilizations (see page 180).

It was not in the lands of the great patrons, however, but in Germany that the greatest quantity and most skilful jewellery was made. The most influential figure was Erasmus Hornick of

Nuremberg whose book of designs, published in 1562, contained ideas which revolutionized brooch and pendant design. *Enseignes* went out of fashion, reflecting the move towards feminine jewellery, and brooches of mermaids, sea serpents, dragons, lizards and other mythological creatures came into vogue. A characteristic feature of these brooches is the use of baroque pearls (large, irregularly shaped ones) to represent parts of the anatomy of the figure or beast being portrayed.

Perhaps the finest example of this is the Canning jewel, to be seen in the Victoria and Albert Museum in London. The jewel, which measures less than three inches overall, depicts a merman. The torso is perfectly represented by one huge baroque pearl, the head is gold with the face enamelled white and the beard and hair gold; the arms are also of white enamel, one being decorated with bracelets; the tail is enamelled in a number of different colours and set with precious stones. In his left hand he carries an openwork shield, again enamelled and set with stones, and in his right a scimitar. Suspended from the pendant are three of the baroque pearls which seem to be almost obligatory for all these pieces.

The workmanship of the Canning jewel is superb and the fastidiousness of the craftsmen of this era is reflected in the setting method of the pendant pearls. The traditional method was to thread the pearl on a piece of wire and twist it at the bottom, but with almost all these figurative pendants a much more complex method was employed. A piece of thick wire is threaded through the pearl, sawn through the middle like a split-pin and a tiny wedge driven up through the middle, forcing the wires against the sides of the hole. The wedge is equipped with a head like a drawing-pin, which finishes the stone with a neat rivet.

Another new development reflected in this Canning jewel is the use of cut stones. Firstly, they are cut square with a table (a flat top) and secondly, they are used to highlight the design in linear patterns rather than to supply the richness of the piece. In other pendants of this time the rigid geometric use of stones is even more pronounced – for instance the cockerel brooch in the *Museo degli Argenti* in Florence. Again this is modelled round a baroque pearl which forms the bird's chest and neck. The face and body are enamelled gold but the tail feathers,

each modelled separately, are studded with square stones, neatly graded for size and positioned with rigid symmetry to emphasize the linear quality.

In Spain birds were preferred to sea monsters and it is interesting to note that the species are often tropical, never seen in Spain until examples were brought from the New World.

The *nef* or ship brooch is generally considered to have evolved in Venice but it was not long before it enjoyed a general popularity, particularly in England, probably stimulated by the nation's sea supremacy. Sir Francis Drake is reported to have given one to Queen Elizabeth I. The designs range from comparatively realistic fully-rigged ships with figures on board, to the highly abstract with the pendant chains forming the mast and the rigging emerging from a stylized hull shape. The materials used also vary from enamelled gold, decorated with precious stones, to simple pieces of crystal held in a gold framework.

The movement of jewellery from country to country again confuses the origins of individual objects but the great jewels are thoroughly documented and represented in portraits. Jewels changed hands by inheritance,

Right: the Danny jewel, a simplified nef made from a section of narwhal's tusk (unicorn's horn) mounted in enamelled gold, English, c.1560. It was owned by the Campions of Danny in Sussex. (Victoria & Albert Museum) Below: Venetian nef in gold, enamel and precious stones, late 16th century. (Victoria & Albert Museum, London)

but more often they were pledged as surety against loans. The great pearl necklace worn by Elizabeth I (shown in a portrait in the National Portrait Gallery, London), for instance, was originally given to Catherine de' Medici by Pope Clement VII in 1533 when she married Henri, second son of François I. When their child, François II, married Mary Queen of Scots, Mary inherited the pearls on his death in 1560 and took them back to Scotland. On her death they passed to her son James I and were later purchased for £3,000 by Elizabeth I. The same string of pearls, therefore, had been in the possession of four European Royal Houses in the space of a generation and a half. And since then they have been in the possession of the Houses of Holland, Bohemia and Hanover.

Despite these complications, however, it is almost certain that the majority of noteworthy jewellery continued to be made, or at least designed, in Germany and Flanders. After Hornick came Hans Collaert of Antwerp. He too produced designs for pendants based on mythical monsters but they were considerably less lumpy and grotesque than the earlier ones. They tended to be well balanced

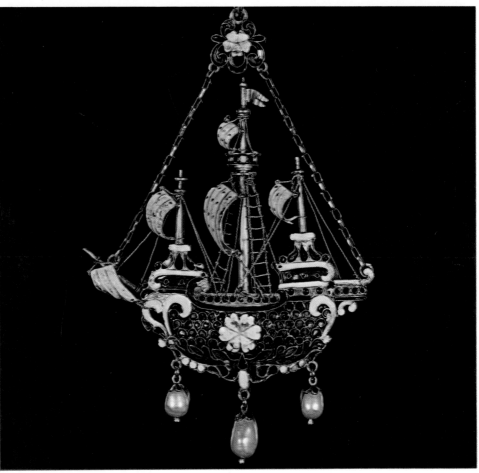

One of the most beautiful 16th century jewel to have survived is the Heneage (or Armada) jewel made for Elizabeth I to give to her Treasurer at War, Sir Thomas Heneage in recognition of his services at the time of the Armada. It is believed to have been designed by Nicholas Hilliard, c.1588 Right: the front of the Heneage jewel shows a raised profile of the Queen against an enamelled background and the rim is set with rubies and diamonds Below: the enamelled back of the jewel depicts the Ark being tossed at sea and bears the legend (taken from the contemporary Naval Award medal) Saevas Tranquilla Per Undas *(Steady in rough seas)*

compositions with figures riding on the backs of animals. Other designs by him revert to religious and mythical subjects, many pear-shaped, not unlike those produced by Virgil Solis, more than 40 years earlier. Again, however, stones are used to provide a linear frame for the figures rather than being incorporated in the figures themselves.

By the 1590s religious, pear-shaped brooches were produced in light openwork, the main similarity with brooches of the previous decade being the overall shape and the three pendant pearls.

At the turn of the century, the design was taken one stage further by a French jeweller, Daniel Mignot, who was working in Germany. His engravings retain the overall pear shape, and in some cases the pendant pearls, but they are for the most part non-figurative, pure geometric designs of fretwork set with precious stones chosen by shape and colour to preserve a perfect symmetry. Aigrettes, for holding hat feathers, were designed by him and his followers in the same manner and mark a return to good taste from the extravagance of the previous 50 years.

Despite the decline of the *enseigne*, portrait cameos retained and if any-

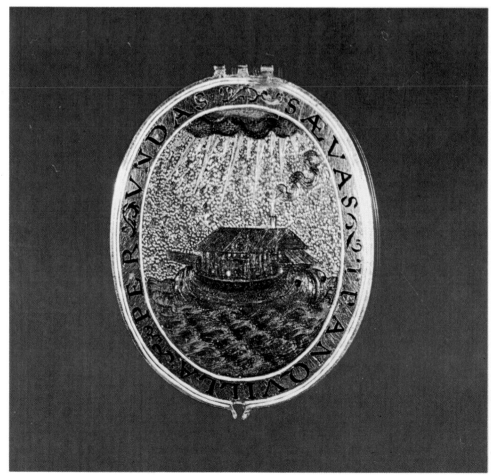

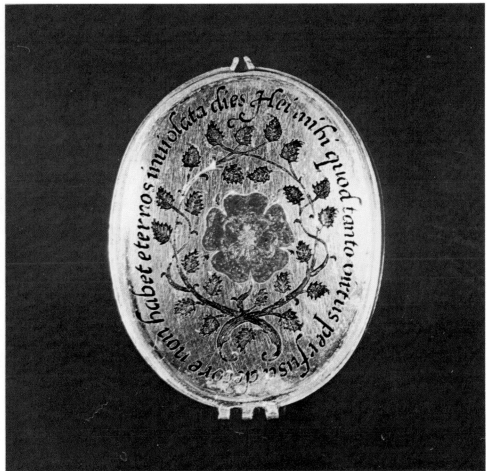

thing increased their popularity in the latter half of the century. A custom, introduced by Elizabeth I, was to give cameo brooches or pendants as gifts to her subjects for favours or services rendered.

Many of these have survived to this day and the most magnificent, the Heneage or Armada jewel (possibly designed by Nicholas Hilliard) is now in the Victoria and Albert Museum, London. It is a two-sided pendant; on the front there is a cameo of Elizabeth in profile, showing her extraordinary sloping forehead and long angular nose; this cameo is mounted on a ground of polished lapis lazuli, the outer framework being formed like a ring-brooch of the 14th century, and enamelled and set with diamonds and rubies. The back of the pendant is gold engraved and enamelled with an ark in a storm, and round this there is a motto; this whole panel is hinged and lifts up to reveal a delightful miniature of the Queen painted by Hilliard himself and dated 1588. Inside the lid there is an enamelled rose surrounded by foliage and another inscription.

Heart pendants appear to have lost favour after the death of Henry VIII but there is one startling exception,

Right: finger-ring in gold, enamel and pearls with box bezel which opens to reveal a secret compartment, late 16th century. (Museo Poldi-Pezzoli, Milan)
Below: pendant in gold with enamel, rubies, emeralds and diamonds, late 16th century
Below right: pendant in gold and enamel, English, late 16th century. (Victoria & Albert Museum, London)

the Darnley jewel which is one of the most highly praised single items of jewellery produced in the late 16th century. The pendant, now in the collection of Her Majesty Queen Elizabeth II, is a true *tour de force* of the enameller's art. It was commissioned by Lady Margaret Douglas on the death of her husband and is shaped as a heart not only for romantic reasons but also because the heart was the crest of the Douglas family. The front of the pendant is set with a heart-shaped cabochon sapphire, surmounted by a crown of enamelled gold and surrounded with four figures representing four of the Virtues in white against a coloured background. The sapphire and its setting are hinged and when opened reveal two clasped hands; the crown is similarly hinged and shows two hearts joined by a knot. The reverse is a panel of delicate enamel covered with symbols; the sun, moon, a phoenix and a human figure, which presumably had some secret significance. This panel opens and would originally have held, like the Heneage jewel, a miniature – probably of the late husband.

The rigid mode of dress severely limited the forms of jewellery which could be worn; broad lace cuffs ruled out bracelets in most cases but the cuffs themselves were often sewn with pearls; high necks made the wearing of ear-rings difficult and the only examples portrayed are similar to those described in the last chapter – simple pearl drops or clusters.

Rings, on the other hand, enjoyed an even greater popularity. They are basically the same forms as those produced in the early Renaissance but more complex and sophisticated; box bezels open to display scenes enamelled *en ronde bosse*; two rings intertwined are used as tokens of betrothal; and other purely decorative themes are developed for traditional bezel rings.

In different parts of Europe, craftsmen were developing new techniques to arouse their patrons' interests. In Spain motif jewellery was produced by a technique known as *verre églomisé*, a piece of glass or rock crystal decorated from behind with religious scenes in black enamel highlighted with gold leaf. These panels were usually housed in a border of enamelled gold and worn as pendants.

The workshops of Prague, which had been in existence since the early Middle Ages, gained new prominence under

175

Left: gold and enamel badge of honour set with a medal of Wilhelm, Count Palatine of the Rhine, German, 1572. (Victoria & Albert Museum, London)

Below: the Barbor jewel, enamelled gold and set with rubies and diamonds, housing an onyx cameo of Elizabeth I. It was said to have been made to commemorate the intercession of the Queen in saving William Barbor from the stake in Smithfield, London. English, late 16th century. (Victoria & Albert Museum, London)

Rudolf II, Emperor of Germany, and became famous for a technique which is generally known as Transylvanian enamel. This is an incredibly delicate version of the *cloisonné* enamel of the Middle Ages; detailed geometric or floral designs are mapped out in fine wire on a backplate and filled with coloured enamel. Unlike previous *cloisonné* enamel, however, the remainder of the backplate is covered with transparent enamel and gives the impression that the designs are appliqué.

In Venice fine filigree came back into fashion towards the turn of the century. The best example of this is a string of beads in the *Museo Poldi-Pezzoli* in Milan. Each bead is constructed of a fine web of open-work filigree and decorated with stylized flowers in green and blue enamel.

It could be said in summary that the late Renaissance was a period where excess preceded good taste and aesthetic appreciation, but it was a state of mind which lasted for no more than 40 years. By the start of the 17th century, there was a move towards symmetry and discipline by goldsmiths designers – and presumably patrons – in every country.

Venetian filigree and enamel work towards the end of the 16th century was extremely fine Below: necklace of hollow beads constructed in fine filigree and coloured enamels, Venetian, late 16th century (and right) enlargement of a single bead from the necklace (Museo Poldi-Pezzoli, Milan)

Obsession for Pearls

When describing a piece of jewellery the phrase '. . . set with pearls and precious stones' is used frequently. The reason for this, of course, is that a pearl is not a stone; it is one of four organic substances widely used in jewellery, the other three being coral (the skeleton of a marine animal), jet (a very hard coal), and amber (the fossilized resin of pine trees).

Pearl is produced when a foreign body such as a grain of sand is introduced into an oyster. The irritation causes the mollusc to pour fluid over the invading particle until it is totally encased in pearl tissue. The resultant pearl comes in an enormous variety of sizes, shapes and colours. The rarest and most sought after (until the introduction of cultured pearls) were perfectly spherical, but other shapes such as the button, pear, seed, blister, freshwater – and the baroque pearl – offer jewellers great scope to incorporate their irregularity into designs.

Apart from the familiar pink, grey, silver, yellow, green, bronze, blue and black pearls are all found from different oyster beds.

Because of their appearance, pearls have generally been associated with raindrops. The Chinese, for instance, believed that they were formed from drops of liquid issued from the mouth of their rain-god, the Sky Dragon. Even comparatively sophisticated western writers such as Pliny expressed a view that they were formed when raindrops fell into an open oyster.

In the west pearls were generally considered to have medicinal properties, particularly for heart complaints 'since they came from the hearts of oysters'. They were also recommended as a cure for insanity, when they were either dissolved in lemon juice, taken in powdered form or crushed and mixed with milk. These various concoctions were attributed with the power to alter the course of nature in a great number of ways ranging from curing stomach ulcers and epilepsy to improving the voice and preserving chastity.

In France, during the 16th century, it was held that pearls improved the complexion and so became a popular indulgence of the aristocracy. In Classical Rome they were considered to be the jewel of Venus and thus became an essential ingredient in love potions. The legend of Cleopatra toasting Anthony with a dissolved pearl (which cost more than the entire banquet she had provided in his honour) is well known.

While pearls were available in Western Europe in the Middle Ages, it was not until the mid-16th century that they arrived in such enormous quantities. The English Court's demand for them (exemplified by vast expenditure such as £3,000 for the necklace of Catherine de Medici) was so great that Elizabeth was forced to buy artificial ones at a penny each to sew onto her dresses. A little later a report tells us that when the Duke of Buckingham visited Paris to collect the bride of Charles I, he was dressed in satin, decorated with pearls worth £20,000.

The fascination of pearls is based not only on their intrinsic beauty and their commercial value, but also on their elusiveness. With every oyster shell you open there is always the chance that it will contain mud – or a pearl (possibly worth several thousand pounds), or it could be a freak like one found in Ceylon (Sri Lanka) which contained no less than 87 pearls.

To retain lustre and avoid eventual decomposition, pearls must be worn regularly.

Pre-Columbian America

Throughout the history of jewellery we have seen personal gain take precedence over aesthetic historical considerations but there has never been such an exercise in sheer greed and stupidity as demonstrated by the 'noblemen' of Spain during the 16th century. When Columbus opened up the American continent in 1493 he exposed for the first time two of the great races of goldsmiths ever to have existed – the Aztecs of Mexico and the Incas of Peru.

The story of the brutality of the Conquistadores is well known and does not concern a work of this type but the fact that in the space of less than 100 years more than 30 tons of pre-Columbian American jewellery was pillaged and melted can only be viewed with amazement and sadness. Our knowledge therefore of their jewellery, particularly that of Mexico, depends largely on the reports of contemporary diaries and the evidence of isolated objects that had been overlooked for centuries but retrieved in recent years.

When Cortés landed in Mexico in 1521 he knew that he had found the 'land of gold' which he had been promising his sponsors in Spain. He found a sophisticated civilization with brilliant architecture and a high level of intellectual and religious development. The earth was rich with minerals – silver, tin, copper and lead, but, above all, gold could be found in abundance. Aztec goldsmiths were skilled in all the technical processes developed in the Old World and were producing objects of great craftsmanship. This quotation from Jacques Soustelle's book, *Daily Life of the Aztecs*, will give some idea of the level of self-adornment: 'Women wore ear-rings, necklaces and bracelets on their arms and ankles. The men had the same ornaments but, in addition, they pierced the septum of their nose to hold a gem or metal jewels; they also made holes in the skin beneath their lower lip so as to wear chin-ornaments of crystal, shell, amber, turquoise or gold; and they placed huge and splendid structures of feathers upon their heads or their backs.

'In this display of rank and luxury everything was strictly regulated in conformity with hierarchic order. Only the Emperor might wear the turquoise nose-ornament and the division between his nostrils was perforated with great ceremony after his election; and only warriors of a certain rank had the right to wear such and such a jewel, whose kind and shape was exactly laid down. The emblems or feather ornaments, dazzlingly coloured head-dresses, bronze-green plumes of quetzal feathers, immense butterflies, cones made of feathers or gold, cloth or feather–mosaic banners to be fixed to the shoulders of the Chiefs, decorated shields – all these were reserved for those who had won the right to them by

their exploits and death was the punishment for any man who should presume to attribute to himself one of these marks of honour.'

The unsuspecting Emperor of the Aztecs sent generous gifts to Cortés which according to reports included: '. . . shields, helmets, cutlasses embossed with plates and ornaments of pure gold, collars and bracelets of the same metal, sandals, fans, panaches and crests of variegated feathers intermingled with gold and silver thread and sprinkled with pearls and precious stones; imitations of birds in wrought and cast gold and silver, of exquisite workmanship . . .'

Of all this nothing remains. Not one item dutifully shipped back to the Spanish Court escaped the melting pot. Ironically, one of the few true Aztec pieces remaining is the head-dress Montezuma is said to have presented to Cortés (now in the *Museum für Völkerkunde* in Vienna). It is an extravagant object made from green quetzal feathers woven and studded with gold.

The only remaining Mexican jewellery is in fact Mixtec, an earlier culture absorbed by the Aztecs. It is clear from this that they were conversant with all the metalwork techniques known in the Old World and particularly skilful at lost wax casting. The best single hoard of Mixtec objects was found in a re-used tomb at Monte Albán. One pendant from this tomb demonstrates the obsession with astronomy: it is in four panels, the top one showing two ball players with a skull, the second a sun disc, the third a moon glyph and the fourth an earth symbol. Below this are suspended four gold bells. Each component has been cast separately, assembled and articulated.

The Andes

Thirty-four years after Cortés entered Mexico, Pizarro and his ragged band of 165 mercenaries defeated a great Inca army of more than 30,000 and entered the capital of Cuzco in Peru. The sight that greeted them must have been beyond the wildest dreams of the most romantic adventurer.

A contemporary writer described the palaces of Cuzco as: '. . . the walls were lined with gold plates and, in preparing the stone they left niches in which they put all sorts of animals and human figures, birds or wild beasts . . . all of which were made from gold or silver. The imitation of nature was so consummate that they even produced the leaves and little plants that grow on walls. They also scattered here and there gold or silver lizards, butterflies, mice and snakes which were so well made and cunningly placed, that one had the impression of seeing them run about in all directions.' Even more fantastic was the Temple of the Sun: 'All four walls were covered from roof to floor with plates and slabs of gold . . . at harvest time the temple terraces were carpeted with artificial cornfields made entirely of gold.'

Gold to the Incas, like the ancient Egyptians, held the power of the sun. This belief is illustrated in their version of the creation: 'Three eggs fell from heaven, one gold, one silver and one copper. From the three came the nobles, the princesses and the common people.'

The story of how Pizarro looted and murdered is well known. Vast quantities of Inca jewellery were lost forever and it is fortunate that the inhabitants of Peru had for centuries subscribed to the view that the 'ferryman of darkness' had to be well paid if the passage into the after-life was to be assured. Their dead were buried with vast treasures, treasures which escaped the attention of the Spaniards. Paulo Inca confessed in Cuzco that: '. . . if all the treasure of the tombs, the temples, and burial grounds was put together, the amount which the Spaniards had would appear as but a drop of water taken from a large jar or as a fistful of grain taken from a measure of maize . . .'

The reason that this vast buried treasure was overlooked is twofold: firstly, the complexity of the Inca burial rites and, secondly, the disapproval with which the Church viewed the plundering of burial grounds be they Christian or pagan.

The Inca Empire, covering Peru, Ecuador, Bolivia and North Chile, had been in existence for 200 years when it was destroyed in the 1520s. Cultures familiar with sophisticated goldworking and lapidary techniques had existed for more than a thousand years earlier. Hoards discovered in the present century have provided us with a vast quantity of jewellery from three of these cultures, the Mochicas, the Nascas and the Chimu, all of whom were conquered by the Incas and might well have been responsible for the bulk of their goldwork.

The Mochicas, who inhabited the Peruvian coast, were probably the earliest metalworkers of the Andes. Certainly by the 4th century AD they had mastered welding, repoussé, smelting, gilding and lost wax casting.

In the graves, along with the idols, weapons and vessels of gold, quantities of jewellery have been found designed for the use of both the living and the dead. Bracelets, diadems and breast-plates, all beaten in repoussé from a single sheet of gold, are decorated with geometric, zoomorphic designs. Three-dimensional brooches of gold and turquoise represent human faces; pendants and ear-rings of the same materials depict strange creatures and birds; but the two most fantastic Mochica objects ever found are pieces of clothing rather than jewellery in its strictest sense. The first, a ceremonial cloak, is made up from more than 1,600 gold discs sewn onto a piece of cloth. On the lower edge there is a border of plates in echelon with eyes in high relief. From these hang discs portraying animal figures. In the centre is the face of the sun with eight rays radiating from it, some terminating in snakes' heads, while the remainder of the discs are covered in zoomorphic motifs.

The other extraordinary pieces are gloves of sheet gold which were placed on the hands of nobles and priests when they were buried. The craftsmanship in these is brilliant down to the finest detail of the simulated fingernails.

The Nasca graves were discovered in 1901 and, although it is for ceramics that this culture will be remembered, a large quantity of exciting goldwork was also produced. Very little is known of this civilization save that it lasted from about the 7th century until the 9th. The Nascas produced jewellery in various forms; bracelets, nose-ornaments, neck-pieces and, while the workmanship is generally inferior to the Mochicas', the design is fascinating. The obsessional sun-worship is much more pronounced in the Nasca pieces, particularly in the funeral masks which represent grotesque faces with rays emanating from them, once again terminating in serpents.

The most spectacular and numerous finds of pre-Columbian jewellery were made by Brunning in the 1930s in the Lambayeque district belonging to the Chimu culture. Tens of thousands of objects have been recovered and represent the greatest find of goldware from any ancient civilization. The Chimu goldsmiths surpassed anything achieved by the Mochicas or Nascas.

In addition to perfecting the techniques
used by their forerunners they evolved
a technique of their own which was to
hammer and weld gold of different
colours in one object to give a vibrant
polychromatic effect. They employed
a large range of precious stones in their
jewellery, including emeralds, lapis
lazuli, turquoise, pearls and rock
crystal which they cut and polished
with great precision. The range of
jewellery they produced is equally
impressive: bracelets, necklaces, ear-
rings, pectorals, crowns, belts, nose-
ornaments, burial masks and clothing
have all been found in large quantities.

The overall form of each category of
jewellery is standard but the decoration of each piece is unique. Ear-rings
for instance are large circular discs,
some simple with designs beaten in
repoussé, some in filigree with stones
inlaid, and others having small three-
dimensional birds attached to them.
Nose-ornaments are crescent-shaped
but again a variety of techniques are
employed to ensure that no two pieces
are the same. The Chimu believed that
to repeat a design would offend the
Gods who were responsible for their
craft.

Chimu burial masks are perhaps the

183

Right: gold funeral mask with emerald eyes and tears of pendant strings of polished emeralds. The flecks of red suggest that the gold was originally decorated with colour, Chimu period, c.12th/13th century AD. *(Coll. Miguel Mujica Gallo, Lima)*

most haunting and impressive pieces. A highly stylized face is beaten out of an oblong sheet of metal, curved at the bottom. In some cases the eyes are picked out with precious stones, nose-ornaments are added and invariably the mask is equipped with circular earrings, which were symbols of rank.

Necklaces come in several styles but are basically strung beads of gold and precious stones with pendants added. The design of the gold beads varies considerably from simple spheres to bells, animals and gods.

Jewellery has always been considered a minor art form but the objects from the Chimu culture are at last treated with the same reverence as the major arts, an attitude which happily is now being applied to contemporary goldsmiths. It is amazing to think that in the 19th century the Bank of England was still melting pre-Columbian goldware to bolster its reserves and that the British Museum was able to buy pieces for as little as ten per cent above scrap price. It is fortunate that the great Chimu finds were not made any earlier or they might have suffered the same tragic fate as those from other ancient civilizations.

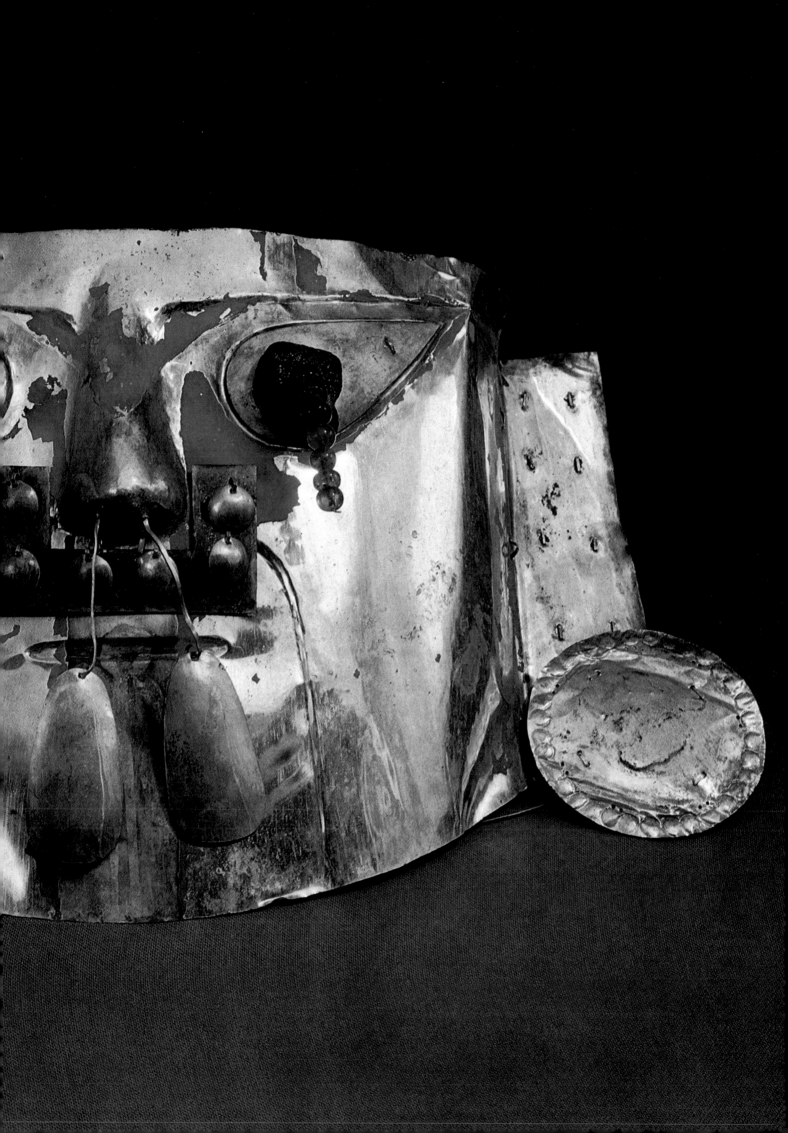

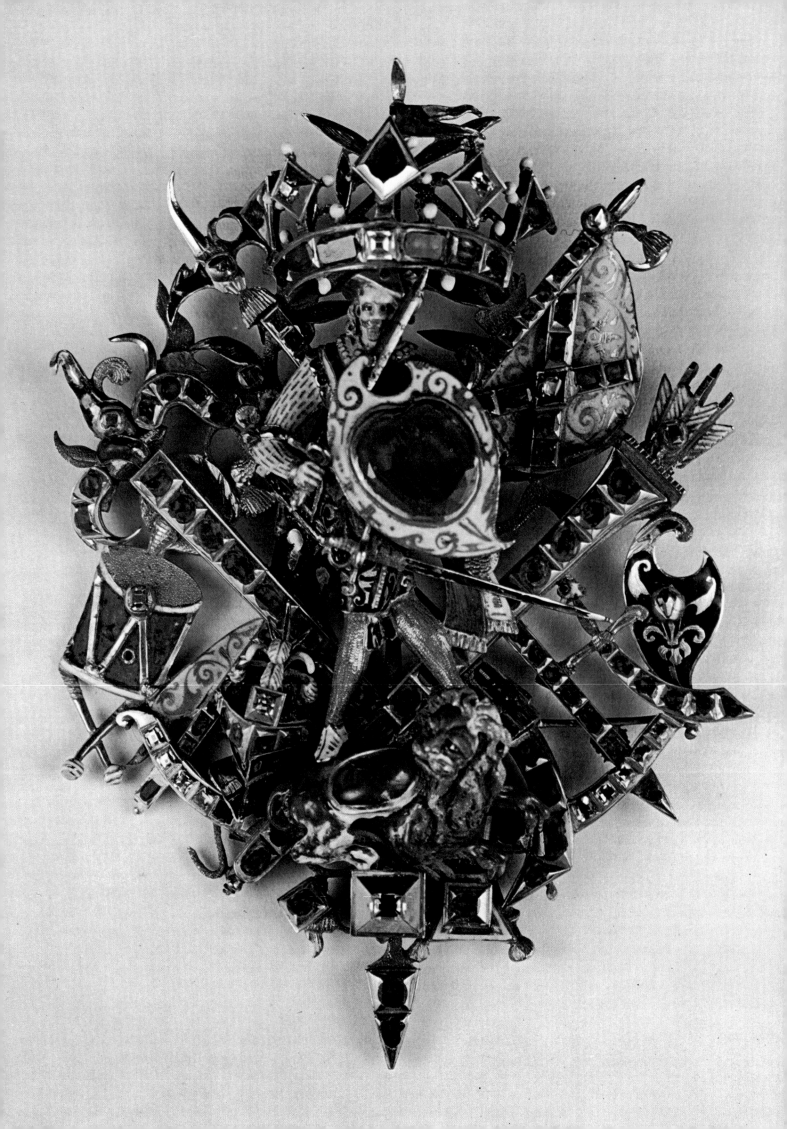

*Under the Commonwealth
Government any form of
ostentation was actively
discouraged and the centre for
fashion was once again Paris.
The 17th century was the era of
baroque design and stone-
cutting – both of which had a
great deal of effect on jewellery
design and craftsmanship
Left: 17th century German
pendant known as the Naseby
jewel. It was looted from the
baggage of Charles I at the
battle of Naseby in 1641 but
was probably made about the
turn of the century. It
represents the transitional
period between Renaissance
and true 17th century design.
(Sir John Soane's Museum,
London)
Below: 17th century French
cross in gold set with emeralds
and decorated with black and
white enamel and pearl
pendants*

The 17th Century

Age of Baroque

Like so many of the terms chosen to describe a period of art history, 'baroque' was originally a term of disparagement (in French *baroque* means grotesque or exaggerated). The term was introduced by critics of the 18th century to describe the art and architecture of the 17th century, which they considered to be vulgar and self-indulgent. It is obviously ridiculous to write off the artistic endeavours of a century which produced painters such as Rembrandt, Velasquez and Georges de La Tour, yet it was not until the early 20th century that baroque art was generally accepted for its true worth.

The whole of Western Europe was racked with war and political upheaval for the first half of the century; the Thirty Years War had the continent of Europe in turmoil and the Civil War raged in England from 1642 to 1646. It is understandable, therefore, that the amount of jewellery produced was considerably limited both for the impoverished Royal houses and the private sector. What little has survived from this time is a continuation of the trends set by engravers like Mignot at the end of the 16th century.

Two new forms, not strictly jewellery, captured the jewellers' imagination – watches and lockets. Watches were in existence in the 16th century but were extremely inaccurate and little more than expensive toys for the rich. With the invention of the balance wheel, they became comparatively reliable and were produced in enormous quantities. The 16th century watch movements had been incorporated into existing styles of jewellery but now watches became the forerunners of today's pocket watches. The forms of embellishment were very varied. One particularly fine example, now in the British Museum, has an enamelled face and an open-work lid set with one enormous cabochon sapphire and eight smaller ones.

A later example, also in the British Museum, by Daniel Bouquet is set with facet-cut rose diamonds and enamelled with flowers. It demonstrates two of the most significant design developments of the 17th century. Towards the end of the previous century a Frenchman, Jean Robin, opened a hot-house in Paris where he grew all kinds of exotic plants. He invited to his garden, now the Botanical Gardens of Paris, fabric designers who he believed could draw

187

inspiration from elegant natural forms. This started a vogue for floral motifs which, at its height, became obsessional and jewellery as much as any other art form reflected this fashion. Every type of flower was used and even vegetables enjoyed a brief popularity, but the firm favourite became the tulip which had been introduced to France fifty years earlier.

The other major influence was the introduction of facet-cut stones. Cardinal Mazarin, a senior minister at the Court of Louis XIV, sponsored a number of lapidaries to develop the rose-cut (see page 379). This cut, with its increased brilliance was adopted by jewellers throughout Europe with the result that the emphasis on gold diminished and jewels were designed to display stones to their best advantage. Emeralds, rubies, topaz and sapphires were all popular but it was diamonds that really caught the patrons' imagination.

The vastly increased intrinsic value is one of the reasons that so little 17th century jewellery has survived. As fashions changed, pieces containing precious stones were, not unnaturally, broken up and remade. Fashions in dress also altered dramatically. Gone are the extremes of the Elizabethan times: starched linen ruffs give way to soft lace collars. Gone, too, are the enormous hooped skirts – overall there is a new feeling of relaxed elegance and good taste.

In general, jewels were still predominantly made for women, with one dramatic exception – the French Court. Whereas his Queen showed little interest in them, the Sun King, Louis XIV, was obsessed by jewels and became one of the greatest patrons of all time. The King had been brought up with jewels by his mother, Anne of Austria. As a child his toy soldiers and guns were made from gold and silver by the Court jeweller and it is hardly surprising that he developed a passion for precious things. So determined was he to outshine everyone that he disapproved of any showiness by members of his Court. He even went to the extreme of sacking Nicolas Fouquet, his minister of finance, after Fouquet had thrown a party in his honour at which he gave jewels to the guests. Even when France was on the verge of bankruptcy he would not sacrifice his jewels to support the economy. He bought as many of the great stones reaching Europe from India and Brazil

Above left: memorial pendant
carrying a portrait of Charles I.
In silver gilt, probably
English, 1660
Above: late 17th century
pendant depicting the
Resurrection. Silver mount
with verre églomisé enamel
Above right: Dutch enamelled
pendant locket, c. 1630
Left: late 17th century
French ruby and diamond
pendant cross
Right: reminiscent of the late
Renaissance style in jewellery,
this gold and baroque pearl
dragon pendant dates from the
early 17th century

*Left: typical 17th century mourning jewel, English, in gold, enamel and pearls
Below: 17th century pendant jewel with Virgin and Child painted miniature under crystal, set in a sunburst of gold and surrounded by a border of enamel, pearls and precious stones*

as he could lay his hands on. His immense collection was further bolstered when he inherited the entire stone collection of the acquisitive Cardinal Mazarin.

Contemporary reports describe a *parure* which was one of the most prized items in his possession. It comprised 191 jewelled buttons, 396 eyelets and 90 frog-fastenings; the entire outfit was so heavy that the King is said to have stooped from its sheer weight. Also in the King's possession were jewelled shoe-buckles which, later on, were to become very fashionable with the bourgeoisie.

The pattern books of the 16th century became even more numerous and such publications as the *Livre de fleurs propre pour orfèvres et graveurs* published in 1680 did much to spread the floral motif from France to neighbouring countries.

The wars, plague and the movement towards Calvinism laid a firm emphasis on death and brought about a fashion of macabre 'death jewels.' The inventory of the Marquis de Rémouville mentions a chain of black ambergris beads, divided by nine skulls each set with 15 diamonds, and a pair of diamond skull ear-rings to match.

190

Left: 17th century gilt reliquary cruciform in rock crystal
Right: 17th century German pendant in gold with rubies. The carved wood Crucifixion is set behind rock crystal
Below: 17th century German fish pendant in gold with enamel (Kunsthistorisches Museum, Vienna)

Even more sinister were the *memento mori* which were fashionable in England. These were coffin-shaped pendants of plain or enamelled gold, sometimes decorated with skulls. The best, if that is the right word, example of *memento mori* was made at the beginning of the century, and is in the Victoria and Albert Museum in London. The coffin lid of enamelled gold opens to reveal a full skeleton and is inscribed: 'Through the Resurrection of Christe we shall be sanctified.' The workmanship of this gloomy object is quite superb. Another effect of this death jewellery was the introduction of jet, later on to become a fashionable material.

Although cut stones were the dominant feature of jewellery, enamelling continued to be used and several new techniques were developed. One, started by the Toutin family of Châteaudun, became particularly fashionable; a monochrome background was fired, the design painted on with a brush and the whole object then fired for a second time.

Another more complex process used by French enamellers was called *émail en résille sur verre*; the design was first engraved on a piece of glass and the cavities then lined with gold foil and filled with low melting point enamel. The problem with the process was to generate sufficient heat to fuse the enamel without melting or cracking the glass base. It was perhaps this problem that accounted for the short life of the technique, for in those days thermostats were unknown. These new enamelling processes were applied mainly for the decoration of snuff-boxes, miniature cases and watches rather than jewellery. Stones were destined to dominate jewellery for the next 250 years until the Art Nouveau craftsmen made enamelling fashionable once again.

In the second half of the century Europe was comparatively stable and more jewellery was produced for general wear. There were no dramatic changes in design but jewels, for the most part, were rather lighter and more open. Again, because most of the jewellery was set with precious stones, very little has survived and we must refer to the pattern books of great designers such as Gilles Légaré (published *c*.1663). He illustrates the two most fashionable forms of jewel: the *Sévigné*, (named after Madame de Sévigné), a bow-shaped brooch with pendants; and girandole ear-rings, which were a similar shape to the brooches, with three or five pendant stones. In many of his designs Légaré indicated the way in which the individual stones should be cut to make the most of the composition.

Necklaces were popular, again with the emphasis on precious stones, and in some cases the ribbon theme was the central design, while in others it was used to construct the links. Bracelets also enjoyed a renewed popularity; one surviving example, certainly designed and possibly made by Légaré, admirably illustrates the new delicacy. It consists of six plaques of floral openwork decorated with diamonds, emeralds and rubies. The gold of the plaques is enamelled but forms a sympathetic backcloth for the facet-cut stones rather than bringing colour to the piece.

In Portugal it was fashionable to wear a large brooch on one shoulder, shaped as a knot. This vogue was brought to England after Charles II married Catherine of Braganza but the fashion was later adapted to incorporate English tastes and the knot was replaced by girandole brooches, similar to the ear-rings.

Diamonds

As late 16th century was inevitably associated with the extravagant use of pearls, so the second half of the 17th century was the time for diamonds. There are reasons for this development: firstly, the increased trade with India (the traditional source of diamonds) and establishment of contact with Brazil, which vastly increased the supply of the stones in Western Europe; secondly, the improved lapidary techniques which revealed the extraordinary optical properties of this mineral and enabled goldsmiths to harness the diamond's glittering beauty.

Diamonds had been used in all jewellery-making nations since classical times and reports from the great Indian epic *Mahabharata*, set in the 3rd millennium BC suggest that the heroes wore diamonds, but these were uncut and polished only in their rough state. The problem had always been the fantastic hardness of the material which would not even yield to steel tools.

The diamond stands aloof from other stones as gold does from other metals. It is the hardest mineral ever discovered (10 on Mohs scale), has the highest refractive index, and is immune to attack from acid. It is yet another miracle of nature that turned an insignificant lump of carbon into the most prized material in the world by subjecting it to great heat and enormous pressure, a process which in recent years has been simulated, thus allowing minute artificial diamonds to be manufactured.

From the 15th century onwards European lapidaries had been struggling to master the material. The strides forward from polishing the natural octahedral crystal to splitting a single crystal and producing the table-cut were made thanks mainly to Indian lapidaries who taught the Europeans to cut diamond with diamond chips.

By the beginning of the 16th century there is evidence that they had learned to locate the cleavage point in a stone and split it. It was not until 1640, however, that the breakthrough was made. Cardinal Mazarin saw diamonds from India with random facets inflicted on the stone to cut out flaws or impurities. He saw the flashes of colour when the stone moved and determined that this was a property which could be harnessed. Consequently, he agreed to

Above left: 17th century Portuguese silver gilt triptych pendant set with boxwood carvings of Virgin and Child, the Annunciation, Visitation and Birth of Christ on a background of humming-bird feathers
Above right: 17th century rose-cut diamond pendant with an enamel portrait of Charles II
Above, far right: gold pendant set with crystals and decorated with coloured enamels. (Victoria & Albert Museum, London)
Right: 17th century pendant with figure of the Holy Child in wax behind glass and bordered with gold and precious stones
Far right: mid-17th century German brooch in gold set with diamonds. (Victoria & Albert Museum, London)

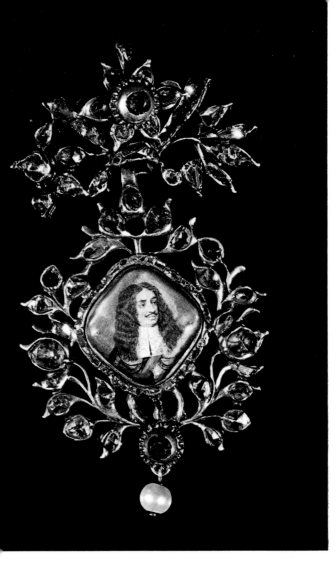

*Pattern books which had
emerged in the previous century
became even more important
during the 17th century
Left: design by Gilles Légaré
in 1663 for a similar pendant to
the one illustrated above. The
criss-cross lines on the stones
are to show the lapidary how
they should be cut
Below: 17th century Spanish
bow brooch with pendant in
gold set with emeralds*

*Right: 17th century Italian
enamelled gold pendant with
portrait under glass. (Victoria
& Albert Museum, London)
Far right: early 17th century
portrait pendant of a woman in
costume for a masque, by Isaac
Oliver
Below right: early 17th century
Spanish gold and enamel
pendant*

sponsor a number of lapidaries to
experiment with different combina-
tions of facets to see which would
produce the most brilliant result. The
outcome of the work was the rose-cut
or Mazarin-cut which remained standard for more than a century and a half
when the brilliant-cut – used to this
day – was discovered. The Mazarin-cut
had 16 facets and two tables which
made use of the light passing through
the stone. The appearance of these
stones had a devastating effect on
jewellery. The demand for them was
immediate and enormous. Gold and
pearls, which until then had been the
most precious materials known to man,
were relegated to a poor second and
third.

The fascination of diamonds stays to
this day and it was during the 17th
century that most of the great legendary diamonds were either found or
came to light in the west. Each has a
tale to tell: theft, murder, revolution
can all be attributed to a handful of
stones.

Perhaps the mightiest of these stones
was the Great Mogul, discovered at the
Gani mine in India in about 1650. The
stone, which was estimated to have
weighed nearly 800 carats, was first

mentioned by the great diamond merchant, Jean-Baptiste Tavernier, who had seen it in 1665 in the possession of the Great Mogul of Delhi. He described it as being as big as an egg cut through the middle. Later that century, the Mogul sent the diamond to a cutter in Venice, Ortensio Borgis, who apparently made a mess of the job and reduced the stone to a mere 280 carats and for his efforts was relieved of all his property. What happened to the diamond after it left the unfortunate Borgis's hands is uncertain; some say it was split into smaller stones, others that it was lost during the Persian invasions of India.

One of the most famous stones to have survived is the Koh-i-noor, now with the English Crown Jewels. This enormous diamond was first mentioned in 1304 when it was in the possession of the Rajah of Malwa. Two centuries later it became the property of the Sultan Babar, founder of the Mogul Empire. When Nadir Shah led the Persians into India and sacked Delhi in 1739 he acquired the stone. On seeing it he is reported to have cried out in admiration – 'Koh-i-noor' (mountain of light). It brought him bad luck: he was assassinated during his journey

back to Persia. From then on the diamond passed through many hands until it was finally acquired by Ranjit Singh (Lion of the Punjab), in 1833. It remained in the Jewel House of Lahore until 1849, when it was accepted by the East India Company as partial payment after the Punjab Wars. A year later the stone was presented to Queen Victoria as part of a ceremony to celebrate the 250th anniversary of the Company. It was shown at the famous Great Exhibition of 1851 at Crystal Palace but anxious spectators were disappointed with its dullness and lack of fire. This prompted Queen Victoria to have it recut. The job was entrusted to a cutter named Voorsanger of Amsterdam, already the diamond centre of the world, and he spent more than a month in London cutting it. A brilliant diamond of more than 108 carats, it is perhaps the most magnificent stone in the world.

All the great diamonds have stories attached to them but none can be considered as unlucky as the great blue diamond brought from India by Tavernier. This stone, generally called the Hope diamond, originally weighed 112 carats when he sold it to King Louis XIV in 1668. Immediately after selling the stone, Tavernier lost his entire fortune and died on his way back to India in an attempt to recoup his losses. Louis gave this diamond to his mistress, the beautiful and infamous Marquise de Montespan who was involved in a group of magicians led by the Abbé Guibourg. He performed a series of black masses at her instigation to ensure her supreme power over the King. During the ceremony an infant was sacrificed and the Marquise is reputed to have been naked throughout the ceremony save for the famous stone which she wore round her neck. Instead of advancing her cause, it in fact brought about her downfall.

A hundred years later the Hope diamond was in the possession of Louis XVI's Queen, Marie-Antoinette, and again disaster struck; she had lent it to her intimate friend, the Princesse de Lamballe, and almost immediately the princess was butchered by a revolutionary mob. Nothing was heard of the stone for a century and a half, then suddenly a diamond of the same deep-blue colour came on the market in London. Its reduced weight, now 44½ carats, and its presence in London suggests that it might have been smuggled out of France during the Revolution for re-cutting and never claimed. The stone was bought by Henry Philip Hope, a London banker, in 1830. Subsequent owners of the stone seem to have been dogged with misfortune. Suicide, bankruptcy, public disgrace and accidental death have never been far away.

In 1947 it came into the possession of the New York jeweller, Harry Winston, who bought it for nearly $180,000 dollars and some ten years later presented it to the Smithsonian Institution, Washington, D.C.

The Orloff diamond is another huge stone originating in India. Legend has it that this rose diamond was one of the eyes in a Brahmin temple statue and was stolen by a French soldier who entered the temple in disguise. He then sold it to an English sea captain who sold it to a Persian in London. Eventually the stone turned up in Amsterdam, where it was purchased for £90,000 on instalments by Prince Gregory Orloff, a favourite of Catherine the Great. After the death of her husband, Peter III, in 1762, Catherine had been contemplating marrying Orloff but he fell from favour and, it has been said, he bought the diamond to try to reinstate himself. Catherine

There were two main reasons for the sudden popularity of diamonds in Europe during the 17th century. Increased contact with India meant that bigger and better stones were available, and improved stone-cutting techniques allowed lapidaries to take advantage of their unique optical properties. Many of the largest diamonds came to Europe from India during the 17th century but some of the most exciting ones, illustrating the wide variety of colours displayed by these extraordinary stones, emanated from South Africa during the late 18th and early 19th centuries

Right: the Eugénie Blue, a 31 carat blue diamond thought to have once belonged to the Empress Eugénie, wife of Napoleon III and Empress of France from 1853–1870. (Smithsonian Institution, Washington, D.C.)

Below: the Tiffany at 128 carats is the largest golden diamond ever found. It was first exhibited in Chicago in 1893 and has been on almost continuous display at the New York store, Tiffany's, for more than 80 years

accepted the gift but it appears to have done Orloff very little good. This rose diamond, nearly 200 carats, is still the most prized possession of the USSR Treasury.

At just over 55 carat, the Sancy diamond is modest in size compared with the others described here but it is a stone of exceptional beauty with a long and fascinating history. Once again this gem was found in India around the turn of the 16th century and was bought in Constantinople by a Frenchman, Nicolas Harlay, Seigneur de Sancy, Henri III's ambassador to Turkey. The French Court was short of funds to raise an army and de Sancy offered them the stone to pledge against a loan. But the diamond very nearly failed to reach France, as the servant carrying it was set on by thieves. However, de Sancy was convinced of his servant's total loyalty and certain that nothing would let him allow the thieves to find the diamond. His trust was well founded; the unfortunate man had swallowed the stone rather than give it up and so it was recovered from his stomach. The French, in gratitude, appointed de Sancy Colonel in Chief of a regiment and his help was further recognized with his appointment as

Minister of Finance, a position which he used to redeem the diamond.

The Sancy stone, still presumably uncut, was sold to Queen Elizabeth I in England and pawned in France by Charles I who found himself in financial difficulties. He never redeemed the pledge and it was eventually sold to Cardinal Mazarin, the father of diamond-cutting. On his death in 1661 Mazarin left the Sancy diamond, together with all his other stones, to Louis XIV who kept it in the Garde Meuble in Paris (the French Crown Jewel treasury) where it remained until 1792 when it was stolen along with the other French regalia. The next time the stone is mentioned is when it was pawned by the Marquise Iranda to finance the Battle of Marengo in 1800. It was then handed on to Queen Maria-Louisa (wife of Charles IV) who is portrayed wearing the jewel in a portrait by Goya. From then on it had an uneventful life, passing from owner to owner at higher and higher prices and when it was on the market in 1906 it was purchased by William Waldorf Astor as a gift for his son's wife, the late Nancy, Viscountess Astor.

Another diamond with a history tainted with blood is the Regent (or Pitt). It is reputed to have been found by a slave working in an Indian diamond mine about 1700 who, realizing the value of the stone, wounded himself in the leg, hid the stone under the bandage and smuggled it out. A sailor offered to help get him abroad but murdered him en route and sold the diamond for £1,000. It was later purchased by Thomas Pitt, while Governor of Madras, who in turn sold it to the Duc d'Orléans, Regent of France. Like the Sancy it was also stolen from the Garde Meuble, but it was later found in the attic of a house in Paris and restored to the French Treasury. As with so many of the great diamonds, it was pledged – this time by Napoleon Bonaparte – to bolster up an unstable economy. It escaped the great auction of the French Crown Jewels and the Nazi occupation and is now on display in the Louvre in Paris.

The Florentine diamond is one of the most beautiful to survive. The history of this extraordinary citron-coloured stone is uncertain. One version is that it was worn uncut in the cap of Charles the Bold, the last Duke of Burgundy (1433–1477) who lost it during a battle. Others say it was brought to Venice by Tavernier from India some two cen-

turies later. The stone passed through many hands until it came to rest as part of the Crown Jewels of the Austrian Royal family. It remained in Vienna until World War II, since when it seems to have disappeared. According to Tavernier not only was the colour of this stone magnificent, but it was also cut in an unusual way, a double rose-cut of overall pear-shape with 126 facets.

Finally, there is one very unusual stone – the Shah diamond – now preserved in the Kremlin. It is uncut and weighs about 90 carats but the unusual thing is that it is engraved, a feat which must have taken incredible skill and patience. The engraved writing is Persian script and gives the names and dates of three rulers: Nizam Shah – 1000 (c. AD 1591), Jahan Shah – 1051 (c.1641) and Fath Ali Shah – 1242 (c. 1826).

Other famous great diamonds such as the Cullinan came from South Africa and belong to the 19th century and later. Said to be the largest gem diamond crystal to be discovered (3,106 carats before cutting), it was given to Edward VII in 1907 and two of the nine major gems from it are with the English Crown Jewels.

From the 17th century onwards trade and diplomatic relations were strengthened between the West and East. Europeans were travelling to India where the Moguls had a great love of jewels. Their supply of precious stones was apparently limitless and their technology, both as goldsmiths and lapidaries, was impressive Left: enamelled turban-ornament and pendant necklace of gold, diamonds, rubies, emeralds and pearls. Mogul, mid-19th century. (Victoria & Albert Museum, London)

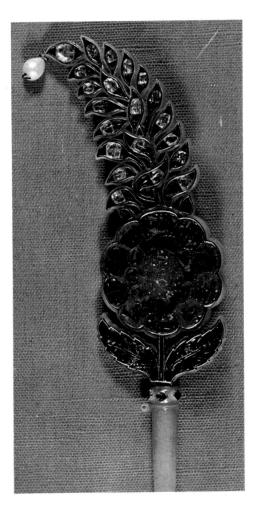

Left: turban-ornament of jade with carved rubies, emeralds and zircons, Mogul, 17th century. (Victoria & Albert Museum, London)
Below: detail of the back of a Mogul jewelled throne, early 18th century. (Topkapi Palace Museum, Istanbul)

The Moguls

The 17th century was a time of greatly increased trade between the West and the sub-continent of India. All the major powers of Europe set up Embassies there, resulting in a regular traffic of foreigners on a scale never before envisaged. To the lover of jewels it was the time when the travelling merchants such as Tavernier brought back great gemstones, including four of the largest diamonds ever found.

India was one obvious omission from the study of the development of metalwork techniques and styles of self-adornment in ancient civilizations (pages 20–99). In the 3rd millennium BC, at the same time as the Sumerians were founding their civilization in the Mesopotamian valley, another equally significant culture was evolving at Harappa in the Indus Valley.

Unlike Western contemporaries, the Harappa culture did not follow the custom of burying the dead with their worldly goods, so little evidence remains of this ancient world. However, there can be little doubt that the Indian civilizations were, from the earliest days, enthusiastic jewellery patrons. One or two pieces were found during excavations in the Indus Valley region but they are too few and too isolated to provide any picture which could form the basis for intelligent criticism. One interesting item found at Harappa, a long string of beads of cornelian, lapis and other gemstones, is almost identical to one depicted hanging from the waist of a statue dated as from about the end of the 3rd millenium BC. But several hundred years may have elapsed between the making of the piece of jewellery portrayed and the statue.

Another find, a sandstone carving from the same period, shows a man wearing his hair tied with a band from which is suspended a gem resting above the forehead (not unlike what was later called a *ferronnière*). He wears a bracelet and his clothing indicates that jewels were sewn onto the fabric.

Actual finds of Indian jewellery were made at Taxila and date from the Hellenistic period (330–27 BC). These show a distinct influence from the Classical lands both in form and workmanship but the Indian love of embellishment is obvious even in these pieces and they lack the order and symmetry of true Hellenistic work. Every possible surface is engraved with pictorial themes – elephants, peacocks and floral

205

Left and right: enamelled pendant jewel with emerald drop. The reverse of the pendant is of carved emerald and small diamonds. Mogul, 18th century. (Museum of Indian Arts and Archaeology, Banaras University, Uttar Pradesh, India)
Below: gold and enamel turban-ornament, Mogul-style from Rajastan, 18th century. (Victoria & Albert Museum, London)

designs, and dozens of different coloured stones are used in a single piece.

For later jewellery we have to return to pictorial evidence. The frescoes from the Ajanta caves, dating from about the 5th century AD, show women literally festooned with jewels. On their heads are huge jewelled head-dresses of turban design, enormous hoop ear-rings, necklaces from which hang several rows of multiple pendants, arm bands reaching to the elbow, and row after row of leg-ornaments.

What differentiated early Indian jewellery from that of the rest of the Ancient World was not so much its extravagance as its obsession with colour. Gold, when it was used, was used sparingly. The reason for this is obvious. India, together with its immediate neighbours Burma, Thailand and Afghanistan were, and indeed still are, rich in mineral deposits. Gold, on the other hand, was in short supply. From the first 4,000 years of this nation of jewellery-lovers we have no more than a handful of pieces from which to draw our conclusions.

It is with the 16th century and the establishment of the Mogul Empire that jewellery came into its own. The

Mogul rulers brought with them the sophisticated design and technical knowhow of the Persians. They did not, however, destroy the existing fashions but absorbed them into their own, forming an amalgam. From the late 16th century, and under the Emperors Jahangir and Shah Jahan in the early 17th century, jewels assumed an even greater importance and became, as they had so often before in other countries, a status symbol and portable display of personal wealth.

The actual forms became more rigidly controlled by convention. The main item for men was the turban, itself heavily encrusted with jewels and fastened with a gem-set kalgi (aigrette); men also wore necklaces of pearls and precious stones, ear-rings, jewelled sashes round their waists, and several rings on every finger.

For women the fashion was even more complex. There were, for instance, at least half a dozen different types of hair-adornment, worn together – each with its own name and specific function. Wreaths of gold flowers were supplemented with jewelled pins, plaited gold strips and rows of pearls intertwining the hair. Encircling the head was a gold band hung with gold leaves, and a

Right: central plaque of a Mogul gold armlet with carved emerald, precious stones and enamel, early 18th century
Below: jade hilt and enamelled scabbard of a dagger belonging to Haider Ali, 18th century ruler of Mysore. (British Museum)

bunch of gold flowers was worn at the nape of the neck.

What is remarkable about the Mogul jewellery is the size and quality of the gemstones used in the pieces. There are numerous contemporary reports which amaze us with stories of emeralds the size of hen's eggs and rubies as big as walnuts. What little has survived, together with stones brought back from India throughout the 17th century, would appear to justify these extravagant reports.

Even after the British officially took control of India (1858) the magnificence did not come to an end. Many of the princes were appointed to political office by the British Government and their personal wealth, far from diminishing, increased.

An account in *India of the Princes* by Rosita Forbes, the late English writer and traveller, wandering through India in the 1930s illustrates this admirably.

'. . . in a southern Indian Palace, I saw the ruling Maharani in full dress. The weight of her jewels was so great that she could not stand without the support of two attendants. Her anklets of gold studded with emeralds weighed 100 oz each and were valued at £1,400. Over her slender feet she wore flat strips of gold attached by chains to jewelled toe rings. The same precious metal covered the backs of her hands and was held in place by diamond links attached to her rings and bracelets. She could not bend her elbows because her arms were covered solidly from wrist to shoulder with wide bracelets of precious stones. Diamonds blazed upon her breast and hung in a multitude of chains far below her waist. Her throat was stiffened by collars of emeralds and rubies.

'Down the full length of her plaited hair, from the crown of her head to her knees, hung a sort of fishtail of gold set with jewels. It was about three inches wide at the top and it tapered to the point where a pear-shaped diamond hung.'

Rosita Forbes calculated that the 18-year-old queen was wearing more than her own slight weight in treasure and the value of at least £250,000. Today, however, to display your wealth is considered to be in bad taste and not without hazard both from the point of view of taxation and political resentment. While much priceless finery does no doubt survive it is for the most part concealed in safe deposit boxes.

The 18th Century

The 18th century saw many developments which were to have a profound and lasting effect on jewellery design. New materials were introduced, together with other new technical developments, and for the first time jewellery was brought within the reach of a mass audience. At the beginning of the century forms and styles were little different from the end of the previous one but the emergence of rococo design in the mid-1700s – together with changes in dress design and social behaviour – brought about significant developments Left: portrait of Queen Charlotte of Mecklenburg-Strelitz by Allan Ramsay, c.1762, which shows her wearing a choker of very large diamonds and a diamond stomacher – the large corsage ornament covering the bodice of her dress. (National Portrait Gallery, London)

If there was ever a century of change and contrast it was the 18th century; at the outset there was as great a division between the rich and poor as had ever been experienced; by the end, the great Industrial Revolution had led to the emergence of a new middle class. In between there were drastic changes in the structures of the Royal Houses of Europe: the death of Louis XIV in 1715; the Bourbons ousted by the Hapsburgs in Spain and the Stuarts of Scotland rejected in favour of the Guelphs of Brunswick; Peter the Great of Russia and Frederick the Great of Prussia moulding their own empires. For the first half of the century all eyes were on the French Court where the magnificence of the Sun King shone long after his death. The French were the barometer of good taste for the rest of the Western world. Even in England, where open disdain for the French character and manner was a matter of course, the nobility did not hesitate to copy her fashion and patterns of social behaviour.

With the accession of the boy King Louis XV the elaborate and feminine 'rococo' style became fashionable. Women's dress assumed a degree of exaggeration which had not been seen since the Elizabethan times. Tightly corseted wasp-waists reappeared and skirts were once more hooped, parting at the front to reveal huge underskirts. The ironmongery required to achieve this bell-shaped appearance must have been grotesquely uncomfortable. The *considération*, as it was known, comprised a full-length corset with three metal hoops strapped on either side to fill out the skirt; necklines plunged and sleeves were worn at half-mast; wigs and powdered hair surmounted porcelain-tinted complexions highlighted with patches and beauty spots. The whole effect was one of contrived elegance.

Men's fashion was no less self-conscious; tight knee breeches, long frock coats, jazzy waistcoats, lace jabots and white-powdered periwigs. Even children were not spared the discomfort of these extremes and were dressed as miniature adults. Looked at today the frivolity of the rococo fashion would seem ludicrous, but the designers of the 18th century had an awareness of proportions which lent the fashion a unique elegance; and their restraint from decorating the material too elaborately allowed it to fall short of foolishness.

209

It was, however, as much the change in social behaviour as in dress that affected the jewellery fashion of this century. Conversation became the most sought after of the social graces, and it was the habit of the nobility to entertain in the evening with luxurious dinner parties. The only form of lighting available for such occasions was, of course, candlelight and it was in this flickering light that great jewels were worn and had to be appreciated. What better stone under such conditions than the diamond, already established as a firm favourite in the previous century?

Diamonds proved their worth and were used to the almost total exclusion of other stones until the 1750s. At the turn of the 17th century the brilliant-cut (a Venetian lapidary, Vincenzo Peruzzi, is popularly credited with the invention) had made even more capital from the diamond's remarkable optical qualities than the Mazarin-cut. For this the stone was cut with 56 facets instead of the 16 of the Mazarin, and exploited the reflective and refractive properties of diamonds to a far greater extent than ever before. The increased brilliance was considerable and the cut has never been bettered to this day.

So, for the first time, different jewellery was designed for wear during the day and at night-time. It differed in form, style and the materials employed in manufacture and needless to say the evening jewellery was the more extravagant, valuable and impressive.

The jewels from the first half of the century have a lightness and delicacy about them. The metal used for setting was reduced to a minimum. In fact the goldsmith's art was reduced to that of a stone-setter and, for the best part of a century, he and the enameller had to turn their talents to the production of snuff-boxes, miniature cases, watches and chatelaines. Diamonds were frequently set in silver which, when polished, detracts less from the diamonds than does gold. During the second half of the century open-back settings were introduced to allow more light into the stones. Again the *pavé* setting was favoured for smaller stones (abutted like paving stones).

Symmetrical floral designs and the bow theme continued to be popular until about 1740 when the rococo vogue temporarily favoured the asymmetrical and reintroduced the love of colour. As always, dress dictated the forms of jewellery worn and, while the idea of *parures* continued to be fashionable, the component parts changed considerably. Predictably none of these great diamond *parures* has survived. Rapidly changing fashion meant that they were broken up and remade with increasing regularity but our knowledge, derived as usual from portraits, is supplemented by contemporary copies made in 'paste' (the fine glass substitute for gemstones which can be cut in the same manner).

The most unusual item was the stomacher, an enormous corsage brooch which covered the entire front of the dress, tapering to a 'V' and highlighting the pinched waist. A portrait of Queen Charlotte by Allan Ramsay, now in the National Portrait Gallery in London, shows her dress covered with a three-dimensional floral pattern in diamonds. A similar piece is worn by Marie-Louise de Bourbon in a portrait by Lorenzo Pécheux.

One surviving example of a stomacher in precious stones can now be seen in the *Schatzkammer der Residenz*, Munich. This is rather lighter and more open than the other two, with an abstract floral motif set with diamonds and pendant pearls. Other paste copies show stomachers

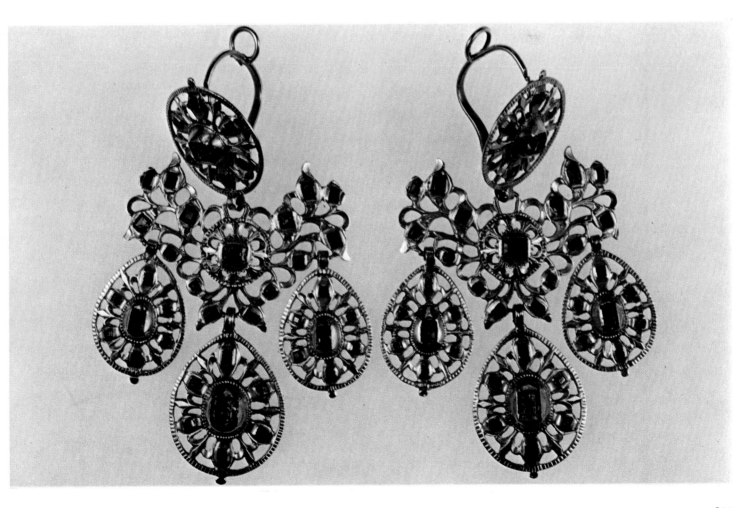

Throughout the 18th century one of the most popular brooch designs was the Sévigné or bow brooch. The simple bow theme was usually decorated with one or more pendants
Left: Sévigné brooch with drop pendant in gold and emeralds, Spanish, 18th century

One form of ear-ring design adopted almost universally in Western Europe during the 18th century was the girandole, typified by its three drop pendants
Below: girandole ear-rings in pierced gold with emeralds, Spanish/Portuguese, mid-18th century

with both floral and bow themes, some constructed in several interlinking parts which could be added to or subtracted from according to the lavishness of the occasion.

Two portraits by Anton Raphael Mengs, the German painter, show us other items of jewellery which were fashionable halfway through the 18th century. The first of Maria Amalia Christina, Queen of Spain, shows her with a *Sévigné* brooch set with large diamonds, worn as a choker on a velvet ribbon; on her left breast there is a similar brooch with a decoration suspended below; her hair is studded with diamond stars; and on both wrists she wears four rows of pearls secured with an enamelled portrait medallion clasp. The other portrait shows the Infanta Maria Ludovica wearing a tiara and necklace of diamonds designed *en suite*; again she has a decoration on her breast but in this case it is held by a velvet bow; she has diamond rings on both fingers and is wearing bracelets almost identical to those described above. One feature common to both portraits is the enormous girandole ear-rings which consist of a central cluster of four large diamonds with three drop pendant diamonds designed

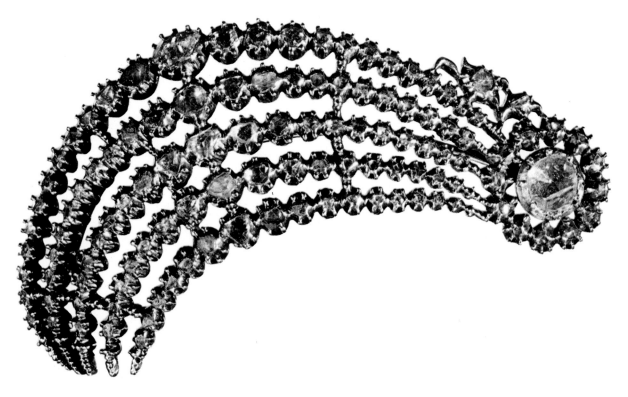

While diamonds held their popularity throughout the 18th century, rococo design demanded more colour and more flair than diamonds could offer. Coloured stones and enamel were widely adopted to give life to asymmetrical floral designs
Left: floral brooch in gold, enamel and precious stones, Spanish, late 18th century. (Victoria & Albert Museum, London)
Above: diamond and silver brooch, probably made in 1759 to commemorate the sighting of Halley's comet, English
Right: diamond memorial ring, inscribed 'In Memory of Dolly Gundry 1748', English

to catch the light with every move of the head.

Another popular item in the *parure*, the aigrette, is depicted in a portrait of Matilde Querini by Pietro Longhi. The delicate spray of diamonds is worn above the right ear and is complemented by other diamond brooches in her hair. On her left breast she is wearing a matching aigrette brooch which is being used to pin a long, knotted string of pearls.

After about 1760, the reintroduction of colour and the effects of rococo considerably change the appearance of jewellery. Again very little has survived, even in paste form, and the few examples available to us are either Spanish or Russian. One particularly fine brooch made in Spain about 1770 depicts a spray of flowers. The interpretation is much more naturalistic and fluid; the leaves and stems are enamelled and held at the base with an enamelled gold bow *pavé*-set with diamonds; and the petals of each flower are also set with small diamonds. This piece has both realism and a charming elegance which typifies the influence from the major arts, an influence soon to be curtailed by a renewed interest in Classicism.

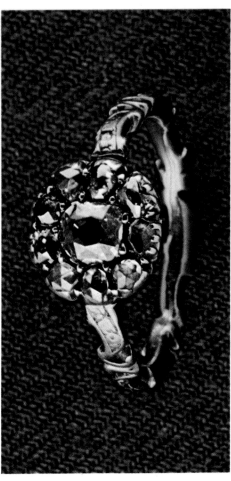

After Catherine the Great became Empress of Russia in 1762, St. Petersburg became one of the great centres of patronage for jewellers – not that the jewels were made by Russians. Talent was drawn from craftsmen throughout Western Europe. Happily some of the examples surviving include the Russian Imperial jewels.

One very fine necklace is a typical example of the *rivière* (a chain of separately set stones) which became popular in the last quarter of the century. This chain is made up from 12 huge emeralds, each bordered with small *pavé*-set diamonds; between each setting there is a link made from five small claw-set diamonds shaped as a cross. The necklace, which can be seen in the Victoria and Albert Museum in London, has a pair of matching earrings, each with one medium-sized emerald surrounded by diamonds and a large pear-shaped drop pendant of the same construction. It has a classic simplicity, which demonstrates a move away from the frivolity of the previous decade. It was a similar, but rather more complex *rivière* which brought about the most famous scandal in history, an event which has become known as *l'affaire du collier*.

Above: another typical rococo brooch in gold and precious stones, Russian, late 18th century. (Kremlin, Moscow)

Smaller and less expensive pendants and jewels were frequently bordered with small pavé-*set diamonds or paste*
Above right: pendant brooch with rose diamonds, enamel, ivory, seed pearls and hair. English, 18th century
Above, far right: paste-set brooch inscribed 'Honour, the Reward of Virtue', English, late 18th century
Right: miniature portrait pendant set in silver and gold, decorated with diamonds, English, 1760
Far right: finger-ring with silhouette surrounded by diamonds, French, late 18th century

The Necklace Affair

This necklace scandal, its extravagance symbolizing the hated aristocracy, was thought to have helped spark off the French Revolution. It was originally commissioned by Louis XV for his mistress the Comtesse du Barry, and made by the Court jewellers Boehmer and Bassanges in 1785.

Carlyle, the historian, reported on it: 'What a princely ornament it was. A row of seventeen glorious diamonds, as large almost as filberts, encircle, not too tightly, the neck, a first time. Looser, gracefully fastened thrice to these, a three-wreathed festoon and pendants enough (simple pear-shaped, multiple star-shaped, or clustered amorphous) encircle it, enwreath it, a second time. Loosest of all, softly flowing round from behind in priceless catenary, rush down two broad three-fold rows; seem to knot themselves, round a very Queen of Diamonds, on the bosom; then rush on, again separated, as if their length in plenty; the very tassels of them were a fortune for some men. And now lastly, two other inexpressible threefold rows, also with their tassels, will, when the necklace is on and clasped, unite themselves behind into a double inexpressible six-fold row; and so stream down together or as under, over the hind neck, we may fancy, like lambent Zodiacal or Aurora Borealis fire. All this on a neck of snow, slight-tinged with rosebloom, and within it royal life.'

The plans for this, perhaps the most extravagant gift ever, went wrong when Louis XV died before its completion; the necklace was offered to Louis XVI but he thought it too expensive and his wife Marie-Antoinette, who had many jewels already, preferred to spend her money in other ways. The jewellers were left with a vastly expensive white elephant on their hands and offered it several times for sale without success. Its existence was soon common knowledge and an officer's wife, Jeanne de Saint-Rémy, devised a scheme to get hold of it. Pretending to represent the Queen and carrying forged letters, she went to see Cardinal de Rohan, saying that the Queen wanted to buy the necklace without the King's knowledge. The Cardinal, who was temporarily out of favour at Court, was only too happy to act as an intermediary. The jewellers handed the necklace to de Rohan who in turn handed it to another of the conspirators who was disguised as the Queen. Madame de Saint-Rémy then sent the necklace to England where it was broken up and the individual diamonds sold.

When the Queen was faced with a bill for £90,000 she quite naturally refused to settle it, never having seen the necklace. The scandal which followed rocked the very foundations of the French Court. Cardinal de Rohan was tried and found not guilty of conspiracy, but lost his position. Jeanne de Saint-Rémy and her husband La Motte were imprisoned, and the husband flogged and branded. Shortly after her arrest Madame de Saint-Rémy escaped to England, from where she conducted a campaign of blackmail against the King. She must have had some good information because her husband was immediately released. The public outcry which followed was enormous.

Left: diamond floral spray, English, 1860
Right: demi-parure of enormous emeralds surrounded by brilliants, Russian, late 18th century. (Victoria & Albert Museum, London)

Right: collection of five 18th century finger-rings. From left to right: diamond cluster; two-row diamond and ruby hoop; agate cameo surrounded by small diamonds; monogram ring in blue enamel surrounded by diamonds; diamond cluster

The bow theme was sometimes adopted for finger-ring design Left: finger-ring with large central ruby decorated with small diamonds, English, late 18th century Opposite, right: stylized floral necklace in diamonds, French, mid-18th century

Orders and Decorations

Extravagantly elaborate jewellery for men would probably have gone out of fashion much earlier if it had not been for Louis XV's passion for dressing up. By the middle of the 18th century diamond jewellery for men was virtually unknown; the nobility demonstrated their wealth by dressing their wives rather than adorning themselves. There were, however, a few isolated examples of jewellery made for men which are of great beauty. One is the magnificent hat-brooch made for Augustus III, Elector of Saxony; it is constructed from intertwining ribbons of gold, *pavé*-set with small diamonds and tied in a ribbon at the top. At the bottom there is a floral arrangement of

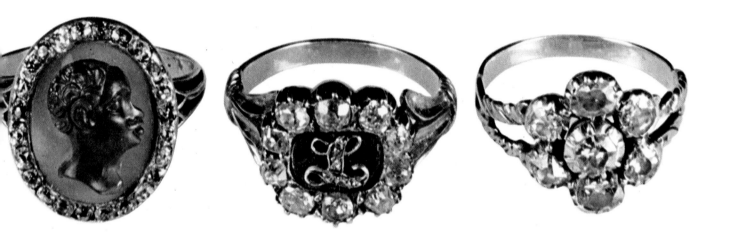

rather larger diamonds which acts as a framework for one enormous green diamond.

The other items of jewellery for men worth mentioning are orders and decorations. Several examples have survived and undoubtedly represent 18th century craftsmanship at its best. Some Orders of the Garter still exist but they do not compare with the three Orders of the Golden Fleece which are still preserved in European collections. All are of similar construction, based on the original design instituted by Philip the Good, Duke of Burgundy (1396–1467): three jewelled plaques with a fleece dangling below, but the jewellers have worked within these limitations with great skill and imagination to produce three very different jewels. One made in Dresden, again for Augustus III, has three enormous table-cut rubies surrounded by dozens of diamonds of various sizes and shapes set in geometric patterns, and below a golden sheep dangles limply. In contrast, one in the *Schatzkammer der Residenz* at Munich is entirely constructed from pink and white diamonds and the sheep is completely covered with smaller *pavé*-set stones.

Other pieces produced for men tended

to be functional and designed primarily for daytime use.

Snuff-boxes, watches and walking sticks were often heavily jewelled.

The Chatelaine

The most interesting development in day jewellery for both men and women, however, was the chatelaine. This was generally constructed from a decorated plaque or series of decorated plaques which clipped onto the belt and from which a watch was suspended. Usually the watch was decorated *en suite* and worn face inwards so that the back, the main area for decoration, formed an integral part of the overall design.

All the rules for night-time jewellery are broken with chatelaines; diamonds are seldom if ever used; cabochon-cut stones once again fulfil the role of providing colour; semi-precious stones and even base metals are perfectly acceptable, and at one stage in some countries the use of precious materials was actually considered to be ostentatious. Consequently the number of examples which have survived is greater than any other form of jewellery from the period, giving perhaps a distorted idea of their popularity. There is no

doubt, however, that the chatelaine provides us with an unbroken picture of the changing styles of ornament in the 18th century.

An example at the Fitzwilliam Museum in Cambridge, dating from 1705, shows the chatelaine at its most basic construction but with decoration more reminiscent of the mid-17th century. The hook is covered with a plate of gold open-work with a single garnet; below this is a hinged, oblong plaque of open-work set with garnets and mother of pearl, the watch below that has a similarly decorated back, and on a simple chain to one side of the central plaque is the key, also inlaid with mother of pearl. The whole composition is geometric and highlighted with red and black enamel.

Twenty years later not only had the design of the chatelaine altered but also its function. Some chatelaines were now fitted with an *étui* – a small case used to carry needles, scissors, pencils and other small items needed in emergencies – and the watch was sometimes eliminated. Other chatelaines retained the watch and were equipped with a number of chains and hooks which could be used to carry a variety of small objects. The whole piece now

became known as an *équipage*. The style of ornamentation favoured from the 1720s to the 1740s was heavily decorated with scenes from classical mythology in gold repoussé plaques. Some base metal chatelaines were made up from identical plaques which were obviously cast, already showing an element of mass production.

By 1760 the taste for colour was returning and this is reflected in the decoration of chatelaines. Various techniques were used to introduce this, and perhaps the most common was to chase the metal with a linear or floral design and fill the channels with enamel. An approach which was particularly fashionable in England was to construct the chatelaine in carved mineral and decorate it with gold. A superb example of this technique can be found in the Victoria and Albert Museum in London; the chatelaine and *étui* are carved from agate and decorated with borders of delicate gold floral tracery.

In 1770 there were two significant developments. One was the introduction of the 'macaroni', a form of chatelaine which, instead of having a hook, was constructed in two hinged sections and merely folded over a tight belt. The watch which hung from one

223

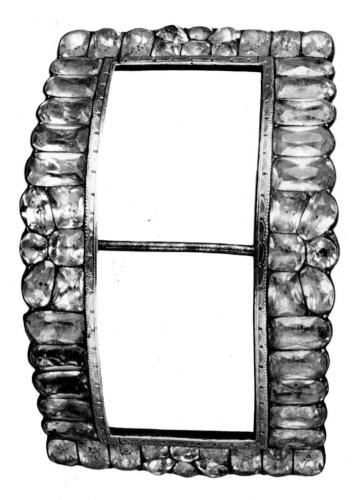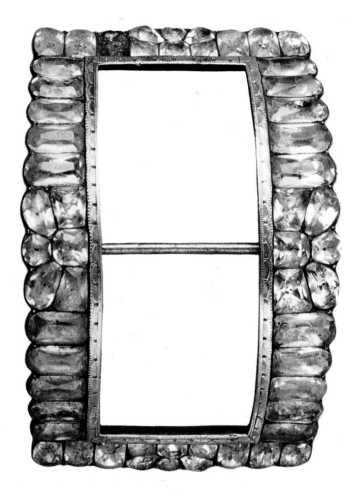

end of the macaroni was frequently balanced by a dummy watch at the other. The second new feature was the introduction of pictorial enamel plaques. This was particularly fashionable in France and the subjects ranged from family portraits to hunting scenes.

Some ten years later the renewed interest in Classical art was making itself felt and the subjects depicted in the enamel plaques moved away from the domestic and sentimental towards scenes from classical mythology. It was about this time that the great Swiss neo-classicist, Angelica Kauffman, moved from Italy to England and while there is no proof that she produced panels for chatelaines her influence is very obvious in some of the pieces made in England, France and Italy.

Buckles and Finger-Rings

Today we live in an age of rapidly changing fashions and while the 18th century fashions were not quite as ephemeral as that, the introduction of the woman's magazine not only reflected fashion but also influenced it to a certain extent. This new self-aware-

Another form adopted for day-time wear was the buckle. Buckles became virtually obligatory and were produced in a wide range of materials to cater for different income brackets
Above: pair of paste buckles, English, late 18th century
Above right: silver buckles, English, late 18th century
Right: silver buckles, English, 1770

ness cannot be better illustrated than by the changes in attitude towards buckles. An article printed in a newspaper at the end of the 17th century commented: 'Certain foolish young men have lately brought about a new fashion. They have begun to fasten their shoes and knee-bands with buckles instead of ribbons, wherewith their forefathers were content and moreover have found them more convenient. Surely every man will own that they were more decent and modest than those new-fangled, unseemly clasps or buckles, as they will call them which will gall and vex the bones of these vain cox-combs beyond sufferance, and make them repent their pride and folly. We hope all grave and honourable people will withold their countenance from such immodest ornaments. It belongeth to the reverend clergy to tell these thoughtless youths, in solemn manner, that such things are forbidden in Scripture.'

Our guardian of public morality cried in vain. Forty years later the complete change in public opinion is reflected by theatre tickets which were printed 'Gentlemen cannot be admitted wearing shoe-strings.' The snobbery attached to buckles was extremely complex and

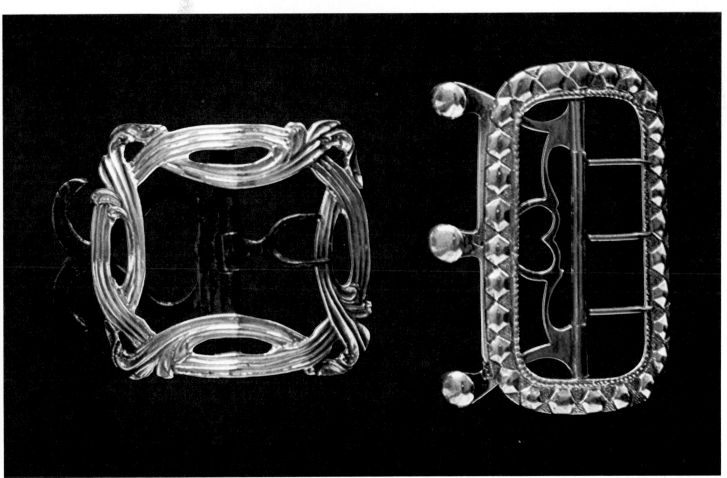

the exact type of buckle worn and the materials from which it was made was a statement of rank or status. A nobleman would wear buckles of silver, *pavé*-set with small diamonds; landed gentry would have a set of silver buckles for Sundays and gilt ones for everyday wear; and a dandy would invariably wear cut steel.

This off-the-cuff method of classifying people is best illustrated in a passage from the Dutch classic, *Camera Obscura*. The writer is observing two fellow passengers in a railway carriage. '. . . whereas one of them had a pair of large round silver spectacles, a silver cigar box, a silver pencil, a silver watch as well as silver brooch and shoe-buckles, from which I concluded that he was a silversmith; the other had a copper kerchief pin, a copper tobacco box, a copper watch chain round his stomach from which I gathered he was no less than a baker's foreman.'

Initially, buckles were used solely for fastening shoes and breeches. Their basic construction was identical to buckles produced today; an oblong or circular border with a rivet down the centre on which the prongs were hinged. It was the size and style of decoration which changed considerably. At the

beginning of the century they were quite small, about two and a half inches across, and the decoration was comparatively simple, but by 1770 enormous ornate buckles which covered the entire instep were fashionable. The border of these later buckles was generally open-work set with semi-precious stones.

By about 1730 smaller buckles were being produced for purely decorative purposes. They were generally pinned onto ribbons of velvet and worn as chokers or bracelets; the central area, left open in shoe-buckles, was often used to accommodate a miniature or cameo. A typical example, using strings of pearls as a band, can be seen in the portrait of the Infanta Maria Ludovica, by Anton Raphael Mengs in the *Kunsthistorisches Museum*, Vienna. Madame de Pompadour is reported to have had two such buckles with portraits of Henry IV and Louis XV.

The demand for buckles in every material continued unabated until about 1790 when the fashion reverted once more to laces. By this time so many people were employed in the buckle industry that this constituted a threat to the livelihood of a considerable number of craftsmen and, in 1791, a group of buckle-makers from Birming-

ham were granted an audience with the Prince of Wales, the arbiter of Court fashion. He agreed to help them out by making buckles compulsory wear in the Court, but fashion cannot be tampered with in this way and by the end of the century the vogue for buckles finally died.

The only other jewellery form adopted in the first 80 years of the century was the finger-ring which was worn by both men and women. The most popular style was a single large oval stone, facet-cut and surrounded with a circle of small brilliant diamonds. The central stone varied greatly; diamonds were, of course, favoured at the beginning of the century but by about 1760 coloured stones, particularly sapphires, came into vogue; at the same time the rococo influence affected the setting and shank design which became rather more ornate with foliated, or scroll, work.

For those who could not afford diamonds or sapphires, the choice was limitless and rings have been found with rock crystal, onyx and many other clear semi-precious stones. Sentimental rings were very popular towards the end of the century, as were the cameo rings produced after the revival of interest in Classical art.

By the end of the 18th century the hunt for cheaper materials was under way to cope with the increasing demand for inexpensive jewels. Better types of paste were invented to substitute for precious stones and an alloy called pinchbeck was developed and became the most effective cheap alternative to gold
Above: pinchbeck bracelet set with coloured paste, English, c.1790
Left: pendant cross in turquoise and diamonds, English, late 18th century

New Patrons and New Materials

So far we have covered 18th century jewellery in terms of the great jewellery commissioned by the royalty and nobility of Europe, for centuries the sole patrons of the goldsmith's art. By the middle of the century, however, a new class was emerging. The onset of the Industrial Revolution was just round the corner and anyone with entrepreneurial flair could lift themselves out of the rank and file and join the new bourgeoisie. They could not afford diamonds or precious metals but the developments which produced the class also provided the technical know-how to cater for their demands for cheaper substitutes.

The most important single development was the manufacture of artificial precious stones. This was already well established in the mid-17th century. In 1676 George Ravenscroft, owner of the Savoy Glass House in London, discovered a method of producing 'paste' glass with lead oxide which had a much higher refractive index – the quality which gives diamonds their unique sparkle – than traditional materials.

While he did not achieve the sparkle of the diamond, this method did provide a very acceptable substitute when viewed by candlelight. Another property of Ravenscroft's lead glass was that it was better for cutting and the brilliant-cut, introduced at the turn of the last century, was easily achieved. Glass or paste gems had been made since the Classical period, and had been highly prized at one time, but in Paris during the 17th century several lapidaries had made a fortune defrauding inexperienced patrons with their paste/glass jewels. Now they were to find a huge legitimate market for their wares which could be sold on their own merit.

Developments on Ravenscroft's technique instigated by Joseph Strasser at the beginning of the century improved the optical quality still further and by 1767 there were reported to be 314 craftsmen in Paris alone producing paste jewellery. While the main object of paste was to cater for a new market interested in jewels but unable to afford traditional materials, these substitutes were not looked down on. Many of the royal houses owned whole *parures* in paste and Messrs. Wickes and Netherton, the English crown jewellers, announced on their visiting card that

they made a variety of 'false-stonework'.

Two other substitutes were widely used for diamonds. Iron pyrites (marcasites) and fragments of rock crystal were facet-cut. So artificial stones started their life fraudulently in the 17th century, then gained respectability, and by the end of the 18th century they moved a stage further to become an art form in themselves. As colour crept back into jewellery every type of stone was copied and some, which could not be found naturally, were invented. A presentable substitute for the real thing was coming to be appreciated in its own right. The other advantage to the jewellery historian is that because of the comparatively modest intrinsic value of the pieces produced many of them have survived to give us a comprehensive picture of the fashions of the Court jewellery upon which they were inevitably modelled.

If paste was the most important innovation then metallurgy came not far behind. A similar situation developed to that described above; the new fashion-conscious bourgeoisie wanted metal for their jewellery and could not afford gold or silver so two main substitutes were developed which by the end of the century, with the

229

Left: pair of cut steel buckles and cut steel brooch, English, early 19th century
Right: cut steel pendant ear-rings, mid-19th century

declining favour of gold, became readily acceptable to the nobility. Some time between 1800 and 1820 an Englishman called Christopher Pinchbeck developed a new alloy which later took his name. It was composed of 17 per cent zinc and 83 per cent copper and proved a very passable substitute for gold. Its cheapness and malleability made it immediately popular with the customer and the craftsman respectively.

Soon all types of jewellery were being produced in pinchbeck, some to individual order and some multiple-cast for speculative sale. Its obvious advantages were in the manufacture of heavy objects and it was widely used for chatelaines, watch-cases and buckles. Unlike paste, pinchbeck never rose above the level of a substitute.

Cut Steel Jewellery

The very word steel smacks of the Industrial Revolution and indeed cut steel jewellery, which started early in the 18th century, survived for more than 150 years. Unlike pinchbeck it substituted for both stones and metal. Perhaps the inspiration came from the vogue for marcasites which were being widely used as a substitute for dia-

monds. Steel workers traditionally producing swords and boxes realized that steel, cut in facets, could achieve the same metallic gleam. In fact, it is quite easy to mistake some steel jewellery for marcasite at a glance but you have only to look at the back of the object to tell the difference. The cut steel studs are always riveted to the background whereas marcasites are always set by conventional stone-setting methods. This reflects the different traditions of the blacksmith and the jeweller, each using his own techniques.

The steel used was extremely soft. Some reports claim that old horseshoe-nails were melted down and re-used and, while this would have been a very economical source in the early days, it is unlikely that so haphazard a method of supply could have fed what was to become a considerable industry. However, it is interesting to note that contemporary reports state that a ferrier would never use a nail which he could not bend against his forehead. So soft a metal would be easy to facet-cut. The steel-cutters adopted a simplified method of the brilliant-cut, using about 15 facets and the studs were *pavé*-set to ensure the maximum reflection over the whole area of the piece.

The most famous workshops were at Woodstock, a small town outside Oxford, a town with many royal associations surrounding the royal manor built there by Henry I in the 12th century. There are several 18th century references to the pre-eminence of the cut steel produced in Woodstock. An extract from the diary of Count Kielmansegge in 1761, for instance, tells us: 'Woodstock is a small town which however is renowned all over England for fine workmanship in steel. The Woodstock workmanship is preferred to that of Salisbury and it is not unusual to find steel buckles and watch-chains, etc.' Again there is an extract from a letter by Horace Walpole to his friend Horace Mann ten years earlier which, while not so openly flattering, gives us an idea of the acceptability of cut steel in the first half of the century. He wrote: 'I have sent away tonight a small box of steel wares which I received but today from Woodstock. As they are better than the first, you will choose out some of them for Prince Craon and give away the rest as you please.'

These steel wares were obviously produced to different degrees of sophistication and this was reflected in their price. Some, produced for the new

middle class customers, were comparatively cheap but others, where the workmanship compared with precious jewellery, were overwhelmingly expensive. A pair of steel scissors, elaborately decorated in open-work, are reported to have cost 15 guineas a pair whereas plain ones cost only two shillings and sixpence (a considerable sum in 1778).

Steel jewellery became fashionable in France and a shop opened in Paris by Monsieur Granchez, Marie-Antoinette's jeweller, was reported in 1760 to have been selling steel jewellery which was more expensive than gold. Decorated steel chains were much sought after and again the cost was incredibly high, one weighing less than two ounces was sold in France for £170. It was perhaps this enormous cost which made steel jewellery so readily acceptable to the nobility. Financial one-upmanship has been with us as long as the money itself.

The forms produced in steel varied a great deal. Initially steel was used primarily for functional items such as buckles, sword-hilts, scissors etc., but in the second half of the century, the craftsmen widened their range considerably and chatelaines, bracelets, necklaces, ear-rings, brooches – all

were produced in steel to designs established by jewellery in other materials. As in precious jewellery, the floral theme remained dominant throughout the century and even the rococo asymmetry was adopted by the steel-cutters when it became fashionable. By the turn of the century the range available and its unquestioned acceptability is obvious.

Napoleon, on his second marriage to Marie-Louise of Austria, found his resources stretched; all the original jewels had been kept by Josephine, and he commissioned a whole parure of cut steel for his new bride and her retinue.

In 1775 Matthew Boulton, the great industrialist, moved his workshop from London to Birmingham. By this time steel wares were a major export industry to every country in Europe and even America. This trade, started by public taste, was encouraged by the sumptuary laws operating in both France and Switzerland, which restricted the use of diamonds and precious metals. Boulton, realizing the renewed interest in colour and the return towards Classical subject matter, got together with that other great industrialist, Josiah Wedgwood, who agreed to produce cheap cameos in jasper-ware

which could be incorporated in steel jewellery. The result of this partnership was some of the most beautiful steel jewellery pieces ever to be produced before or since. A necklace, now in the Lady Lever Art Gallery at Port Sunlight, Cheshire, England, admirably demonstrates this; it has six rows of decorated beads which fasten behind the neck, and at the front is a large Wedgwood cameo; below, hung from four more decorated chains, are two other smaller cameos. Another example, now in the Victoria and Albert Museum in London, is a chatelaine and watch in which the entire back of the watch-case is covered with a cameo and a smaller one is the centrepoint of the chatelaine itself.

By the 1790s the industry was producing its finest work but the French Revolution robbed the British workshops of their best customer. Many had to close down and even when peace returned to France the business was not easy to regain. French steel-cutting workshops had opened in the meantime and were catering for the majority of their domestic demand. The best, however, survived and continued producing jewellery of considerable delicacy until the turn of the 19th century.

Above: cut steel bracelet decorated with blister pearls, French, early 19th century

The vogue for cut steel survived well into the 19th century
Right: early Victorian cut steel brooch

After the French Revolution

The French Revolution touched every nation in the West and put an end to the magnificence of a French Court which had survived for so many centuries. This was a time for neither luxury nor display. The few traditional patrons of the jewellers' art, lucky enough to survive the guillotine, were in no mood to wear anything ostentatious lest they be labelled 'aristocrat'. In the years of terror which dominated France from 1789–95, the only jewellery produced was directly designed to emulate the new 'liberty' of the French people. Women wore their hair in a style which became known as *à la victime*, cropped close to the skull as a condemned woman en route to the guillotine; they wore thin red ribbons round their necks as a symbol of the same fate. Triangular ear-rings of base metal symbolized reason; other earrings of steel were produced in the form of miniature guillotines; memorial finger-rings known as *bagues à la Marat*, were designed to commemorate the three martyrs of the Revolution: Marat, Chalier and Lepeletier. These rings were produced solely in base metals.

The Revolutionary wars overstretched the French Treasury and many aristocrats, hoping to appease the guillotine-happy revolutionaries, surrendered their jewels; in 1891 the entire French regalia which had been put away for safekeeping by Louis XVI was stolen and broken up. In France it was unquestionably the worst time for jewels the country had ever experienced.

With the establishment of the *Directoire* in 1795, comparative stability returned to the country which allowed a gradual easing of austerity, nothing dramatic but definitely noticeable. In England democracy was also on the increase, but through commercial and industrial rather than political revolution. Fashion there had continued to develop during the years of the revolutionary wars, reflecting the renewed interest in Classicism. At the beginning of the Directorate, Paris adopted this interest and, perhaps because of the relief after years of fear, a mode of dress was adopted which was frivolous beyond belief. *Les merveilleuses du Directoire*, as the bright young things of the day referred to themselves, dressed in *la mode à la grecque*: a sleeveless tunic, inspired by the *peplos* worn in classical Greece, made from extremely flimsy fabric gathered under the bosom and with a plunging neck-

line; on their feet they wore open sandals and completed the outfit with a most incongruous bonnet.

La mode à la grecque was not conducive to the wearing of jewellery; the object was to accentuate the curve of the figure and any appendages would only clutter the line. Women continued to wear the ribbon *à la victime* but gradually other jewels were adopted. The most fashionable items were long chains worn either round the neck or waist; these were often of a complex construction, decorated enamel plaques linked by multiple chains, a style which owed much to the design of chatelaines of the previous century. These decorated chains were known as *sautoirs*. The only other jewels generally worn were very long pendant ear-rings known as *poissardes* (fishwives).

It was not until Napoleon Bonaparte seized power in 1799 and established the Consulate that jewellery came back into its own and, as is so common, it was the taste of one man which dictated a revival. The internal peace of the country led to greater financial and political stability within France and, as always after times of trouble, there was emphasis on the pursuit of pleasure; once again there was a wide demand for

jewellery and many of the goldsmiths who had been patronized by the French Court of Louis XVI came out of retirement. The result was a rejuvenation of late 18th century design. Diamonds, however, were still associated with the *ancien régime*, and so most jewels were made from semi-precious stones. The neo-Classical mode of dress continued in a somewhat modified form and the items of jewellery adopted included long necklaces, pendant ear-rings, and now rings were not only worn on every finger and thumb but also on toes – which continued to protrude from open sandals.

Napoleon was a great one for display and had a deep love of jewels but this was a mere passing fancy compared with the obsession of his wife Josephine. By 1804, when Napoleon named himself Emperor, he had recovered the bulk of the French Crown Jewels which went into *parures* for his Empress. From this time on, things changed radically; it was no longer an insult to wear diamonds and soon tiaras were glistening in the candlelight. The Emperor was fond of great social events and evening *parures* became virtually obligatory for anyone connected with the Court.

Josephine continued to spend vast

Left and right: pair of gold brooches set with cameos, pearls and gemstones. French, c.1855. (Victoria & Albert Museum, London)

Below and opposite page: this late 18th century portrait by Vigée-Lebrun of Marie-Caroline, Queen of Naples, and her daughter illustrates the way in which cameos were incorporated into various forms of jewellery. (Musée de Versailles)

sums of money on jewels after the Coronation although this would seem to have been rather tactless when you remember the public outcry after the 'necklace affair' less than 20 years before. One diamond parure alone purchased by her was valued at 350,000 francs. Napoleon, with his flair for organization, founded a school where deaf and dumb children could train as goldsmiths or lapidaries and his generals were given an open brief to gather precious materials during their campaigns overseas.

The style and forms employed were a mixture of 18th century fashion and Classical tradition. Most important was jewelled headwear; tiaras were the richest form employed, some made as gold laurel wreaths set with precious or semi-precious stones; aigrettes were also popular, some articulated with springs so that they would shimmer in the candlelight; but the most common form for the less affluent was the jewelled comb. Necklaces became shorter and were frequently of the *rivière* type, matching bracelets were worn on either wrist or on the upper arm. This complete about-face of public attitude towards jewels cannot be better illustrated than by François Gérard's

portrait of Josephine painted in 1803, the year before Napoleon's Coronation. She is wearing a three-piece *parure*, a diadem of enormous table-cut emeralds set in diamonds with huge pendant pearls; her *rivière* necklace is also of emeralds and again hung with pearls and the matching ear-rings are single emeralds. A portrait by the same artist of Queen Marie-Caroline shows her similarly adorned but in this case the *parure* is of comparatively inexpensive materials – pearls, turquoises and gold.

By 1805 the fashion for cameos reached unprecedented heights, an edition of the *Journal des dames* of that year reported: 'A fashionable lady wears cameos in her belt, on her necklace, on both of her bracelets, in her tiara. Antique stones are more fashionable than ever, but in default of them one may employ engraved shells.' These were cameos cut from shells which were executed with great skill, particularly in Italy. Another substitute evolved to cope with the enormous demand from both nobility and the bourgeoisie, came from Germany where cameos were made from fired porcelain and coloured glass.

It was not long before entire cameo *parures* were being produced for the French nobility. The best examples

While Napoleon Bonaparte flourished in France and expanded his Empire, Germany was under constant threat of attack and desperate for currency. A scheme was devised in which patriots surrendered their jewels made of precious materials and in return were given jewellery made of iron. This proved not only to be an expedient but also the foundation of a whole new art form – Berlin ironwork

Left: the fineness of the metalwork of some Berlin ironwork is illustrated by this necklace and brooch, designed en suite. The medallions in the necklace show the emphasis on Classical design Right: two matching bracelets in Berlin ironwork

of these can be seen in many contemporary portraits, in particular the painting of Napoleon's sister Pauline, Princess Borghese, by Robert Lefebvre, executed in 1806 and now in the *Musée de Versailles*. She wears a wide gold belt of Greek fret design, *pavé*-set with diamonds; the buckle is a large Classical portrait cameo surrounded by diamonds. Her head-dress is of identical construction, interspersed with several diamond-set cameos; above this she wears a comb of five cameos in diamonds, her ear-rings are single cameo pendants; the only part of the *parure* which does not follow this pattern is the double *rivière* necklace. This is also true of the portrait (painted in the same year) of Marie-Caroline, later Queen of Naples, with a *parure* of pearls and cameos but only a simple string of pearls round her neck. One cameo *parure* from the period which has survived, attributed to Empress Josephine, is now in a private collection in England. It includes a crown, coronet, ear-rings, bracelet, slide and comb; all are of gold set with cameos cut from onyx, shell and cornelian. Napoleon himself is reported to have been crowned with a simple band decorated with cameos. He was presented with a rosary by the Pope and

it became fashionable to wear rosaries, necklace-style, and often jewelled.

A romantic gift form was introduced after the Emperor gave his sister a bracelet to mark the birth of her child; it was set with different stones, the initial letters of each stone spelling the name of her child. When Napoleon married his second wife, the Archduchess Marie-Louise of Austria in 1810, he allowed Josephine to keep most of the jewellery she had acquired during their marriage. His new wife was not particularly interested in jewels but this did not prevent the Emperor from spending 6,000,000 francs on jewellery for her as wedding presents. By 1812, Napoleon realized that all his resources were needed for campaigns and no great *parures* were ordered

Berlin Ironwork

So far we have only looked at the early 19th century from the French point of view. Under Napoleon the French were the arbiters of fashion throughout the western world and, with improved communications, fashions became virtually indistinguishable from country to country. One interesting development, however, was happening in Ger-

many but even this was in part the result of Napoleon's foreign policy.

The origin of Berlin iron jewellery is somewhat vague. It was almost certainly a development by iron craftsmen anxious to extend their range of products. As the steel-cutters in England moved from the manufacture of boxes and sword hilts to shoe-buckles and chatelaines, so the German iron-casters turned their attentions to jewellery.

The first place which definitely produced jewels in iron was the Royal Prussian Foundry which opened in 1804. This factory manufactured every type of ironware ranging from ornate mirrors to bridges and it is apparent that jewellery was part of their repertoire from the start. The earliest pieces were geometric patterns of fine woven wire, enamelled black, but it was not long before ironwork started to show the neo-Classical influences which were dominating European fashion. Repoussé medallions of various sizes, sometimes bordered with gold, were linked together in a chain to form a necklace and bracelets. In 1806, however, just two years after the factory opened, Napoleon captured Berlin and confiscated the moulds used for casting the medallions and sent them to France

where production was set up. From
then until 1815 it is virtually impossible
to say whether a piece is of German or
French origin since very few pieces
carry the maker's or designer's mark.
It is ironic that this very jewellery
should have later contributed to
Napoleon's downfall. From 1813 to 1815
the Germans were fighting for their
independence and one of the major
fund-raising methods used was to per-
suade the wealthy to exchange their
diamonds and precious metals for Berlin
ironwork. Many surviving examples
carry self-congratulatory messages
such as *Gold gab ich für Eisen* (I gave
gold for iron).

It was during these days of financial
hardship that Berlin ironwork was at
its most popular. But even after
Napoleon's fall, when comparative
stability returned to both France and
Germany, the vogue did not die out
immediately. The public had grown to
like the delicate black tracery. Styles
follow that of jewels produced in other
materials. After 1815 there was a return
to realism and themes from nature were
adopted such as flowers, plants and
butterflies. Gothic themes were also
common in ironwork.

The range of items produced was con-

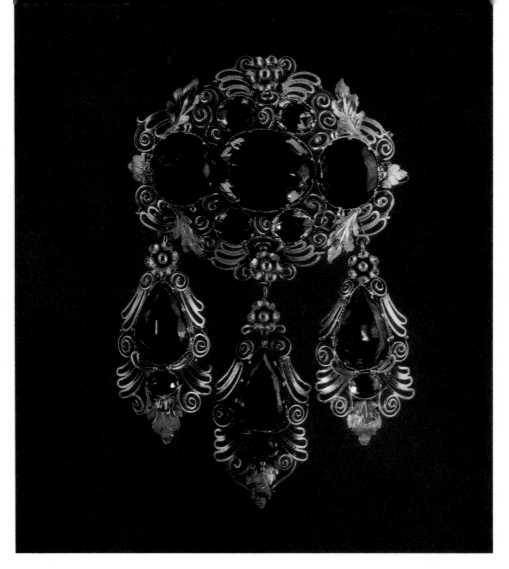

siderable: necklaces, bracelets, ear-rings, brooches, hair-ornaments, together with ancillary objects such as snuff-boxes and buckles. The best collection of Berlin ironwork is in the Victoria and Albert Museum, London.

Fluctuating Fashions

In 1814 the Empire fell, Napoleon was exiled and the Bourbons returned in the shape of Louis XVIII, grandson of Louis XV. Once again royal patronage came to a virtual standstill. The Bourbons had been in exile for a quarter of a century and were both impoverished and out of touch with the fashion trends of the previous 25 years. Also, they preferred to ignore anything to do with, or instigated under, the Napoleonic regime. Other loyalist members of the aristocracy returned impoverished, to find their estates confiscated by the republicans, and many of them had sold or pawned their existing jewels to maintain themselves during the long years abroad. This comparative poverty and the memory of Napoleon's gross extravagances led to a period of austerity which made it temporarily fashionable to wear no jewellery whatsoever. Gradually, however, the natural

French love of display overcame economic considerations and the jewellers of Paris were employed once again. Diamonds, however, were out of fashion as the patrons wanted display but within a limited budget. Amethyst, topaz, aquamarine and turquoise were widely used in the *parures* of the 1820s.

Louis was old when he was returned to the throne and his remoteness from the fashions of Napoleonic France was accentuated by an indifference towards jewels and precious things. He did however recover most of the regalia of Napoleon and had it remade by the jeweller Bapst.

While some classical influences remained, fashion changed dramatically in the few years after the fall of Napoleon. The hour-glass figure was all the rage: huge leg-of-mutton sleeves, wide short skirts and tiny waists by definition restricted the wearing of jewellery. While the King was not particularly interested in jewellery or clothes, the French found their champion in the Duchesse de Berry who started fashionable social gatherings similar to those of the late 18th century. She became the arbiter of fashion and tried to prevent the intrusion of new mass production techniques already

having a profound effect on goldwork on the other side of the Channel.

The most common of these techniques employed machine-stamped components which could be assembled and finished by hand, thus dramatically reducing the man hours necessary for making a single piece. The same stamping process was used to produce standard stone settings which had previously been fashioned by hand. *Cannetille*, a technique which produced matt gold with coarse filigree, also reached France from England and was widely used for the settings of semi-precious *parures*. Perhaps the best example of these parures is now in the Metropolitan Museum in New York; it has seven component parts: a diadem, two bracelets, ear-rings, necklace and brooch, all designed *en suite*. The goldwork is machine-stamped and set with enormous cabochon amethysts. The theme is floral and shows a move towards realism which, together with improved techniques, eventually stultified the jeweller's own flair for design.

In 1824, Louis XVIII was succeeded by Charles X (another grandson of Louis XV) whose tastes were, if anything, even more modest, but his short reign marked the start of the 'Gothic revival'

Left: parure of coral, French, mid-19th century. (Musée des arts décoratifs, Paris)

The renewed Classicism spread throughout Europe and there was a vogue for jewels derived from Gothic and Renaissance styles and techniques
Below: mid-19th century neck-band by A. W. Pugin, the famous 'Medieval-Victorian' architect, in gold and enamel set with ruby, diamonds, turquoises and pearls. (Victoria & Albert Museum, London)

Below: enamelled gold pin by Froment-Meurice of an amazon attacking a panther. Shown at the Paris Exhibition of 1855. (Victoria & Albert Museum)

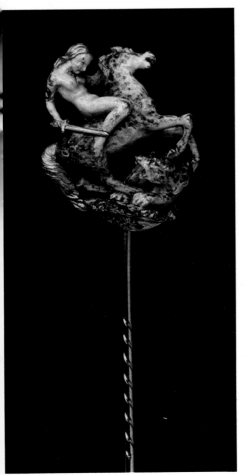

which was to dominate the next few years. It was a time of intense romanticism; women read Byron, fainted, and died of broken hearts.

From the beginning of the 1830s to the end of the century we see the most complex and changeable situation in jewellery fashion ever experienced before or since. Europe was already under the full influence of the Industrial Revolution which affected techniques, social structure, national and international communication. In France Louis Philippe, the bourgeois Monarch succeeded the Bourbons. Son of the Revolution's famous Philippe-Egalité, he in turn was replaced by Napoleon III and finally another Republic. In England the reign of Victoria never looked remotely vulnerable but the outside influences from her ever increasing Empire led to an eclectic and sometimes distorted scale of aesthetic values. We enter the great age of archaeological discoveries where jewels of the Etruscans and the Aegean had a profound effect on design; and, to confuse the matter further, the vogue for Gothic and Renaissance art was prevalent throughout Europe.

It was in France that the move had started towards romanticism and by

1830 it dominated all forms of fashion.
The crinoline was introduced; women
wore their hair parted in the middle and
with long ringlets hanging over their
shoulders. This hair-style led to the
revival of an old form of jewellery,
the *ferronnière* – a jewel worn on the
forehead, suspended from a thin ribbon
encircling the entire head. Later this
fashion was further elaborated by the
addition of two other pendants which
hung down by either temple.

The unquestioned master of the
Gothic revival, the *style à la cathédrale*,
was a Parisian named Froment-Meurice,
a cultured man, who was a trained
craftsman but preferred to design and
have his jewels made up by colleagues.
Unlike many of his contemporaries,
Froment-Meurice drew his inspiration
from the legends of the Gothic era and
the Renaissance tales of knights and
maidens in distress which were ideally
suited to the ultra-romanticism of the
time. His jewels themselves were small
sculptural vignettes. He had been working in Paris since the 1830s but it was
in 1851 with the Great Exhibition in
London, that he gained an international
reputation.

His prominence is summed up in an
obituary in *Le Siècle*. 'No one had ever

demonstrated so clearly that art had a
right to a place in every sphere. Particularly in his jewellery, so simple in
appearance, he showed an inventiveness, a delicacy and a gracefulness of
execution which had been long for-
gotten.'

Froment-Meurice undoubtedly had
all the qualities attributed to him by
Le Siècle, but other lesser mortals con-
tented themselves with straightforward
copies of the few Renaissance pieces
which had survived. Museums were by
this time springing up throughout
Europe and jewellers were able to
study the work of older craftsmen rather
than relying on pattern books. The
result of this was anything but benefi-
cial. When working from an engraving
a jeweller had ample opportunity to
exercise his own interpretation but
when confronted with the actual object,
he tended to follow the construction
rigidly and the result lacked both
warmth and personality.

While Froment-Meurice was building a reputation in France, another
jeweller, Pio Fortunato Castellani, was
establishing a business in Rome. He
drew his inspiration from the Ancient
World. On his own doorstep, treasures
of the Etruscan graves were starting

Left: memorial brooch in gold, diamonds and chrysoprase housing a cut steel cameo. English, mid-19th century Right: memorial brooch in gold, enamel and pearls, English, late 19th century

to come to light, and further afield the works of Classical Greece and Rome. He spent years trying to master the metalwork techniques which had made these objects possible. The main area of difficulty was granulation. Castellani never discovered the secret of Etruscan soldering but he and his two sons produced some very acceptable substitutes. Work from the Castellani family, marketed under the name of 'archaeological' jewellery fetched enormous prices throughout Europe. He later turned his attentions to the Roman, Greek and Byzantine jewels, including enamels and mosaics.

Two Neapolitan craftsmen also became famous for their 'Classical' jewels. Giacinto Melillo who for the most part by-passed the technical problems of reproducing the works of the ancient masters by casting by the lost wax

method. The other, Carlo Giuliano, was born in Naples but moved to London and produced 'Classical' jewels for the British market. However, he was most famous for his interpretation of the forms of the Renaissance which he adapted with enormous skill and taste.

Despite this fanatical interest in Classical and Renaissance art, the interest in motifs derived from nature was far from eclipsed. If anything these motifs became more representational than in the previous decade. At one stage there was a fashion for using green enamel to represent leaves of jewelled sprays. In France there was even a vogue for rings fashioned as old gnarled trees and logs and the new Paris zoo had its effect on jewellery with a brief popularity for brooches enamelled with giraffes. Other themes popular in France were birds protecting their young from a serpent and, after the wars in Algeria, arabic designs and lettering.

In 1848, however, France suffered another revolutionary upheaval and once again saw a sharp decline in the demand for jewellery which was to last until the establishment of the Second Empire by Napoleon III in 1852.

Victorian England

In 1837, Queen Victoria ascended the throne, a position which she was destined to hold for 64 years. Britain was in the throes of industrial euphoria, obsessed by mechanical gadgetry. The technology that was evolving, introduced several new materials and techniques to the craftsman's repertoire. The most significant of these was electro-plating, originally developed by an Italian at the beginning of the century but never applied on a commercial basis until the mid-1840s by the work of Elkington and Wright. Until the process had been discovered, most cheaper jewels were produced in pinchbeck and, while this provided a passable substitute, electroplating covered the entire surface of an object with a film of gold and was superficially indistinguishable from the real thing.

Methods of imitating precious stones were also improved with the refractive index of the new pastes increased considerably since the work of Joseph Strasser. A Midlands factory in Burslem was producing an imitation ivory, parian, which was a type of porcelain. This was carved and used for brooches and clasps. Techniques for stamping

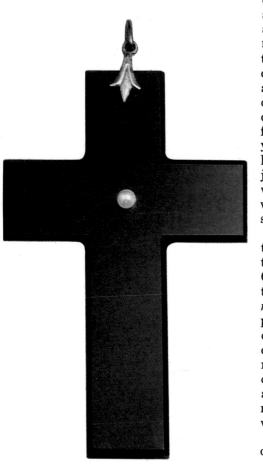

entire pieces of jewellery from thin sheets of gold became easier, quicker and cheaper as more sophisticated machinery was invented. Queen Victoria was fond of jewellery and not only wore it herself but often gave it away as presents, particularly at weddings. She had grand *parures* for state occasions but her true affection was for sentimental jewellery. In the early years of her reign she was happy with her consort Albert and sentimental jewels reflected her *joie de vivre* but with his untimely death in 1861, she went into a deep mourning from which she never fully recovered.

Public mourning was nothing new to the British; it had been a tradition in the country since the execution of Charles I in 1649, and indeed it was on this occasion that mourning jewellery, *memento mori*, was first worn. The practice continued until the early 19th century when mourning became an obsession, reflecting the move towards romanticism. When Queen Victoria came to the throne in 1837 she and all loyal subjects observed a period of mourning for William IV which today would seem excessive.

Mourning became more than a sign of respect, particularly for the bour-

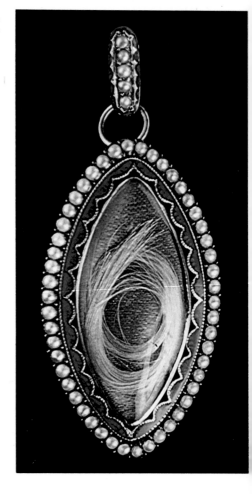

geoisie for whom it was an indication
of position in society; the grander the
funeral the better the man. Fashion
magazines jumped on the band wagon,
illustrating suitable costumes for every
type of event for those in mourning and,
complementing these outfits, there was
inevitably mourning jewellery. The
most popular material for the jewellery
was jet, the black fossil of wood, hard
coal or lignite which was found on the
beaches around Whitby Bay, a small
town in Yorkshire.

Jet is known to have been used since
the Bronze Age; the Romans used it and
called it black amber; but it was not
until the beginning of the 19th century
that it was used for jewellery on any
scale. First there was one workshop
in Whitby, then in 1832 another opened
and the work force grew to 25; by 1850
five new workshops had opened and the
production of jet jewellery was beginning to be a substantial business. It was
not until 1861, however, when the untimely death of the Prince Consort
plunged the whole country into a deep
and long mourning that Whitby came
into its own. By 1870 some 1,500 people
were employed cutting and polishing
jet which at that time constituted a
major industry.

*Even more macabre than hair-set jewellery was the vogue for jewels actually constructed from plaited human hair
Left: a parure of English hair jewellery, c.1865
Right: bracelet in hair with a pinchbeck clasp*

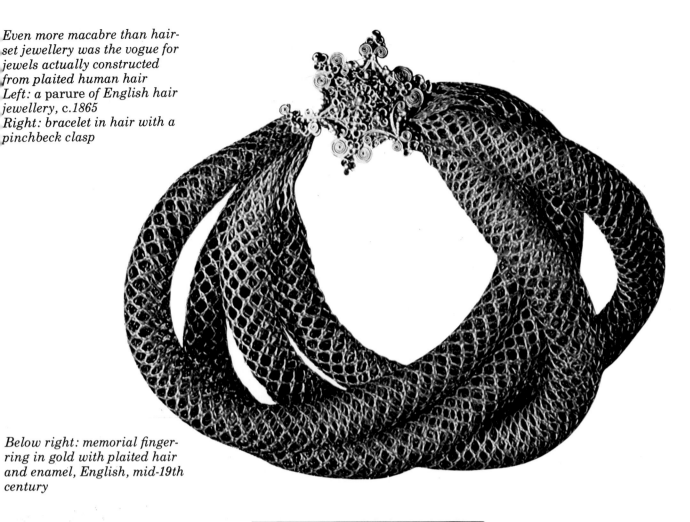

Below right: memorial finger-ring in gold with plaited hair and enamel, English, mid-19th century

A comparatively soft material ($3\frac{1}{2}$ on Mohs scale), jet can be carved or engraved comparatively easily and yet takes an excellent polish. The forms adopted by the jet craftsmen of the 19th century reflected public taste in conventional jewellery: necklaces made from strings of spherical or facet-cut beads; spherical pendant ear-rings, and carved finger-rings; but most fashionable were oval or heart-shaped lockets and pendants decorated with floral motifs. Sad to relate, the boom of Whitby was short-lived and by 1884 the work force was reduced to 300 people. This did not reflect a move away from public mourning but the introduction of other cheaper materials which could produce the same sombre effect as jet. The most common of these was black glass which became known as 'French jet'. In Ireland bog oak was carved in cruciforms and other jewel forms and, while it was not the true black of jet, it was considered a suitable substitute. Another popular, though far from cheap, material was tortoiseshell; but perhaps the biggest single invader was black enamel. This was particularly popular for finger-rings, where it was used in contrast with a gold band to make up floral designs, hearts, or written tributes. Later, even the gold for mourning jewellery lost out to gilt, pinchbeck or base metal.

In addition to jet, hair jewellery continued from the 18th century. The most common form was the brooch constructed from a number of materials, gold, jet, pinchbeck, gilt, tortoiseshell or enamel. This was generally circular or oval with a central panel to accommodate the lock of hair. Unlike the 18th century, when little vignettes were constructed from hair, the Victorians tended to have it simply plaited and held in place with a panel of glass. Others preferred to be more private about their mementos and lockets were produced which concealed the plaited hair. On the border of the brooch or locket there was invariably a commemorative message, often in Gothic script: 'In Memory Of . . .'

Finger-rings containing hair from the deceased were equally popular and followed the same pattern as the brooches. Some displayed the hair under a central glass panel and others had false bezels where the hair could be kept hidden. A more morbid form of commemorative jewellery, known as 'hair work', became popular about the middle of the century. Hair from the

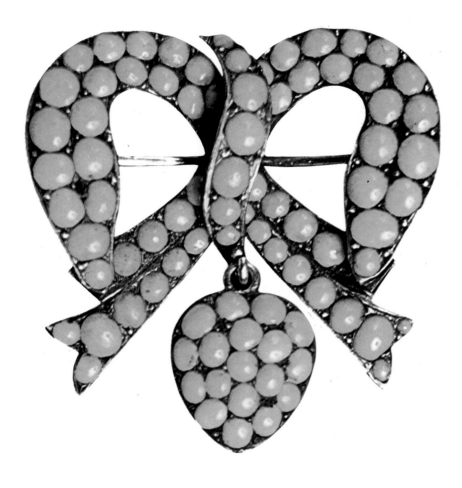

After quarter of a century of mourning the English had had enough. With the Silver Jubilee, Queen Victoria was persuaded to sanction relaxation of the mourning code. The sentimental approach, however, persisted and gloom was replaced as a theme by romance and cloying affection. Jewellery from the late 19th century until the Art Nouveau movement hit on an all time low
Left: bow brooch with heart pendant, pavé-set with turquoises. English, late 19th century
Right: two heart brooches in gold set with turquoises and satin under glass

Photography was within the reach of most pockets by the end of the 19th century and there was a fashion for the use of photographs in jewels
Far right: gold brooch with photograph, English, late 19th century

Machine-stamped sentimental jewels were produced in their thousands, in base metal silver or gold, for the servant classes
Left: two typical low-cost sentimental brooches, English, late 19th century

Right: garnet heart pendant pavé-set with diamonds and mounted in gold. French, late 19th century
Far right: snake bracelet in gold and blue enamel, set with pearls and rubies. English, late 19th century

deceased was woven and plaited into ropes which were fitted with gold terminals and served as bracelets, necklaces or watch-chains.

Towards the end of the century photographic mourning lockets, virtually identical to their counterparts containing hair, became fashionable, but by the time the camera was within the reach of the man in the street, the emotional climate in England had changed and photographic lockets were used more as reminders of the living.

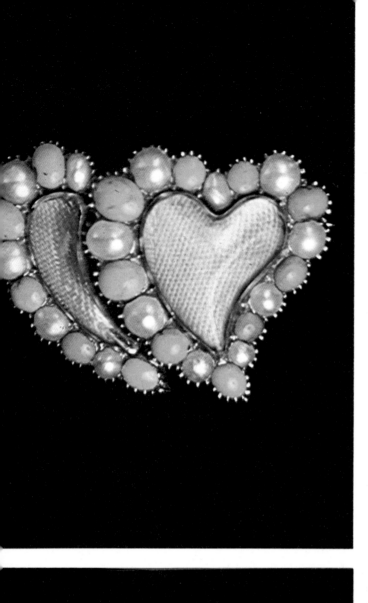

*Perhaps the most vulgar
examples of jewellery produced
in Victorian times were to be
found among sporting and
'doggy' brooches
Right: gold, fabric and crystal
dog brooch, English, late 19th
century*

*In the more expensive bracket
jewels in the form of birds and
insects were extremely popular
in both France and England
during the last twenty years of
the 19th century
Left: two gold bird pendants on
chains, French, late 19th
century*

By 1885, the English were bored with
the constant burden of mourning and
they approached the Palace to see if
the Queen would not give her blessing
to a relaxation of the extremes they had
suffered for nearly quarter of a century
on her behalf. . . . Yet it was not until
1887 that Victoria gave way and agreed
to wear some silver jewellery to commemorate her Silver Jubilee.

The public, and indeed the jewellers,
must have been delighted. Their pre-
dilection for sentimentality shifted emphasis from death to love. The result
was sentimental silver jewellery produced on a vast scale to suit every
pocket. The design of these pieces and
their often shoddy execution may
have little appeal today but they do
reflect the mood of the time and are,

Right: machine-stamped hunting brooch, English, late 19th century
Below: gold brooch with dog in ceramic, English, late 19th century

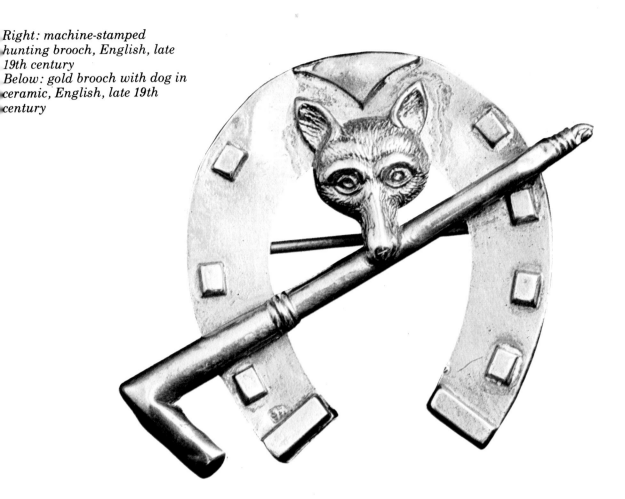

therefore, relevant to the story of jewellery design.

Mass production had never had such a field day in the jewellery industry. Millions of sentimental brooches were stamped from thin sheet, some with special panels in which the purchaser would have a name engraved. Perhaps the most common theme was the name brooch, a simple oblong band of silver with a floral border containing the name of the loved one – an ideal gift 'from the footman to the pantry maid'.

Other themes were hearts, clasped hands, anchors – all symbols of lasting friendship or affection. Almost all these were accompanied by some form of floral decoration. Different flowers had their individual significance which would be chosen to denote some secret message between the giver and the receiver. A book written in 1856 and published at the beginning of this century gives the significance of no less than 700 plants, obviously too many to enumerate here.

Interesting or not, Victorian sentimental jewellery represented a new low in Western European design and craftsmanship and in England it was a situation which took several decades to rectify.

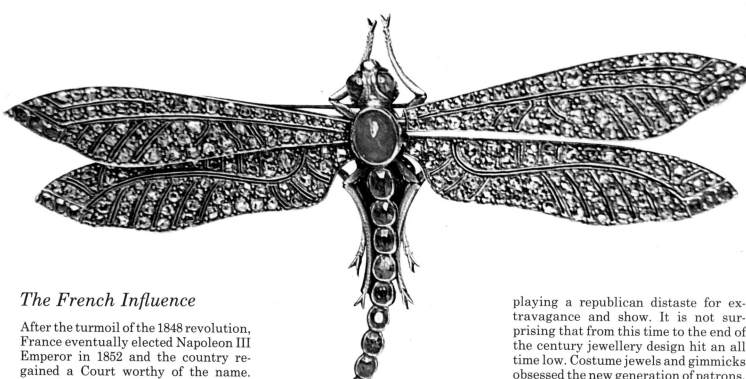

The French Influence

After the turmoil of the 1848 revolution, France eventually elected Napoleon III Emperor in 1852 and the country regained a Court worthy of the name. Like his famous uncle, the young Emperor married a woman whose appetite for jewels was enormous. The Empress Eugénie had a particular penchant for pearls and diamonds and a fondness for the designs of the 18th century. She had all the major crown jewels broken up and reset in the style of Marie-Antoinette.

France was once again the leader in European fashion, whilst England, far behind, wallowed in sentimentality. In 1851 French goldsmiths had made a considerable impression at the Great Exhibition in London. Together with Froment-Meurice, it was another Parisian – Massin – who provided the real new challenge to the 18th century style with his floral sprays of *pavé*-set diamonds.

The renewed glory of the French Court was short-lived. Napoleon III was deposed in 1870 and Europe was left with no leaders in fashion. England was still subdued by a Queen Victoria in mourning, while France was dis-

playing a republican distaste for extravagance and show. It is not surprising that from this time to the end of the century jewellery design hit an all time low. Costume jewels and gimmicks obsessed the new generation of patrons. Paris produced 'electric' jewels, vibrated by the power of a battery concealed under the dress. Coy animal brooches were popular in England, portraying dogs, horses and even house flies. Novelty jewellery showed the trappings of the Industrial Revolution such as steam engines, bridges and tools.

Another fashion which originated in England but soon spread further afield marked the new role of women in society. Previously sport had been a male preserve but by the end of the 19th century it was acceptable for women to try their hand. By 1890, pins and brooches with golf clubs, golf balls, riding crops, stirrups and other sporting themes became as popular as sentimental jewellery had been a decade earlier. The end of the 19th century, however, was not all bad. One great craftsman emerged, to become perhaps the most famous jeweller of them all – Fabergé, and the foundations were laid for the Art Nouveau movement which was to revolutionize European taste.

Right: floral spray brooch in gold and enamel set with diamonds and rubies. French, late 19th century

Below: three diamond floral brooches, French, late 19th century

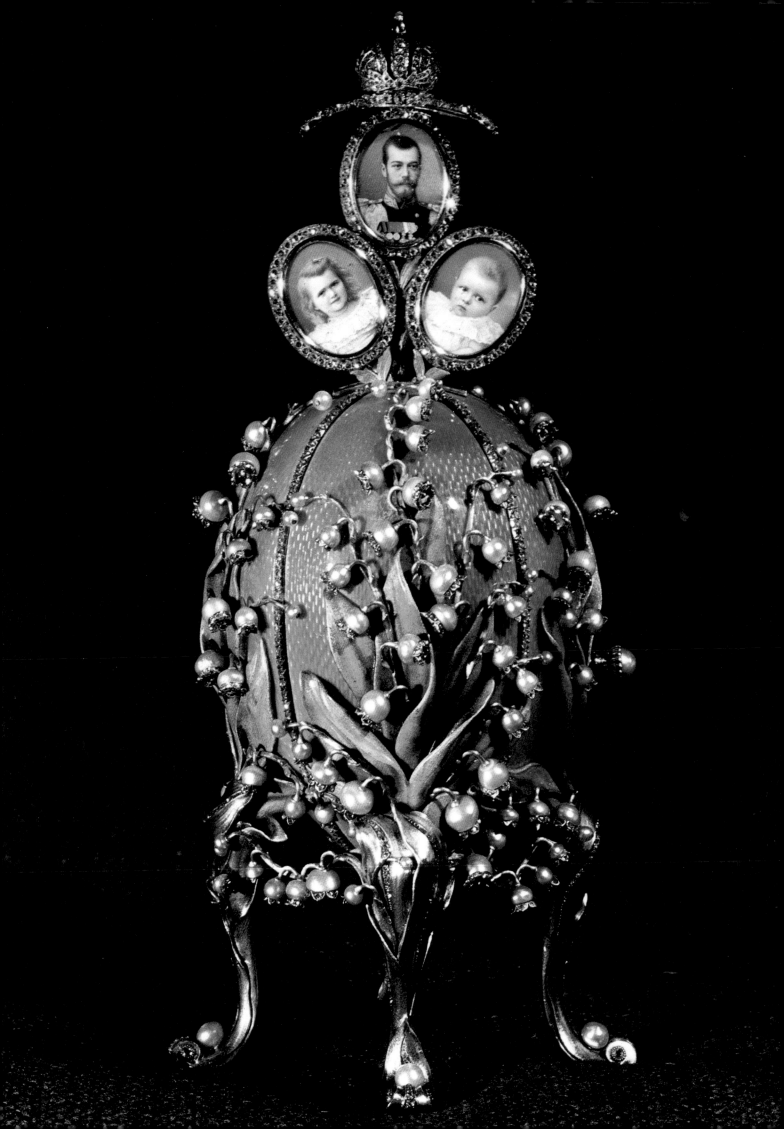

Perhaps the greatest virtuoso in the history of jewellery to emerge since Cellini was Peter Carl Fabergé. Ironically, like Cellini, he produced very little jewellery as such, concentrating rather on objets d'art. He will always be remembered mostly for the jewelled Easter eggs which he made for members of the Russian royal family and it is with these that his genius can best be illustrated

Opposite: the 'Surprise' Easter egg presented by Tsar Nicholas II to his mother, the Dowager Empress Marie Feodorovna, in 1898. The egg, in gold and enamel with pearl and rose diamond 'lilies of the valley,' contains miniature portraits of the Tsar and the Princesses Olga and Tatiana. Made to Fabergé's design by his chief work-master, Michael Perchin Below: the Serpent egg clock presented to his Tsarina, Marie Feodorovna, by Tsar Alexander III, c.1890. (Both, Coll. Wartski, London)

Fabergé

Ask anyone to name three jewellers and nine times out of ten, the first would be Fabergé. Carl Fabergé's inventiveness and his imaginative use of every conceivable technique and material earn him a place of honour in any book concerned with jewellery.

The Fabergé family, were probably originally French Huguenot refugees who eventually settled in St. Petersburg where, in 1842, Gustave Fabergé (Carl's father) set up a jewellery business. He sent Carl to Germany and France to learn his trade and in 1870, when his son was still only 24, he retired and handed over the business.

The firm had traditionally produced jewellery but Carl Fabergé decided to concentrate on producing *objets d'art* which in commercial terms seems a very odd decision to have made. His gamble paid off, however, and it was not long before the house of Fabergé was being patronized by the Tsars of Russia, a situation which ensured it world supremacy until its confiscation in 1918 after the Bolshevik revolution. Fabergé first exhibited at the Pan-Russian Exhibition in Moscow in 1898 where he carried off the top award. Other accolades

followed thick and fast at Stockholm and Nuremberg – but it was not until 1900 and the *Exposition internationale universelle* (World Fair) in Paris that Fabergé's reputation reached its pinnacle. French goldsmiths, traditionally confident of their supremacy, marvelled at the objects he exhibited and he was duly awarded the *Légion d'honneur.* These important exhibitions gained Fabergé an international reputation and the patronage of the Royalty and aristocracy of Europe, India and the Orient.

By 1898 Fabergé employed more than 700 craftsmen and had branches in St. Petersburg, Moscow, Kiev, Odessa and London but despite this vast expansion he never lost control and every piece which left the workshops had his highly individual mark. The range of objects produced was amazing: ikons, boxes, trays, cups, fans, clocks – anything which could be jewelled was tackled. His style, like most other craftsmen of the 19th century, was essentially eclectic. The influence can be seen of Louis XIV, Louis XV, and Louis XVI (presumably resulting from his Paris apprenticeship) as well as that of Renaissance, Old Russian, Byzantine, and Classical design. Yet he seems to

Right: one of Fabergé's most celebrated pieces, the Coronation egg presented by Tsar Nicholas II to his Tsarina Alexandra Feodorovna at Easter 1897, the year after his coronation. The egg, which is 5 inches high, contains a faithful replica of the coronation coach in gold, enamel and diamonds, with rock crystal windows and tyres of platinum. Made to Fabergé's design at Michael Perchin's workshop. (Coll. Wartski, London)

have been able to use all these styles and combine or interpret them until they became his own – all Fabergé.

His technical virtuosity is unparalleled; he used all the traditional techniques and stretched them further than ever before; he used modern machinery without ever becoming a slave to it; he flaunted tradition, not caring about the intrinsic value of materials but only about the visual effect they produced in a piece. Thus he gave his patrons a nudge away from the flashy commercialism which had dogged jewellers for so long. He employed every imaginable precious and semi-precious stone; he disliked the brilliant-cut, which he thought vulgar, and used instead either cabochon- or rose-cut. He was a law unto himself.

It is ironic that the one thing for which he will always be famous was supposed to be a private matter between him and the Russian Court. The Imperial Easter Eggs were first shown at the 1900 Paris World Fair.

It was some years before, in 1883, that the Easter egg saga started. Carl Fabergé suggested to Tsar Alexander III that he should give a jewelled Easter egg to the Tsarina for her Easter present of the following year,

instead of an ordinary piece of jewellery. He promised that the egg should have a special surprise and, despite the Tsar's curiosity, Fabergé kept his secret until the following year. He was something of a practical joker and it must have been with a certain dismay that the Tsar looked at the plain white enamelled egg which confronted him, but Fabergé was as good as his word. When the egg was opened it revealed a gold yolk; inside the yolk was a tiny chicken of different coloured golds; within this there was a model of the Imperial crown and inside this again a tiny egg-shaped ruby. The Tsar was so delighted that he gave Fabergé a standing order for an egg every Easter. It was a tradition carried on by Tsar Nicholas II and, over the years, he must have produced at least 57 of them.

Fabergé is important to the development of jewels. The late 19th century was the start of great retailers, producing objects speculatively as well as by commission. Such companies as Cartier in Paris, Garrard in London and Tiffany in New York had been in business since the first half of the century but it was indisputably Fabergé who brought a lasting new dimension to the retailing of quality jewels.

264

Towards the end of the 19th
century the Art Nouveau
movement swept through
Europe, revolutionizing
architecture and the decorative
arts. In no area was it more
impressive than in jewellery
Left: representational themes
are the very essence of Art
Nouveau design. This butterfly
necklace in gold and coloured
precious stones was designed
and made by René Lalique in
the 1890s. (Victoria & Albert
Museum, London)
Below: pendant-brooch by René
Lalique in ivory, gold, enamel,
brilliants and baroque pearl.
(Coll. M. Périnet, Paris)

Art Nouveau

The second half of the 19th century was a time of unprecedented disillusionment amongst exponents of the applied arts. Saddled with a public interested solely in revamped fashions of the past and trapped by the economics of mechanization, the art had gone from their craft. The new consumers, the ever growing *nouveaux riches*, gobbled up everything that the factories could produce. Aestheticism was not their *forte*. Yet, by the end of the century, we see the most dramatic innovation to fashion ever experienced. Unlike vogues of previous centuries which grew from developments of existing styles, a gradual process often spread over several decades, Art Nouveau was *new* in the true sense of the word. At its height in 1895 it affected every branch of the applied arts throughout the western world, yet by 1914 it was dead, killed as a result of its own excesses.

Art Nouveau was more than a design concept; it was a total philosophy centred round a desire to revive the crafts and to offer good design to a mass audience. It was not so much an attempt to squash mechanization as to make the machine a servant rather than the master it had become.

The expression 'Art Nouveau' derives from Siegfried Bing's shop *La maison de l'art nouveau* which opened in Paris in 1895; it had, however, many other names. In Germany it was known as *Jugendstil* (after the art magazine *Die Jugend*), in France as *style moderne,* in Austria as *Sezession* (Secession), in Italy as *Stile Liberty* (after the famous London store) and in Spain as *Juventud*. Whatever the country or the name, the theme was the same, unapologetically ornamental with free-flowing lines – a total rejection of the rigidity and stiffness of the previous half century. It shocked, it impressed, but above all it was *new*.

One of the most important achievements of the Art Nouveau movement, apart from the works produced by its followers, was the re-establishment of the applied arts. Never since the Ancient World had the great craftsmen of the 'minor' arts been appreciated with such reverence. Walter Crane, the English artist, illustrator and associate of William Morris, said he wanted to 'turn our artists into craftsmen and our craftsmen into artists.'

The division between pure and applied arts for a brief but stimulating period vanished. Great painters such

as Bonnard and Vuillard would decorate furniture; Toulouse Lautrec and Alphonse Mucha produced posters. The poster in fact became accepted as one of the most important major art forms and a fashion for *panneaux décoratifs* enjoyed a brief popularity. These were posters produced for decorating the home rather than as vehicles for advertising, a vogue which came back into fashion in the 1960s, with poster shops springing up in every capital, many of them indeed selling Art Nouveau posters by artists such as Aubrey Beardsley.

To find the origins of Art Nouveau we must go back to the 1850s for, though Art Nouveau was new, it had roots like anything else. The undisputed doyen of the movement was the English designer, William Morris, who started the Arts and Crafts movement to which Art Nouveau owed much. Morris was connected with the pre-Raphaelite school, a close friend of both Burne-Jones and Rossetti, but, unlike them he favoured the applied arts. He formed a company which became the first true interior decorators. He believed rooms should be designed as a total unit and would insist on everything being designed *en suite* from furniture to fabrics

and details such as door handles.

Unlike some of his followers, Morris had a deep loathing for mechanization in any form. He was a man of great social conscience and believed mechanization to be degrading for all involved. He dreamed of a return to the crafts. Paradoxically, the methods he employed required so much manpower – no longer a cheap commodity – that his products became vastly expensive and far beyond the reach of the very audience for whom they were originally intended. Even the work he did produce could not truly be described as Art Nouveau but it was Morris's ideas that provided inspiration for great designers such as Mackmurdo, Crane and Ashbee. While lacking Morris's power as a social-reformer, they had much more success in putting his philosophies into practice. Whistler was another friend of the pre-Raphaelites who helped pave the way for the Art Nouveau movement. He was far too much of an individualist to seek refuge in any movement but it was his love of Japanese art which gave a form to what had previously been a dream. Trade treaties had been signed with Japan in 1859 and large quantities of Japanese goods were flooding into

Philippe Wolfers, a Belgian, was one of the few Art Nouveau jewellers not to emanate from Paris
Right: a somewhat macabre pendant made by Wolfers in 1902 in gold, enamel, ivory, opal and baroque pearl. (Private collection)

Despite the overall freedom of the Art Nouveau jewels, artists like Georges Fouquet were highly disciplined craftsmen
Below: design for a pendant by Fouquet in gold, enamel and pearl. (Musée des arts décoratifs, Paris). Below right: the finished object. (Coll. M. Périnet, Paris)

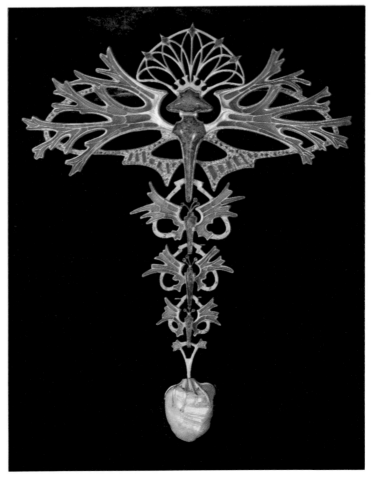

269

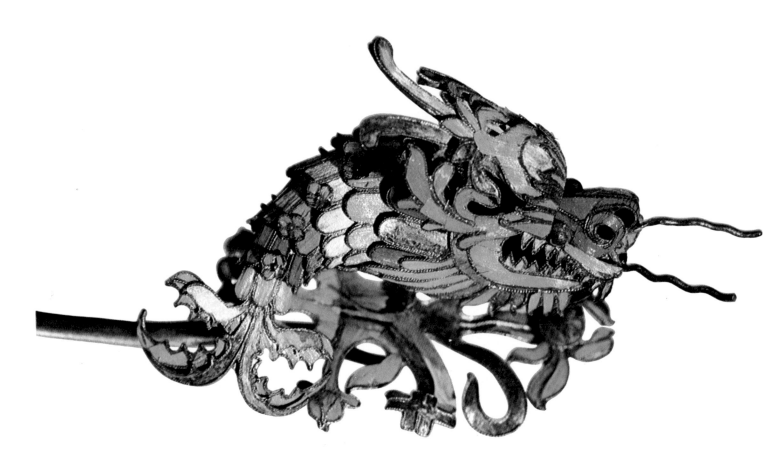

Europe, particularly to Paris where Whistler had studied.

In 1862 a large collection of Japanese fabrics and prints were shown at the second Great International Exhibition in London; the bulk was bought by a Company called Farmer and Rogers who then set up an Oriental department with a young man, Arthur Lasenby Liberty, in charge. Liberty became friendly with Whistler and Rossetti and when Farmer and Rogers closed, he purchased their entire Oriental stock and set up business on his own in Regent Street. His store, Liberty, was destined to become the most important showcase for Art Nouveau, and it is interesting to note that the other two great Art Nouveau stores, Bing of Paris and Tiffany in New York also sold Japanese goods.

The first true member of the Art Nouveau proper was probably Arthur H. Mackmurdo who formed the Century Guild in 1882 whose object was to rid the arts of the influence of industry. His designs, notably for fabrics, were instantly successful and it is a measure of the man that his designs were still being used and adapted 30 years later in England, France and Germany. In fact they were widely adapted for jewellery as well as other things.

Six years later C. R. Ashbee, famous English architect and goldsmith, formed the Guild of Handicraft, again to try and put Morris's social reforms into practice. He was perhaps the first member of the movement to produce jewels but they lacked the excitement and technical virtuosity of artists such as Lalique and Fouquet. For the most part they were rather lumpy and inelegant.

It would be impossible to discuss Art Nouveau without mentioning Aubrey Beardsley who took the symbolism of Japanese prints to their most extreme. He was a precocious young man and by the age of 21 was contributing to *Studio*, the leading art magazine of the day. His reputation was established by his pornographic work on *Lysistrata*, and after illustrating Oscar Wilde's *Salomé*. He was, as a person, largely disliked but his wide, sweeping lines and flat black backgrounds had an enormous influence on all branches of the decorative arts.

It was in Glasgow, of all places, that British Art Nouveau reached its peak. Charles Rennie Mackintosh led a group which became known as the 'Glasgow School', which also included

The most important influence on the Art Nouveau movement was Oriental, despite the fact that neither China nor Japan had any great history in jewellery (in both cases, dress was so elaborate that jewels would have been superfluous). Hair-pins with profusely decorated heads were continually favoured, the fantastic animal shape being typical of Art Nouveau (although the Oriental example illustrated was in fact made during the previous century) Above left: dragon-head pin in gold with bird feathers. (Private collection)

Fantasy was one of the essential ingredients of the Art Nouveau. No one took this further and to greater extremes than French jeweller René Lalique Right: serpent brooch in gold and enamel by Lalique, 1898. (Gulbenkian Foundation, Lisbon)

Left: silver-gilt buckle by René Lalique, 1898. (Victoria & Albert Museum, London) Right: brooch by an unknown French artist in gold and enamel. (Victoria & Albert Museum, London)

his wife, Margaret MacDonald, and Herbert and Frances McNair. Perhaps the most famous example of their work to survive is one of the Tea Rooms in Glasgow, designed by Mackintosh in 1894. Their work brought an order and precision which was to have a long-lasting influence. Like so many of his contemporaries, Mackintosh was an all round craftsman. Unfortunately only one piece of jewellery by him has survived, a silver finger-ring set with pearls, amethysts and rubies. The only other piece to have survived from the Glasgow School is a pendant by Margaret MacDonald, a heart set with rubies, pearls and turquoises. Neither of these two jewels is particularly exciting but it would be unfair to criticize artists, who proved their brilliance elsewhere, on such flimsy evidence.

As is so often true in Britain, these designers had the inventiveness to start an idea but lacked the stamina to develop it and we must move to the continent before we see the true potential of Art Nouveau exploited, particularly in the field of jewellery. We must look to France to find the great Art Nouveau jewellers. After 1895 when Bing opened his *La maison de l'art*

nouveau, Paris took the style to her heart with an unabashed enthusiasm and by 1900 the city was a mass of peacocks, lilies and sensual swirling lines – in posters by Alphonse Mucha, glassware by Emile Gallé, architecture by Hector Guimard and furniture by Louis Majorelle and Eugène Vallin. But it was for jewels that the French Art Nouveau movement will be remembered, with names like Lalique, Fouquet and Vever. In the 20 short years that the vogue survived, they produced some of the most exciting and original pieces ever seen in this century or any other. Sometimes they were exaggerated to the point of being grotesque but at their best they were quite stunning.

The greatest of these three was undoubtedly René Lalique. Lalique originally wanted to be a painter but in 1876, when his father died, he became apprenticed to the eminent Parisian jeweller Aucoc at the age of 16. He served two years and then decided to continue his studies in England and it was there that he became involved with the ever-growing Art Nouveau movement. He returned to Paris in 1881 and opened his own workshop, which he operated with modest success until

1891 when he had his first big break in the form of a commission from the darling of the theatre, Sarah Bernhardt.

He spent the next three years studying glass-making techniques, and this material became the backbone of his finest pieces. It was not until 1895 that he burst on the Paris fashion scene after his exhibition at the Paris Salon. His work was greeted with unanimous acclaim. Like Fabergé (with whom he shared the honours at the World Fair in Paris in 1900) Lalique was instrumental in ending the materialistic attitude which had dogged jewellers for centuries. He believed that the cash value of the materials used in a piece of jewellery was totally irrelevant. He loved his materials, irrespective of their value; he would use glass if that was what would do most for the design. He had a great love of ivory horn and amber which he carved with incredible skill; golds of different colours were used in the same piece, together with silver, silver with patina, copper and steel. But it was for glass and enamel that he had the deepest love, and he became a master of the stained glass technique of *plique à jour*.

Nothing like his jewels had ever been seen yet the Renaissance influence

273

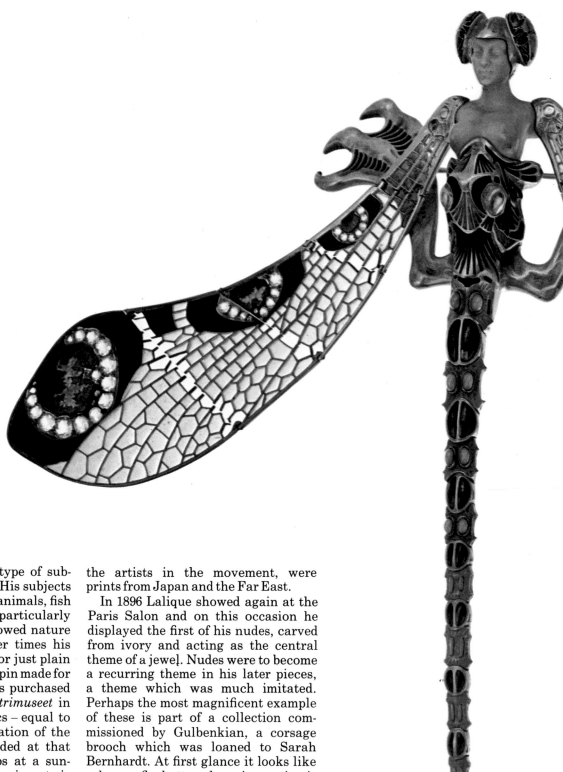

is obvious both from the type of subject matter and execution. His subjects were drawn from nature – animals, fish and plants, and insects, particularly insects. Sometimes he followed nature with great precision; other times his images would be distorted or just plain fanciful. For example, a hatpin made for the World Fair in 1900 was purchased by the *Dansk Kunstindustrimuseet* in Copenhagen for 1500 francs – equal to over £550 today (an indication of the respect his work commanded at that time). It depicts five wasps at a sunflower. The modelling of the insects is masterful and the range of materials – gold, silver, opal, glass, horn and diamonds, illustrates his total freedom from convention.

Other parallels with the Renaissance are obvious in his figurative work, but Lalique could never be accused of being imitative. Henri Vever, a contemporary jeweller, pays tribute to his colleague's integrity: '. . . this resemblance, evident though not intended, proves that an artist can evolve new interpretations, imbue everything with new life; and to be satisfied with imitations is, in fact, tantamount to a confession of impotence.' Another source of inspiration for Lalique, and indeed used by all

the artists in the movement, were prints from Japan and the Far East.

In 1896 Lalique showed again at the Paris Salon and on this occasion he displayed the first of his nudes, carved from ivory and acting as the central theme of a jewel. Nudes were to become a recurring theme in his later pieces, a theme which was much imitated. Perhaps the most magnificent example of these is part of a collection commissioned by Gulbenkian, a corsage brooch which was loaned to Sarah Bernhardt. At first glance it looks like a dragon-fly, but on closer inspection it proves to be a hideous creature with a long, thin body and enormous claws. From the gaping jaws of this creature protrudes the torso of a woman with, instead of arms, huge wings of *plique à jour*. Another style he evolved later was a female profile either in gold or ivory with complex hairstyles which curled and wound in the curvilinear fashion which typifies Art Nouveau.

While Lalique was undoubtedly the master of Art Nouveau jewellers, two other Frenchmen also deserve great respect: George Fouquet and Henri Vever. Unlike Lalique they were both born into the profession, and both inherited established businesses in the

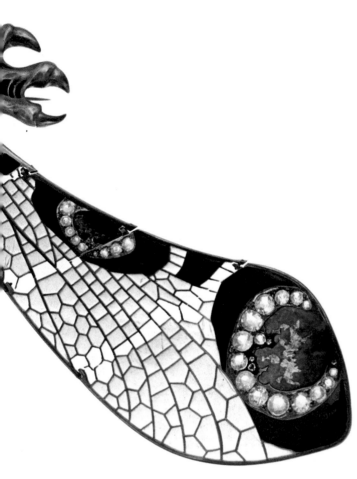

The Gulbenkian Foundation in
Portugal has the finest
collection of Art Nouveau
jewels anywhere in the world.
Calouste Gulbenkian
commissioned René Lalique to
make a collection in 1898
Left: one of the most famous
pieces by Lalique, a flexible
corsage ornament in the form
of a dragon-fly in gold, ivory,
plique-à-jour enamel and
chrysoprase. (Gulbenkian
Foundation, Lisbon)
Below: gold and enamel
repoussé plaque by René
Lalique, c.1900. (Gulbenkian
Foundation, Lisbon)

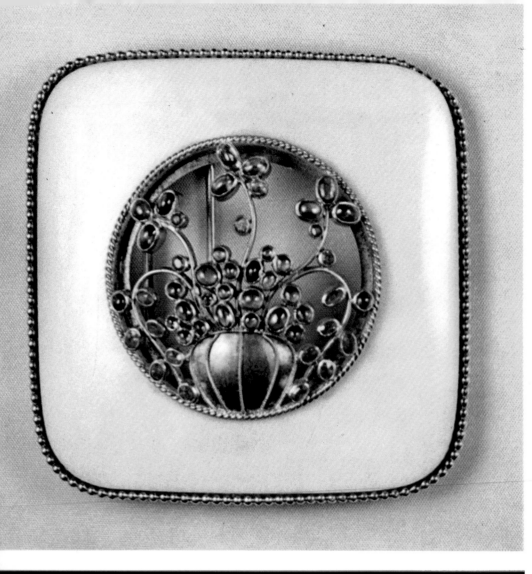

1880s. Fouquet in particular came from a most distinguished family of goldsmiths; his father Alphonse produced some of the best jewellery in the Italian Renaissance style during the 1850s and 1860s; today his son is one of the finest artist-craftsmen in Paris. Fouquet's jewellery was neither as imaginative nor as adventurous as Lalique's, being more symmetrical and heavier. He was at his best when working with the designer and poster artist, Mucha.

Alphonse Mucha left his native Prague for Paris and soon established himself as the leading Art Nouveau poster designer. Amongst other things, he had a contract to design all Sarah Bernhardt's posters, a situation which he exploited to the full. In the early days his designs for Fouquet were unimpressive but later, much influenced by Lalique, this team produced some extraordinary pieces. Most famous of these must be the snake bracelet which was worn by Bernhardt for her role as *Cleopatra*. A great gold and enamel snake encircled her wrist three times, and the carved opal head with ruby eyes rested on the back of her hand; from its mouth a chain joined a finger-ring, also of opal, gold and enamel. The piece is reported to have cost so much that

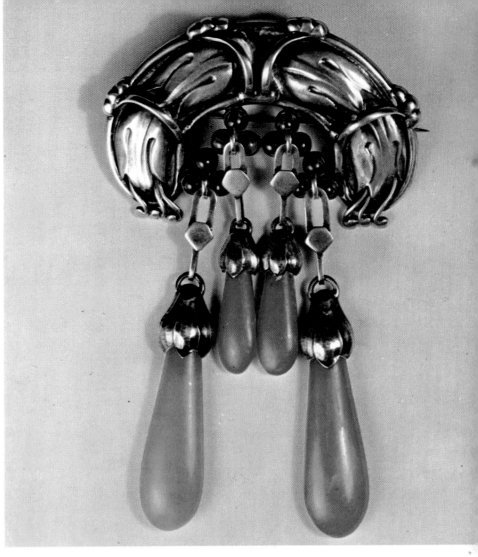

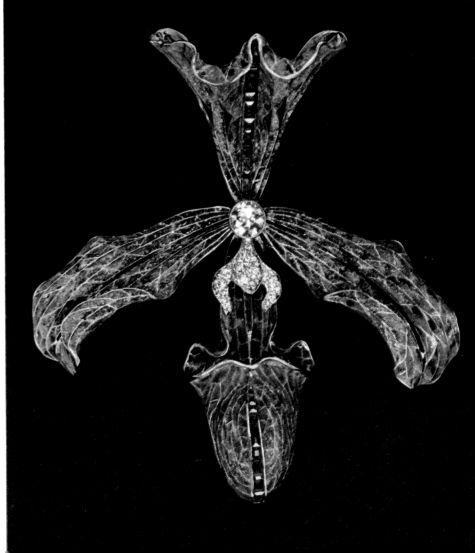

Fouquet had to collect his payment in instalments from the stage door.

Henri Vever had no such distinguished client. His work was much more formalized but it fits firmly into the Art Nouveau movement. Perhaps his greatest contribution to posterity was his book *La bijouterie française au XIX siècle* to which we owe much of our knowledge of 19th century trends.

The effects of Art Nouveau hit other countries in Europe at different times and in different ways. Scandinavia, for instance, virtually did not exist as an artistic entity but during the time of the Art Nouveau movement, the foundations were made for a race of jewellers who were to become the pacemakers for the first half of the 20th century. The name Georg Jensen epitomizes everything that is good about Scandinavian design. Jewellery and metalwork from his factory symbolized the clean, simple design which is today described as modern, but it was with Art Nouveau that Jensen made his initial impression on the public. Several of these Art Nouveau jewels are preserved at the Jensen headquarters in Copenhagen. They are generally more robust and three-dimensional than the work of the French jewellers.

He had a liking for large cabochon-cut stones set in symmetrical, curvilinear designs of silver or tortoise shell. The motifs are undeniably Art Nouveau but the Scandinavian temperament has crept in, bringing order and precision to the sweeping lines. The results are not nearly as exciting as the French work but interesting as forerunners of the Danish designs which were to come in the 1920s and 1930s.

Elsewhere in Scandinavia jewellery had been carried out for centuries at a mundane level, yet with the internationalism of Art Nouveau, Norway emerged as one of the great sources of enamelling, in particular the difficult process of *plique à jour*.

Other countries in Europe followed the vogue but none of them produced jewellery of any particular note with the exception, that is, of Belgium. The Belgians were as shackled with the past as anyone, everywhere there was work in Renaissance and Gothic styles. They had watched the work of Morris and Mackmurdo with interest and in 1884, a group was established under the name of *Les Vingt*, whose aim was not so much to react against mechanization (which still had yet to get a grip on Belgium) but more to react against

Above: hinged bracelet in gold, enamel and pavé-set brilliants by René Lalique, c.1900–05. (Gulbenkian Foundation, Lisbon)
Right: lapel brooch in gold and enamel, made in 1900 by Georges Fouquet to a design by C. Desroziers. (Victoria & Albert Museum, London)

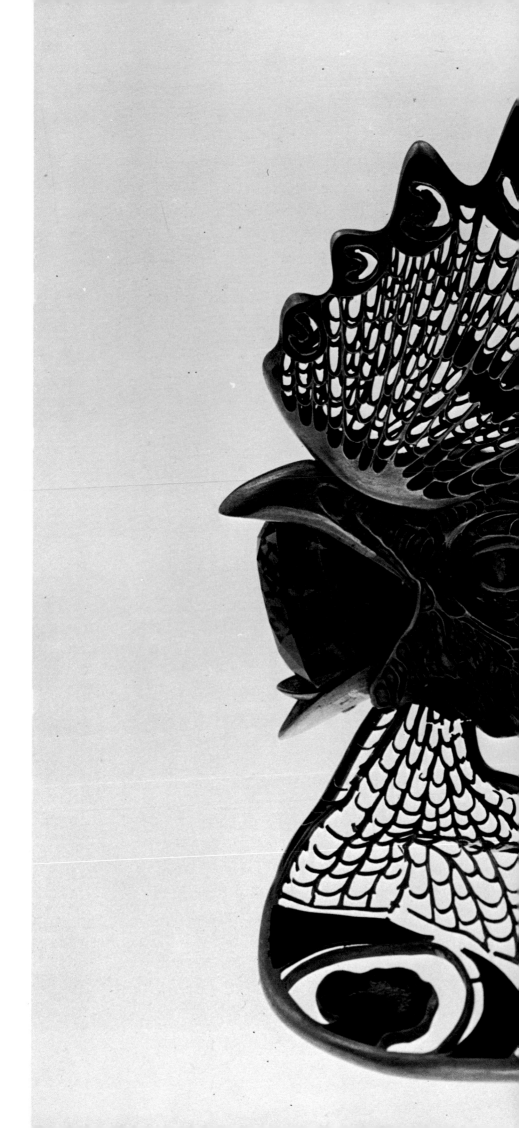

Another of the fantastic pieces made by René Lalique for Calouste Gulbenkian in 1898. His craftsmanship was as staggering as his imagination. This hair-ornament, measuring more than 6 inches across, is in open goldwork and enamel with one enormous facet-cut amethyst in the cockerel's mouth. (Gulbenkian Foundation, Lisbon)

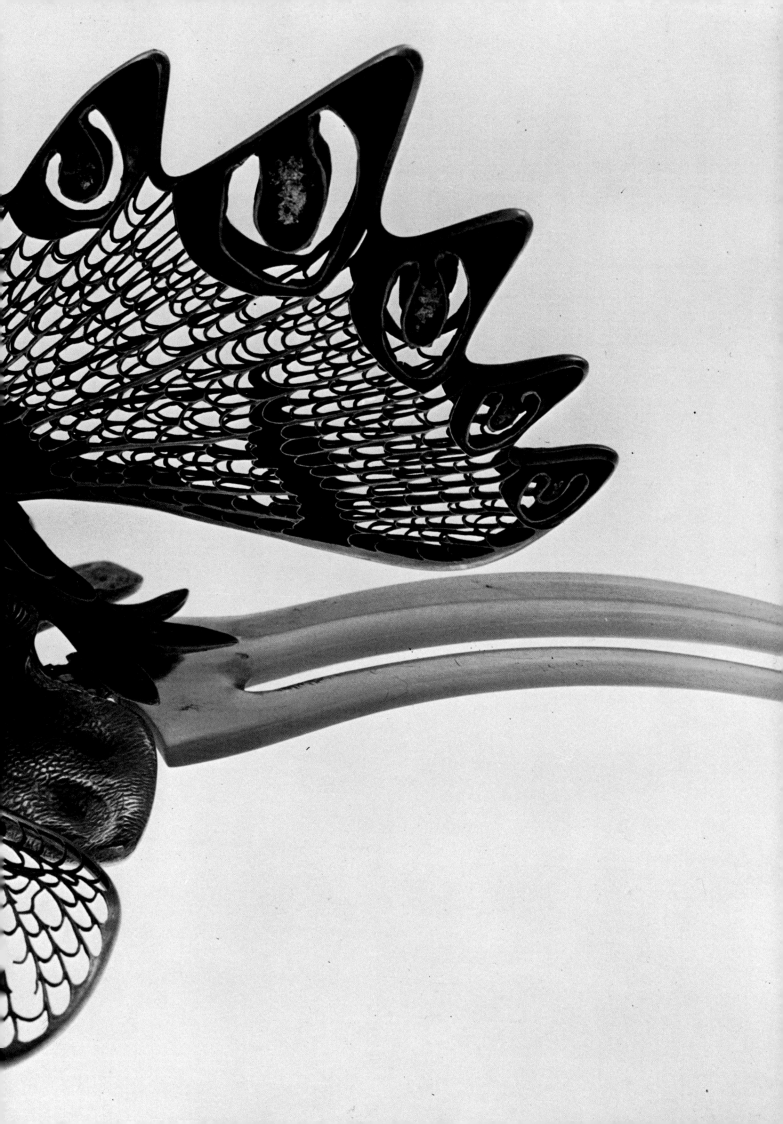

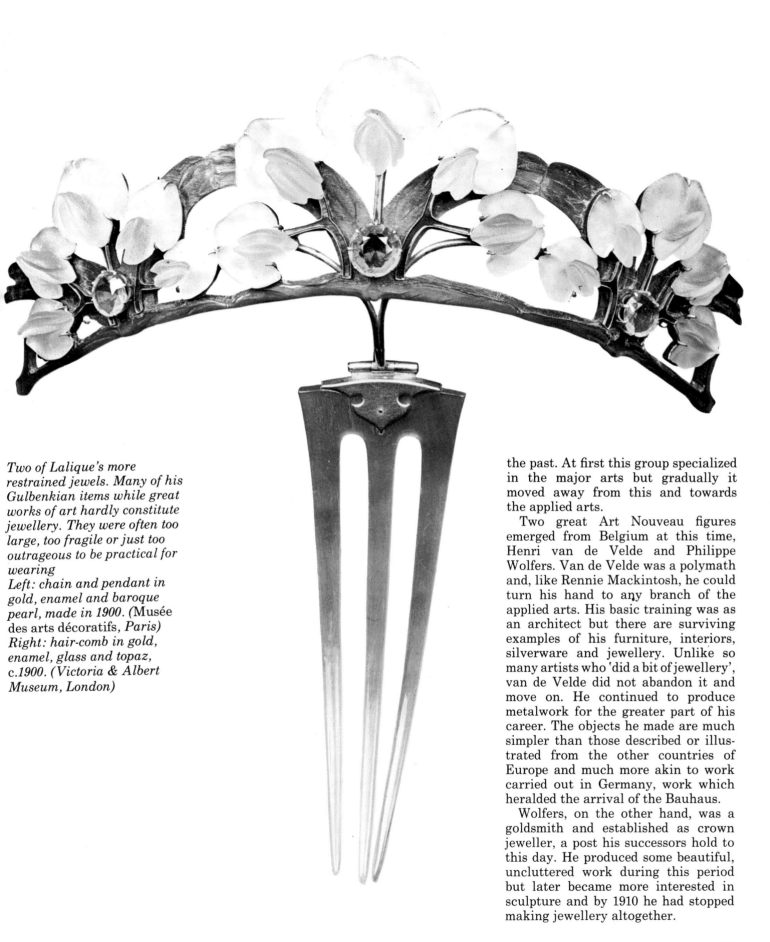

*Two of Lalique's more
restrained jewels. Many of his
Gulbenkian items while great
works of art hardly constitute
jewellery. They were often too
large, too fragile or just too
outrageous to be practical for
wearing*
*Left: chain and pendant in
gold, enamel and baroque
pearl, made in 1900. (Musée
des arts décoratifs, Paris)*
*Right: hair-comb in gold,
enamel, glass and topaz,
c.1900. (Victoria & Albert
Museum, London)*

the past. At first this group specialized
in the major arts but gradually it
moved away from this and towards
the applied arts.

Two great Art Nouveau figures
emerged from Belgium at this time,
Henri van de Velde and Philippe
Wolfers. Van de Velde was a polymath
and, like Rennie Mackintosh, he could
turn his hand to any branch of the
applied arts. His basic training was as
an architect but there are surviving
examples of his furniture, interiors,
silverware and jewellery. Unlike so
many artists who 'did a bit of jewellery',
van de Velde did not abandon it and
move on. He continued to produce
metalwork for the greater part of his
career. The objects he made are much
simpler than those described or illustrated from the other countries of
Europe and much more akin to work
carried out in Germany, work which
heralded the arrival of the Bauhaus.

Wolfers, on the other hand, was a
goldsmith and established as crown
jeweller, a post his successors hold to
this day. He produced some beautiful,
uncluttered work during this period
but later became more interested in
sculpture and by 1910 he had stopped
making jewellery altogether.

283

The 20th Century

During the last decade of the 19th century, the craze for Art Nouveau was supplemented by 18th century-style diamond jewellery produced by the great jewel houses of the West. Cartier and Boucheron in Paris, Asprey in London, Black, Starr and Frost in New York, and Bulgari in Italy all produced work of great technical virtue but of severely limited artistic originality. By 1910, their scope was considerably widened by the use of platinum which rapidly replaced silver for diamond-setting. Unlike silver, the new metal did not tarnish, and, because of its greater strength, reduced the amount of metal required to hold a stone securely. Stars, ribbons and bows were favoured themes for this Edwardian diamond jewellery which for the first time was designed specifically for day-time wear, and under electric light (as opposed to candle-light) which was now an automatic requirement for those who might afford such jewels.

By 1914 the Art Nouveau movement was dead, a victim of its own self-indulgence and lack of discipline, and what promised to be a revival of the crafts appeared to die with it.

The carnage of the 1914–1918 War reached every corner of the civilized

world and brought about a virtual halt in jewellery production for four years. With hindsight it is easy to trace the development of the art of jewellery from the end of World War I to the present day and even call it a logical progression, but for the craftsman in 1918 the outlook must have been black, with a return to the imitative banalities of the mid and late 19th century. Yet he was about to enter the most fascinating and valuable period in jewellery design since the 16th century, with designs by major artists and small craftsmen workshops throughout the world. By 1960 there was to be a revival of the crafts, an escape from mechanization and a narrowing gap between the pure and applied arts – in fact William Morris's dreams were to come true a hundred years after his theories were propounded. But before this a complete change in the structure of the jewellery trade had to take place, and twenty more years of uninspired design had to be tolerated.

Inevitably there was a taste for luxury after the long hardships of the bloodiest war in history. Jewels were in demand but produced for a new, commercially-minded clientèle who wanted a portable, public display of

*Below: bracelet in platinum,
diamonds and lacquer, 1925,
and lacquered powder compact
and cigarette box, the latter
with jade, 1924. The cigarette
box shows the Oriental style
of enamelling characteristic of
the period. All by Lacloche
of Paris. (Private collections)*

their wealth. The emphasis was on the intrinsic value of the component parts and little attention was paid to design; even shoddy workmanship was acceptable provided the stones were big. The *nouveau riche* customers wanted value for their money. But rescue was at hand from other branches of the arts, such as the famous Bauhaus. Originally a school of architecture founded in Weimar in 1905, it rapidly widened its horizons and under its new director Walter Gropius (who took control in 1919) the Bauhaus introduced a school of fine art and applied art. His ultimate aim for the Bauhaus was the collective work of art, the building in which all the barriers between the structural and decorative arts are eliminated.

It is questionable whether Gropius achieved this goal, but the effect of the Bauhaus school at Weimar was enormous. He gathered round him other great innovators from every branch of the arts – painters like Klee and Kandinsky, sculptors like Gerhard Marks, other architects, furniture designers and typographers. The result is still with us, typified by clean and simple designs of beautiful, studied proportions.

Innovations in the major arts
have always had a profound
effect on the design of jewels.
During the late 1920s and
early 1930s, when the Bauhau
flourished and the Cubist
movement dominated the art
galleries, there was a passing
fashion for pure geometric
jewels using a mixture of
traditional and new materials
Left: triangular brooch in
yellow gold made in 1925 by
Georges Fouquet, one of the
leading lights of the Art
Nouveau movement. (Musée
des arts décoratifs, Paris)
Right: brooch by Raymond
Templier in platinum,
brilliants and enamel, 1925.
(Musée des arts décoratifs,
Paris)
Below: brooch in onyx, coral
and pavé-set diamonds by
Boucheron after a design by
René-Charles Massé, c.1925.
(Musée des arts décoratifs,
Paris)

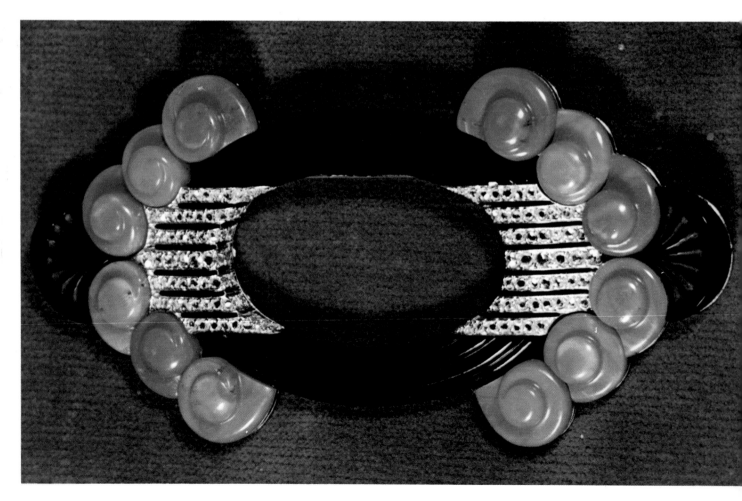

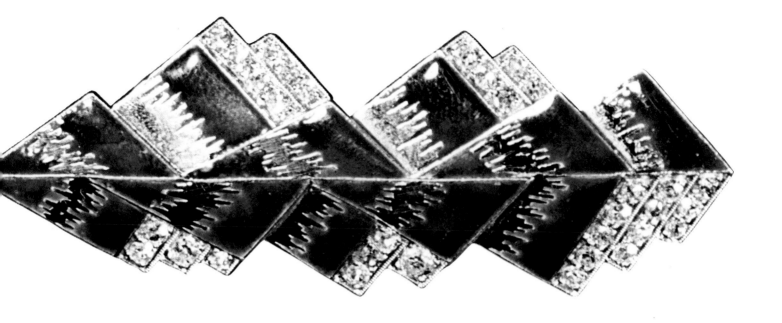

The Bauhaus, together with the pre-World War I Cubist movement flourishing further south under the leadership of Picasso and Braque, had a profound effect on several jewellers during the early 1920s, once again illustrating the time-lag between innovations in the major and minor arts. Pure geometric jewels were now produced; simple studied compositions of squares, oblongs and circles. Perhaps the greatest exponents of this new geometric jewellery were French – Paul Brandt, and Jean Fouquet whose father had been one of the leading lights of the Art Nouveau movement. Purely abstract designs like the paintings of Mondrian relied for their effect on the overall composition and chromatic balance. Semi-precious and non-precious materials were introduced whose value to the jeweller was not commercial but their ability to provide the contrasts needed to complete a composition. Pavé-set diamonds were arranged in geometric patterns in onyx or black enamel and laid alongside polished slabs of platinum or gold.

While this new style was gaining popularity the great commercial houses were not totally sterile. They were reviving styles from the past, notably influenced by an exhibition of *chinoiserie* and the treasures of Tutankhamun whose tomb was opened in 1922. Jewellery on Oriental and Egyptian themes was shown alongside the now inevitable 18th century style. These jewellers also included dog brooches and charm bracelets, not in base metals for children but in gold or platinum decorated with diamonds.

Other less frivolous new forms were also introduced to the field of diamond jewellery towards the end of the decade, notably the double clip. This was composed of two interlocking sections which could be worn either separately or as a single piece. Necklaces and bracelets of platinum and *pavé*-set diamonds were also popular. Stones were still brilliant-cut, but there was a fashion for the emerald-cut, and diamonds with coloured gemstones to give the pieces more variety and contrast. The workmanship of these pieces, especially those by Cartier, was unsurpassed, but the designs are unexciting.

Artist-craftsmen like Fouquet, Raymond Templier, Georges Bastard and Wiwen Nilsson continued to concentrate on geometric forms which became considerably more elaborate by the early 1930s. After the Wall Street crash of 1929, many European countries abandoned the gold standard. By 1936 the economic crisis had passed, but Europe, sensing an impending disaster, moved towards romanticism, bringing back to jewellery the floral themes of the late Victorians.

In 1939 the holocaust of world war returned and jewellery production ground to a halt during six years of conflict, until the mid-1940s.

From World War II on we can consider jewels as originating from two distinct sources: firstly 'commercial jewellery' from the great jewel houses, invariably using precious materials, frequently made to individual commission and usually sold without any reference to the individual craftsman responsible for the design. The great firms already mentioned, together with many others, fall into this category and, while the term 'commercial' is not intended detrimentally, its scope for original design, in fact its whole *raison d'être*, is different from that of the second category, the jewels of the artist-craftsman. Small workshops, run by either professional jewellers or artists-turned-jewellers, are destined to produce the most exciting and inventive jewels for centuries.

After 25 years of comparative sterility, jewellery received a new lease of life when major international painters and sculptors started once again to consider it an art form worthy of their attention
Left: gold brooch designed by Pablo Picasso and made by François Hugo. (Galerie le Point-cardinal, Paris)
Right: one of 133 jewels designed by Georges Braque at the age of 81 and made for him by Baron Henri-Michel Heger de Löwenfeld in 1963. All the jewels were inspired by incidents from ancient mythology. This one (2 inches wide) in gold, diamonds and jasper depicts Icarius returning to marry the naiad Periboea in Sparta (later to become parents of Penelope, wife of Ulysses). (Gimpel Fils, London,

1945 and After

Many factors affected jewellery during this post war recovery period. There was a shortage of money, materials and machinery which made jewellery a luxury few could afford. It was not until the 1950s that things really started to improve. This last section of the history of jewellery will concentrate on jewels made by individual artist-craftsmen. Although they still represent only a fraction of a total market dominated by High Street retailers, these craftsmen, together with a handful of larger companies, are the only sector which has made any substantial contribution towards establishing jewellery as a serious art form.

The first and most dramatic event to affect jewellery design was the interest shown by international figures from other branches of the arts. The first of these was probably the American sculptor, best know for his mobiles, Alexander Calder, and the Swiss sculptor Alberto Giacometti. The latter's surrealist rings and buttons represented no more than a passing flirtation with the applied arts but, in the case of Calder, his jewels, mostly of beaten brass wire, were a logical exten-

sion of the other media he explored and they are of lasting fascination. Calder had studied engineering before turning to art and his understanding of materials and structures formed the foundation of his art, but his interpretation and total disregard for the value of materials involved must have been quite revolutionary when his jewels were first exhibited in 1938.

By the late 1950s dozens of other painters and sculptors had followed these two men's example. Cocteau, Ernst, Arp, Man Ray, Tanguy, de Chirico and Dubuffet were among those who produced collections of jewels in the 1950s–1960s. With two notable exceptions – Braque and Dali – many of them produced but a handful of pieces.

In 1963 the 81-year-old Braque produced designs for more than 130 jewels which were exhibited at the *Musée des arts décoratifs* in Paris. For the most part they represented themes from classical mythology interpreted with his unique metaphysical vision. The form of many of them was similar: textured gold superimposed on slabs of cut stone such as lapis lazuli and rhodocrosite. They are objects of great fascination, more as an aspect of

Braque's total career than a significant development in jewellery design.

The same can also be said of another large collection produced a few years earlier by the Spanish surrealist, Salvador Dali. His jewels in themselves are extraordinary. Dripping watches, elephants with spider's legs, a pulsating heart of rubies and a cross of golden sugar lumps – they are all an extension of his surrealist vision. Some are wearable, others are more in the nature of jewelled ornaments. It is not, however, just the jewels themselves that are interesting but also Dali's reason for creating them. The esteem in which he held the jewellers' art is best described in the words of his own comment in introducing the splendid book of colour photographs of his jewellery, *Dali – a study of his Art-in-Jewels.*

'In the period of the Renaissance, great artists did not restrict themselves to a single medium. Leonardo da Vinci's genius soared far beyond the confines of a picture. His scientific spirit envisaged the possibility of miracles under the sea and in the air – now realities. Cellini, Botticelli, da Lucca created gems for adornment, goblets, chalices – jewel-

Surrealist painter Salvador Dali was another leading contemporary artist to explore the possibility of jewellery as a medium for expression. In 1958 the Owen Cheatham Foundation of New York acquired his collection of jewels (to which they have added new ones) and allow them to be exhibited throughout the world. These pieces were made by Alemany of New York to Dali's designs
Right: 'Man cannot escape or change his time. The eye sees the present and the future . . .' Comment by Dali on his 'Eye of Time' watch, of enamelled platinum set with baguette diamonds and a cabochon ruby
Opposite: 'Cubes of nugget gold form a cross against a sunburst of diamonds – symbolizing the Passion and Sacrifice of Christ . . .' Comment by Dali on his cube cross in yellow and white gold, set with brilliants

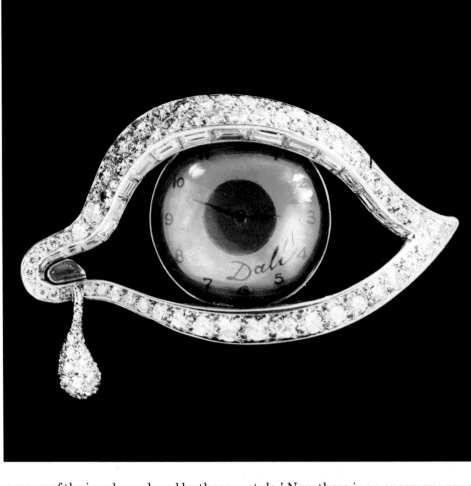

led ornaments of puissant beauty.

. . . Paladin of a new renaissance, I too refuse to be confined. My art encompasses physics, mathematics, architecture, nuclear science, the psycho-nuclear, the mystico-nuclear – and jewellery – not paint alone. My jewels are a protest against emphasis upon the cost of the materials of jewellery. My object is to show the jeweller's art in true perspective – where the design and craftsmanship are to be valued above the material worth of the gems, as in Renaissance times.

. . . My collection of jewels, brought together by the Owen Cheatham Foundation, will be, ineluctably, of historic significance. To history, they will prove that objects of pure beauty, without utility but executed marvellously, were appreciated in a time when the primary emphasis appeared to be upon the utilitarian and the material.'

Jewellery as an art form has never had such a boost since similar claims by Cellini in the 15th century. Dali, Braque and others narrowed the gap between the major and minor arts further than ever before, even though

so many of the jewels produced by these artists failed to come off. With a few exceptions, none of them learned the necessary techniques to enable them to produce their designs; consequently they had to entrust their execution to others. This is said because, without an understanding of the materials and their physical properties, you can never extract from them their full potential; it is the trained goldsmith who is best equipped to design in gold.

In the next few pages, therefore, we shall look at the work of modern jewellers throughout the world.

France

One of the most stimulating trends in jewellery since World War II has been the enormous growth in the number of artist-craftsmen 'doing their own thing', freed from the restrictions of the patronage of the nobility and large retail firms. This freedom has allowed individuals to express their own design ideas in isolation. Plagiarism, of course, still exists, but only by the inferior of the superior. It was once possible to say, 'between such-and-such a date ear-rings were of the girandole

style.' Now there is an enormous range of styles from which to choose without the restrictions of fashion.

France, with its unparalleled history as arbiter of fashion, has sadly failed to allow its artist-craftsmen this freedom. The great family firms such as Boucheron, Cartier and Chaumet, Van Cleef and Arpels are still firmly in control. The very firms which, in the days when the shoddy was considered acceptable never dropped their standards, now make use of talent which individually might otherwise contribute much more original work to contemporary jewellery.

These firms continue to produce work of great technical merit: gold, platinum and precious stones are their materials, and the materials of their clientèle, but, with the exception of Chaumet, who show modern jewellery, nothing of startling originality has as yet come from their workshops.

There are, of course, a handful of independents who stubbornly resist the temptation of a secure salary. Perhaps the most eminent of these is François Hugo, but even he is better known for making up the designs of other artists such as Picasso, Cocteau and Ernst.

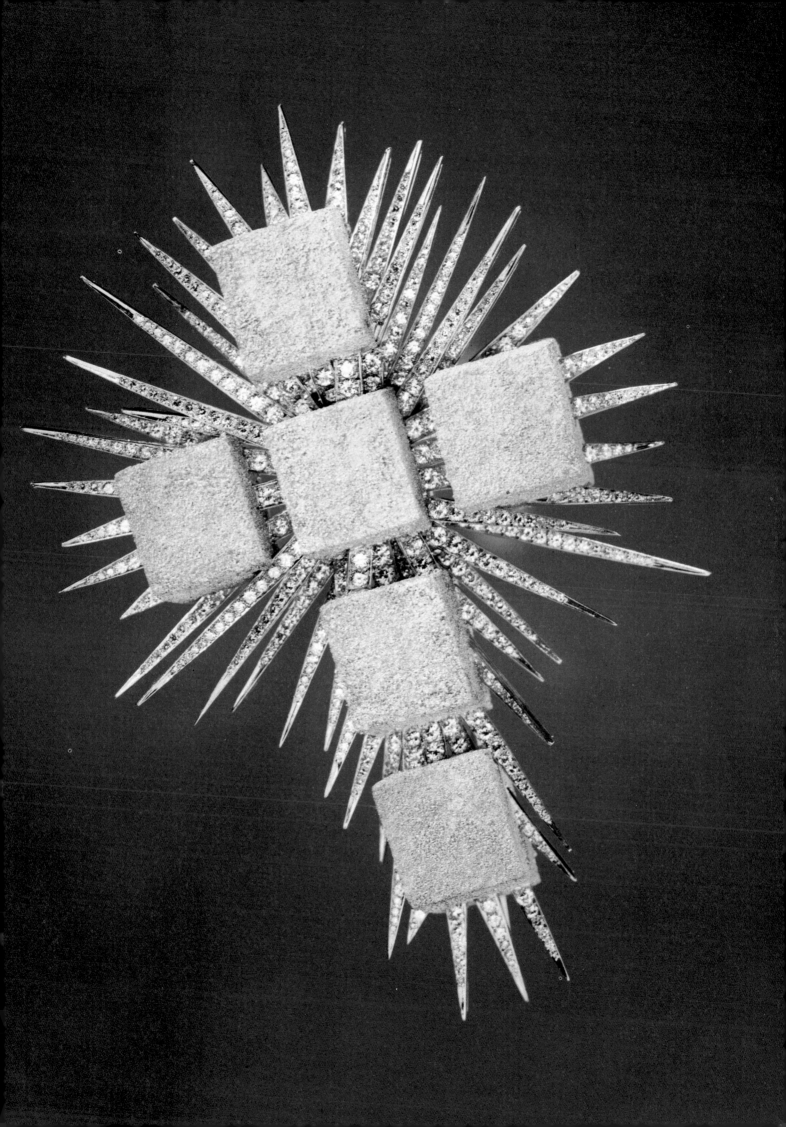

Left: finger-ring in gold and diamonds by David Thomas for De Beers. Thomas is one of many artist-craftsmen now running their own workshops in London, bringing new and exciting ideas to the more traditional outlets

Andrew Grima is one of the most original and successful contemporary jewellery designers and retailers. His style varies enormously, as these two pieces demonstrate Right: watch in white gold from a collection commissioned by Omega of Switzerland. (Private collection) Below: brooch in gold and diamonds, cast from pencil shavings. One of many Grima jewels based on objets trouvés

Pages 296–7: jewels by three international artists Centre: two brooches in gold by César Left: ring designed by Yves Tanguy and cast in gold (from his rosewood model carved in 1937), 1961, made by H. J. Company, London. (Private collections) Right: reversible profile brooch in gold and lapis lazuli by Man Ray

Britain

Perhaps the most knowledgeable person on the subject of contemporary jewellery is Graham Hughes, Artistic Director of The Worshipful Company of Goldsmiths in London. His volume *Modern Jewelry,* published in 1963, resulted from the First International Exhibition of Modern Jewellery (1890–1961) which he had organized two years earlier in London.

This exhibition opened the British public's eyes to a totally new concept in jewellery. More than 1,000 pieces were shown from 28 countries, and from this the British interest in contemporary jewellery has snow-balled. Galleries and small retail outlets, specializing solely in craftsman-made jewellery, have sprung up in London and other major cities.

One of the most important names to emerge from the 1961 International Exhibition was that of Andrew Grima. Born in Nottingham in 1921, Grima at first studied engineering but in 1946 formed the H. J. Company, which originally produced traditional jewellery but gradually under Grima's influence moved towards more free design. Since that time he, as a designer

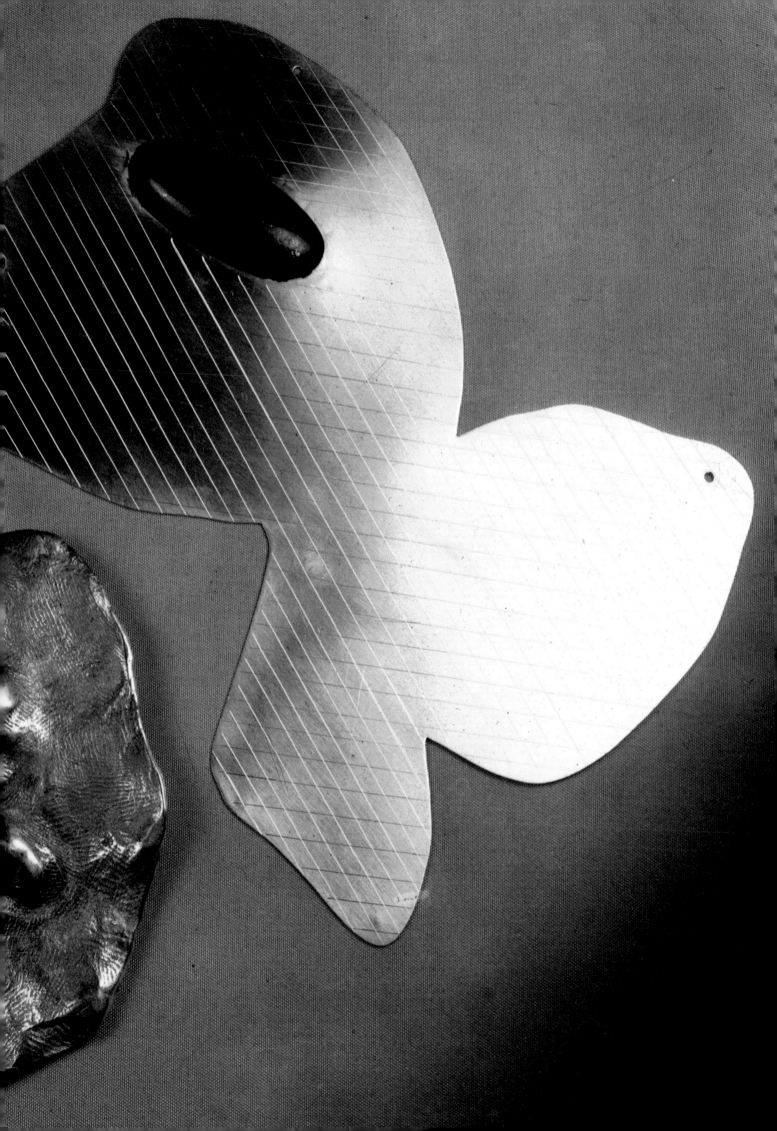

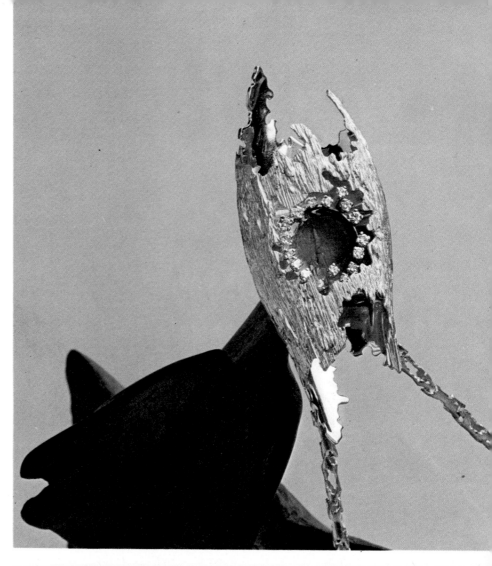

*Right: pendant watch in
yellow gold and diamonds by
Andrew Grima for Omega
Far right: brooch in gold and
diamonds by John Donald
Below right: brooch in yellow
gold with diamonds and a
black opal by Patricia Tormey
Below, far right: ring in yellow
gold and pearls by David
Thomas*

and his company (which employs several other designers) have grown in stature to become Britain's foremost contemporary jeweller. Grima's own designs tend to have a random, free look with great emphasis on textures; much of his jewellery is based on *objets trouvés,* cast in 18 carat gold and set with precious stones. Leaves, twigs, bark have all been reproduced in metal to achieve the unusual textures he required.

Grima, in contrast to many of his contemporaries, is an astute business man and has set up his own retail outlets. The largest of these, in London's fashionable Jermyn Street, has a façade with asymmetrical porthole display windows which reflect the very essence of his design.

Unlike Grima, John Donald is himself a craftsman. His designs are equally concerned with texture, and he shows great skill in harnessing the natural properties of the materials he uses. He has a particular fondness for setting uncut crystals in free, organic gold settings. This style is best illustrated in a group of brooches which he produced specifically for the Worshipful Company of Goldsmiths (Goldsmiths' Company).

298

The work of David Thomas, on display at River of London, is rather more symmetrical and organized but none the less exciting.

The only woman to emerge as a pacemaker from the 1961 International Exhibition was Gerda Flockinger. Born in Innsbruck in 1927 to Austrian parents, she came to London as a child and later attended St. Martin's School of Art and the Central School of Arts and Crafts where she studied jewellery and enamelling. Her work is sensual, feminine in the best sense, and tends to be delicately textured with filigree, or open like lacework, and set with cabochon stones. In 1970 her contribution to the art was recognized officially when she became the first woman to have a 'one-man' exhibition at the Victoria and Albert Museum in London. Britain (with the possible exception of America) has the highest proportion of women goldsmiths among her foremost designers.

Helga Zhan, who is Anglo-German, won a gold medal for her work in Germany in 1966. Unlike most of the other craftsmen mentioned, she prefers to work in silver, with a liking for large, bold shapes, discs of textured silver which, despite their bulk, are both delicate and eminently wearable.

Patricia Tormey from Dublin, also now working in London, has won several international awards. Her early work concentrated on textures, and after years of experiment she developed some extraordinary effects by techniques – some of these rather bizarre and ranging from dropping molten gold into a tray of lentils to slamming it between layers of textured charcoal. Now, however, she is best known for her minute figures cast in gold, which initially appear to be organic textures but on closer examination reveal complex, and often erotic, figurative compositions.

At the other end of the scale there is Wendy Ramshaw who produces her highly disciplined jewels on a lathe. One of her most original designs, a cluster of five rings which could be fitted in any order on the same finger to make up different compositions, won her a London Design Centre Award.

Two other British women designers whose work is strikingly original are Gillian Packard and Catherine Mannheim. Packard favours large, geometric shapes whereas Mannheim's jewels are small, pictorial vignettes produced in different coloured metals.

It would clearly be impossible to describe every artist-craftsman at present contributing to the ever-growing British jewellery scene but there are a few names whose work is particularly worth mentioning. Breon O'Casey, for instance, whose sensual beaten gold evokes the Ancient World, Louis Osman whose crown for the Prince of Wales' investiture in 1969 is world-famous, and Charles de Temple, the son of screen cowboy Tom Mix.

All the artists mentioned have their work displayed in galleries and permanent collections. The finest of these is undoubtedly Goldsmiths' Hall in London; other specialist gallery or retail outlets in London include Andrew Grima of Jermyn Street, the Electrum Gallery in South Molton Street, Hooper Bolton in Sloane Street, River of Hatton Garden, and the Oxford Gallery in Oxford.

The future of British jewellers looks bright. There is an increasing public awareness, new outlets are springing up everywhere, and, thanks to the Goldsmiths' Company, and De Beers (with their generous annual Diamonds-International Awards since 1954), a new financial stimulus has been injected into the industry.

*Below: rings by Wendy
Ramshaw. By altering the
order in which they are worn a
different pattern is achieved.
(Worshipful Company of
Goldsmiths, London)
Bottom: finger-rings in gold
and pearls by Louis Osman*

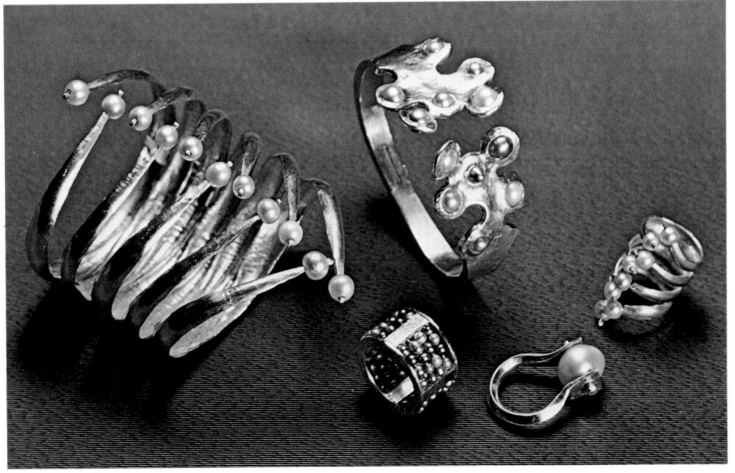

*Right: collection of six
textured gold wedding rings by
Charles de Temple
Below: cuff links in silver gilt,
one set with a pearl, by Gerda
Flockinger, the first of many
women goldsmiths to emerge in
Britain since the 1961
'International Exhibition of
Modern Jewellery 1890–1961'
held at Goldsmiths' Hall,
London
Opposite: brooch in gold and
diamonds by David Thomas*

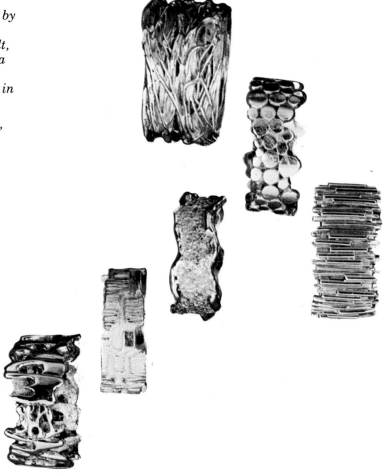

Italy

As with most sweeping statements, there is always an exception which proves the rule. The idea that jewellery produced from outside the craft is unsatisfactory is confounded by the Italians. There, the most inventive and exciting contemporary jewellery comes from the workshops of sculptors and painters. Men like Martinazzi and the Pomodoro brothers have, for more than 15 years, produced some of the most breathtaking contemporary jewellery anywhere in the world. What makes them different is that, realizing the importance of their materials, they learned the goldsmith's craft for themselves rather than producing drawings to be interpreted by others. The result is the best of both worlds: from the painter a profound feeling for colour and composition, and from the sculptor an understanding of abstract and figurative composition in the round.

Perhaps the most exciting of these artists is Bruno Martinazzi who was born in Turin in 1923 and started his higher education by studying chemistry. After qualifying, he decided to pursue a career in the arts and while primarily a sculptor, Martinazzi now

Bruno Martinazzi and the Pomodoro brothers have dominated the contemporary jewellery scene in Italy since the 1950s. All three are sculptors of international reputation yet manage to develop both pursuits without any apparent conflict
Right: 'Apple' ring in yellow and white gold by Bruno Martinazzi. He has recently turned to representational themes for his jewellery
Below: an earlier finger-ring by Bruno Martinazzi in gold set with a baguette diamond, made when he was concentrating on textural effects. (Worshipful Company of Goldsmiths, London)

Right: silver and gold necklace pendant by the Pomodoro brothers. This is an early piece when, like Martinazzi, they were working with textures. Recently their work has become much more disciplined, and in some cases shows geometric influence. (Worshipful Company of Goldsmiths, London)

spends an increasing proportion of his time making jewellery. Understandably his jewels are strongly sculptural and have great emphasis on textures. Unlike so many contemporary craftsmen he does not rely entirely on casting to achieve these effects, but builds up his designs layer by layer. With this technique he is able to use different coloured golds and even platinum in the same piece, giving an exciting metallic colour contrast. The textures are often high-lighted by small precious stones, usually diamonds, frequently *pavé*-set to accentuate the linear qualities of his design; on other occasions a single coloured stone is set to provide the piece with a focal point.

Arnaldo Pomodoro and his younger brother Giò spend a smaller proportion of their time reproducing jewellery than Martinazzi but their contribution to the art has been no less significant. As well as being two of the most influential sculptors in the country, Arnaldo studied architecture and Giò is a painter and graphic designer. The disciplines required for these branches of the arts have had an obvious effect on their jewellery designs which, while they are not unlike Martinazzi's, is rather more orderly,

Bulgari of Italy must now be one of the largest jewellery houses in Europe but, despite their rapid expansion since the beginning of the century, they have never lowered their standards of design and craftsmanship
Left: magnificent pearl and diamond necklace by Bulgari, 1961
Right: two recent finger-rings in different coloured golds by the Pomodoro brothers, demonstrating their move away from free textural effects
Below right: eye brooch in different coloured golds by Bruno Martinazzi, Since 1970 eyes and lips have emerged as favourite representational themes for Martinazzi

suggesting that the total design was planned, rather than evolving during manufacture. This is not to say that their work is stiff. On the contrary, it has a glorious fluid quality which is immensely sensual and feminine.

These three represent only a small cross-section of Italian painters and sculptors who have turned their attention to jewellery in recent years, not producing a few interesting knick-knacks as Christmas presents for their friends but using it as a valuable extension to the media available to them. The list is a distinguished one with names such as Lucio Fontana, Pietro Consagra and Pietro Gentili.

It would be unfair to leave Italy without mentioning the larger jewellery manufacturers, notably Bulgari, who, unlike so many of their counterparts in Western Europe, have managed to harness the advantages of mass production techniques without abandoning their artistic integrity.

Germany

Another important centre for modern jewellery is Germany. Unlike most countries the jewellery centre is not in the capital city, nor even in a major

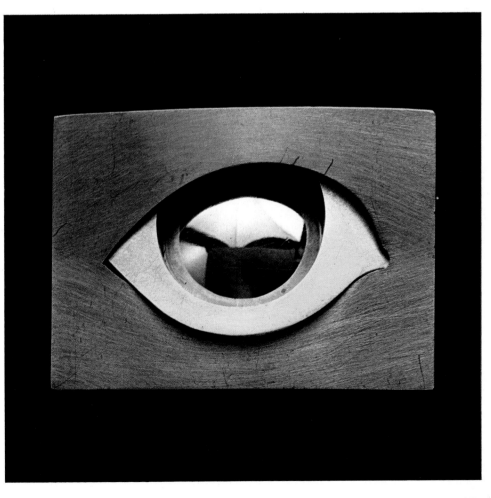

Germany has produced some of the most inventive and technically brilliant jewels to have emerged since the 1950s
Left: kinetic ring by Claus Bury. The gold balls revolve on the flat, highly polished gold bezel which makes the entire composition shimmer when the wearer moves
Right: necklace pendant of silver incorporating a prehistoric arrowhead, by Helga Zahn (Private collection)
Below: kinetic silver finger-ring by Friedrich Becker. The hoop on top of the bezel is precisely balanced to revolve with any movement of the hand

conurbation, but in Pforzheim, a small south-west German town a few miles from the French border. A large number of workshops, ranging from the one-man to those employing more than 100 craftsmen, exist side by side, producing some of the most original jewellery to be found anywhere.

From this enormous complex of craftsmen and designers, a handful of names emerging in recent years have had a profound effect on contemporary jewellery. Perhaps the most original of these is Reinhold Reiling. Born in Germany in 1922, Reiling studied both as an engraver and as a goldsmith. He now divides his time between his workshop and teaching in Pforzheim. His earlier work, such as that shown at the 1961 International Exhibition was of simple geometric forms arranged to make complex repeating patterns, with an orderliness more typical of Scandinavian designers. Recently, however, his work has become more free and asymmetrical; textures have started to appear, and cabochon and facet-cut stones are used in the same piece. One small gold brooch made by him in 1967 contains moonstones, yellow, green and blue sapphires, diamonds, quartz and pearls – yet the

design is so beautifully conceived that the piece avoids looking messy.

Another trend-setter, this time based in Düsseldorf, is Friedrich Becker. He also burst on to the international jewellery scene after the 1961 Exhibition in London. In 1966 Becker had a one-man exhibition at the Goldsmiths' Hall at which he showed more than 150 pieces. At first glance his work appears severe, even hard, but further examination reveals the extraordinary sympathy of his designs. The influence of his training as an aeronautical engineer is obvious. Every piece is composed of geometric forms; gold and stones are highly polished, and he shows no interest in natural textures, but the beautiful proportions of his pieces lend them a fascination and femininity which is unusual for work within the severe restrictions of symmetry. Some of the most interesting pieces are kinetic with moving components.

It has been demonstrated over and over again that nothing is really new in jewellery. The materials and all the basic techniques known to us today were all discovered by the craftsmen of the Ancient World, but, every now and then, attempts are made to introduce

new materials, products of modern technology. Two young German designers, Claus Bury and Gerd Rothmann, together with Austrian Fritz Maierhofer, recently held an exhibition in London at which they showed acrylic jewels. All three received a traditional goldsmith's training but believed that jewellery should reflect the times in which we live. The

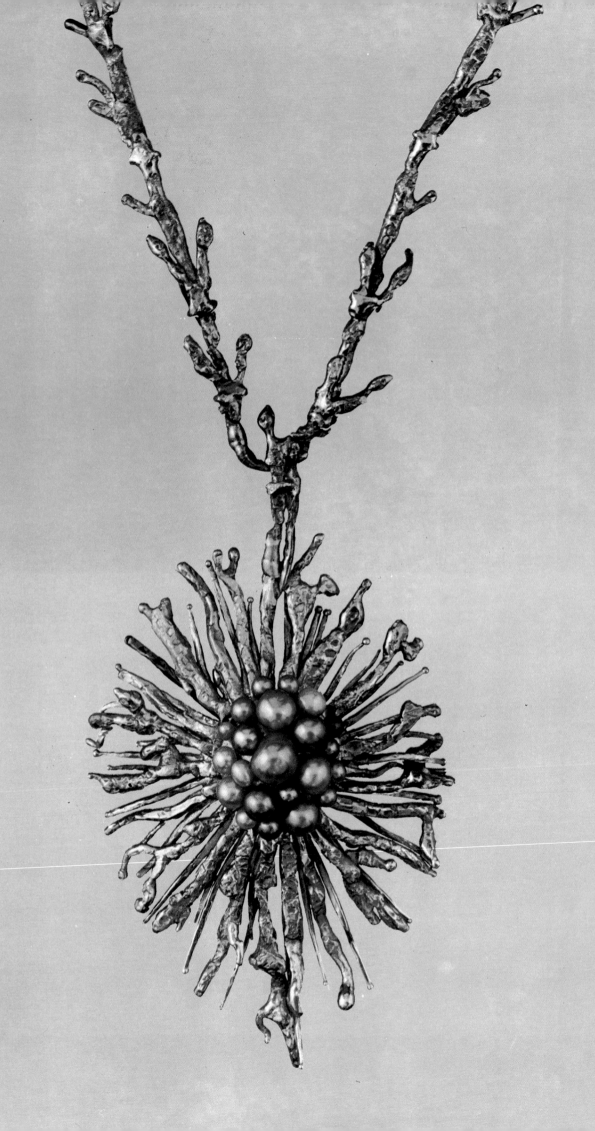

In Switzerland the watch
industry, notably Patek
Philippe and Omega, have
been responsible for
patronizing and promoting
leading contemporary jewellery
designers. The most
distinguished designer in
Switzerland in the past 20
years is Gilbert Albert. He was
at one time chief designer for
both these companies
Left: pendant watch in white
and yellow gold with
coloured baroque pearls by
Gilbert Albert for Patek
Philippe. The pearls form a lid
which opens to reveal the
watch face
Right: brooch in gold, enamel
and step-cut stones by Swiss
designer Günter Wyss, 1961
Below right: finger-ring in
yellow and white gold, with
baroque pearl, sea shell and
brilliant-cut diamonds, by
Gilbert Albert

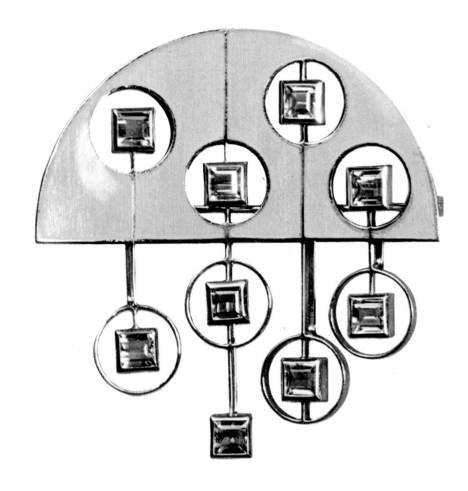

designs, particularly by Bury, are novel and exciting; the materials are colourful, but, despite the absence of more traditional precious materials, their work is expensive and limited sales would suggest that the buying public are not ready for such innovations. There are three possible reasons for this: perhaps 6,000 years of associating jewels with precious stones cannot be broken overnight; maybe, not realizing that workmanship is time-taking and therefore expensive irrespective of materials, the price put off buyers; or it could be that the element of investment associated with jewels is still a factor even with the most enlightened buyer of contemporary jewellery.

Switzerland

It used to be said that the Swiss economy is based on snow and cuckoo clocks, and it is amusing to note that the watchmakers of Switzerland, rather than the jewellers, have fostered their foremost artist-craftsmen.

Gilbert Albert, who is unquestionably the finest jewellery designer ever to come out of the country, and arguably the finest designer working today, was chief designer for both Omega and

Patek Philippe. During the time when
he worked for these two great watchmakers, he established himself an enormous world-wide reputation. No single
person has ever won as many international awards on his own behalf or
that of his employers, including several
'Oscars' from the De Beers Diamonds–
International Awards. Today he is
independent, working with a handful
of other craftsmen and producing
jewels which excite and inspire goldsmiths in every corner of the world. His
jewels are strongly influenced by
nature, without any tendency to imitate
it. At his one-man exhibition at the
Goldsmiths' Hall in 1965, he shocked
some people with his use of meteorites,
in place of precious stones, set in fluid
goldwork. Questioned about the use of
a material of no intrinsic value, Albert
merely laughed, demonstrating an attitude common to all great contemporary
jewellers: a material's value to a designer is its ability to enhance a design,
not the price it would fetch over the
counter.

It is obvious from the work of Gilbert
Albert that he experienced no restrictions under the patronage of either of
his employers; they gave him his head
and were amply rewarded for their

confidence. There are other examples of this; the distinguished French painter Jean Lurçat, for instance, also produced a magnificent collection of jewels for Patek Philippe.

Scandinavia

At the turn of the 20th century, after several hundred years of artistic sterility, Scandinavia started to capture the attention of the design world. Their development was rapid and by the 1930s 'Scandinavian' evoked everything that was 'modern' and good. The clean simple design, uncluttered by an artistic heritage, was adopted in every branch of the applied arts.

For more than 70 years, the name of the Danish master, Georg Jensen, has reigned supreme in the field of Scandinavian metalwork. Jensen established his company in Copenhagen in 1906 at the height of the Art Nouveau vogue and, while the Jensen workshops produced a large quantity of jewellery in this mode, it is for their clean, simple silver jewellery that they will remain famous. Since the founder's death, the company has been run by his family and, while they have always retained several top designers such as Nanna

Ditzel and Henning Koppel, their jewels have always had a house style. Their work is always beautifully designed and executed, but for strikingly original Scandinavian design you must look elsewhere. Not to Sweden or Norway, where design is still affected by the austerity of Bauhaus days, but to Finland – the forest-covered landmass sandwiched between Sweden and Russia. Its population is still less than 5,000,000, yet it is alive with ideas and since the war has produced some of the most exciting Scandinavian designers in every field.

Perhaps the most original jeweller to come from that country is Tapio Wirkkala. Basically a sculptor, Wirkkala produced several *objets d'art* in precious materials during the early sixties, notably two pieces for the 1961 International Exhibition at Goldsmiths' Hall. Since then he has produced a number of jewels, mainly figurative, which are executed in repoussé from sheet gold. Two head pendants by him, illustrated in Graham Hughes' book *The Art of Jewelry* have the startling simplicity achieved by the pre-Columbian American goldsmiths.

The other major figure in Finnish

The name Georg Jensen first emerged in the world of jewellery during the Art Nouveau era but it is for this Danish firm's clean, simple designs that it will remain famous. Over the years Jensen have employed many top designers, yet the work from the factory has a definite house style which is instantly recognizable
Left: necklace in silver from the Jensen 1973 collection, designed by Bent Gabrielsen Pedersen
Right: two finger-rings designed for Jensen typify the company's love for simple shapes; by Nanna Ditzel, 1960, and (far right) Henning Koppel
Below: one of the classic Jensen pieces, a necklace in silver designed by Henning Koppel

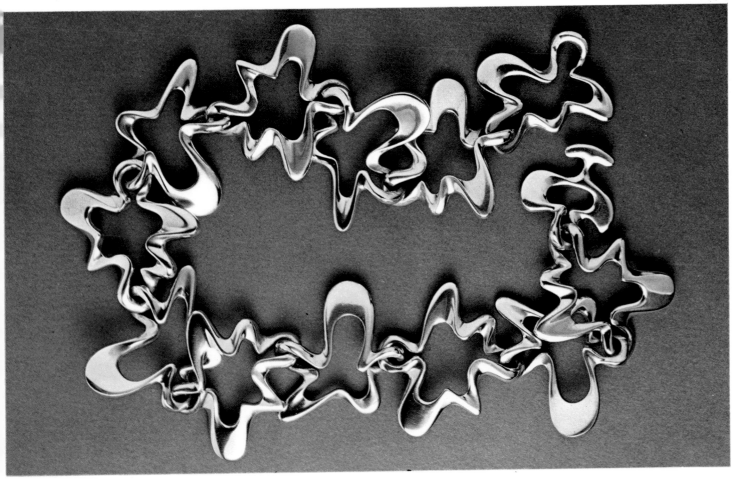

In recent years some of the best jewellery produced in Scandinavia has come, not from Denmark or Sweden, but from the workshops of Finland. Björn Weckström has emerged as one of the great trend-setters. His jewels are multiple-cast and marketed throughout the world by Lapponia Jewellery, bringing quality contemporary jewellery within the reach of most pockets
Right: 'Tourmaline River' gold finger-ring with tourmaline crystal designed by Björn Weckström ....
Below: 'Inari' gold pendant necklace with facet-cut stones designed by Björn Weckström
Below right: 'Opus 381' bracelet in textured gold designed by Björn Weckström
Far right: 'Flowering Wall' pendant necklace in textured gold and tourmaline crystals designed by Björn Weckström

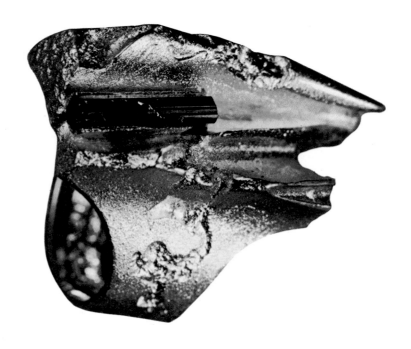

jewellery is Björn Weckström who originally worked alone as an artist-craftsman but now markets his work, cast as limited editions, through the firm Lapponia. His jewels are rough and chunky with exciting textures; stones, when they are used, are unpolished and frequently uncut.

In the USA

Modern jewellery got off to a better start in the United States than anywhere else in the world. The first major exhibition was held at the Museum of Modern Art in New York in 1946. Some 26 jewellers exhibited a total of 135 pieces. The show attracted considerable public interest and two years later a show at the Walker Art Center in Minneapolis showed work by nearly twice as many artists. Since that time national exhibitions have become a regular feature in the American art calendar.

The crafts had virtually died out during the depression of the thirties and it was thanks to the encouragement and backing of one woman, Mrs. Vanderbilt Webb, that a revival became possible. For 25 years she was the champion of the craft cause, and her

In the United States several
exciting designers, who
combine jewellery with
teaching, have emerged
since World War II
Right: brooch in gold by
De la Cueva
Below: electro-formed silver
gilt pendant with amethyst and
purple polyester by Stanley
Lechtzin, one of the most
technically inventive designers
working today

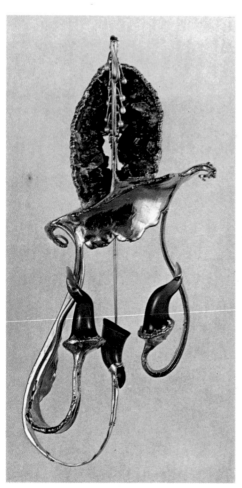

efforts culminated in 1955 with the foundation of the Museum of Contemporary Crafts in New York. Her example was followed in 1960 by the Government who established the American Crafts Council, a body which has opened regional centres throughout America which organize workshops, seminars, exhibitions and institutional centres for craftsmen. Yet, despite this organization (which has no parallel) there are no more than a handful of craftsmen capable of making a living from their work. Most teach or are retained by one of the large retail firms.

Hand-made jewellery is more expensive than machine-made, a problem which faces the artist-craftsman everywhere and those numbers of the American buying public who are interested in contemporary jewellery and are prepared to pay the extra seem to give preference to the work of foreign craftsmen.

Having said that, we should describe the work of the few exceptions. One of the most original is John Paul Miller, who is based in Cleveland, Ohio. He is one of the few contemporary craftsmen with the patience and the skill to use the technique of granulation. His most

exciting pieces are undoubtedly hi
animal pendants which are stylized
three-dimensional creatures of the
more grotesque variety: crabs, scor
pions, octopuses and bats, which are
generally executed in gold decorated
with granulation and enamel. Another
brilliant craftsman with a distinctive
style is Mary Kretsinger, whose mos
recognizable form is a hollow, domed
pendant, not unlike an Etruscan *bulla*
which she forms in silver, gold or base
metal and decorates with complex de
signs in *cloisonné* enamel.

One of the most exciting, in fact one
of the only new, techniques to become
available to the jeweller since the
Ancient World is electro-forming, and
one of the leading pioneers of the
application of the process was Stanley
Lechtzin who was born in Detroit in
1936. His rich asymmetrical designs
make the most of the vast variety of
textures which can be achieved by the
process.

Russian-born Irene Brynner is an
other highly individual designer
Educated in Switzerland, she started
her artistic career as a sculptress bu
later turned to jewellery. Unlike the
other craftsmen mentioned above, her
work is simple, more studied and

Right: the torque, a traditional jewellery form dating from prehistoric times, revived by Stanley Lechtzin in green polyester and electro-formed silver

The idea of parures and demi-parures has been revived by contemporary jewellers in the United States
Far left: matching necklace, ear-rings and ring in gold and semi-precious stones by Harry Abend
Left: matching necklace, ear-rings and brooch in gold and coloured pearls by American designer Irene Brynner

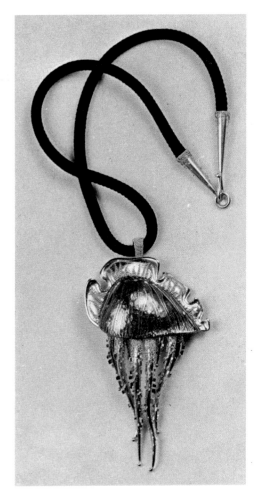

John Paul Miller, based in Cleveland, Ohio, is one of the few contemporary designers with the skill and patience to use the technique of granulation
Left: this 'Octopus' pendant in gold reflects his passion for portraying animals and insects in his jewellery

Below: pendant, electro-formed in silver gilt with amethyst crystals and moonstones, by Stanley Lechtzin

Left: collection of finger-rings set with gemstones by Harry Shawah

symmetrical but her compositions are beautifully conceived and executed.

Other artist-craftsmen working in the United States particularly worth mentioning include Harry Shawah, of Boston, who claims to be the only full-time goldsmith in the USA, Philip Morton, and Sam Kramer who was perhaps the earliest modern jeweller working in the States.

The East

The miracle of Japan's economic recovery since World War II cannot have escaped anyone's attention. From devastation to the greatest industrial power in the free world in the space of only 20 years makes even the colossal achievements of the West Germans look puny.

The Japanese have no tradition in jewels. Their idea of self-adornment was confined to dress: kimonos richly decorated with gold and coloured threads left no scope for additional jewels. Yet, since the war, Japan has become an important element in the world of jewellery both as a producer and a consumer. Her demand for jewels both conventional and contemporary is now vast, and, while a large proportion is still imported, the Japanese jewellery industry is growing fast. It is not true they only copy and thus produce nothing original. You hear this said about Japanese jewellery. True, much of their initial product was imitative, but, at the first Japanese National Modern Jewellery Exhibition held in Tokyo in 1971 there were already a handful of distinctive and original goldsmiths emerging, such as Hiramatsu, Yamada, Suzuki and Hishida. They are not yet great but in the West we have a 6,000-year tradition in the art – they have had less than 20 years.

Moving South to Australia, many will find it surprising to discover a lively and original design movement. In recent years the luxury goods market has grown enormously and, as in most countries, a proportion of this has been captured by contemporary jewellery.

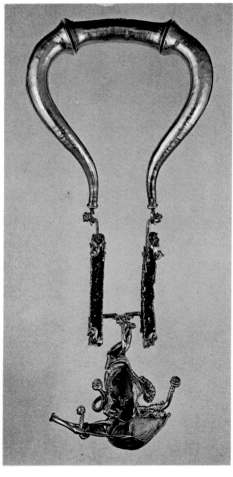

Right: three pendants by Emanuel Raft in cast silver and fragmented black opal. Raft, who for many years lived and worked in Australia, now teaches and has a workshop in England. (Worshipful Company of Goldsmiths, London)

The inevitable law of supply and demand has come into play and an increasing number of artist-craftsmen are setting up shop throughout the country. Like Japan, Australia has no domestic tradition in jewellery and the young craftsmen of Australia are not hampered by worn-out traditions dictating the public taste: they enjoy a freedom for which others in the West have had to fight. Sadly for the Australians the most exciting jeweller to have worked there, Emanuel Raft, is now living in London – a loss an embryonic community cannot afford.

Tomorrow

We have looked at the past and the present. What does the future hold for jewellery? There will always be Apostles of Doom among us. Every branch of the arts has had its period of glory and periods of sterility. Some of the fine art galleries are happily displaying canvases painted pure white, and crushed motor car engines in the name of art; this may indeed be art but few can claim to appreciate its value. On the other hand, jewellery designs, however *avant-garde,* are accepted much more easily.

In some ways the story has hardly begun; only since the turn of the century has the full potential of jewellery as an art form been appreciated or explored. There is no shortage of avenues to explore. The main danger must be seen from the commercial end of the business. Truly modern jewellery has been with us for only a few short years, yet already the shops are cluttered with cheap imitations. Present mechanical methods make this all too easy and the protection of copyright is a difficult legal procedure and in the end seldom commercially viable. Only when a large company is involved, that could afford to pay compensation to the artist, would it be worthwhile for an individual to protect himself in this way. The best form of defence, as with the dress designers, is to be one step ahead of the field. Designers will still be copied but it is to be hoped that a discerning public will not make do with the second best. The increasing number of specialist outlets, equally discerning, will continue to offer a shop window for the exponents of this exciting branch of the arts. Will the public start collecting jewellery for art's sake and not solely as self-adornment or for investment? Only time will tell.

Jewellery has never been a traditional craft in Japan or China, the elaborate nature of their clothing rendering it superfluous. In recent years, however, with increasing westernization, the demand for jewels has increased to the point where Japan is one of the world's greatest importers, and a number of admirable designers and craftsmen have emerged in Japan itself Right: three silver finger-rings for De Beers by Hiramatsu

322

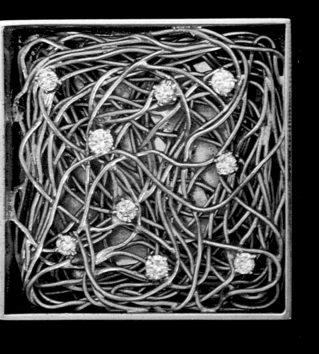
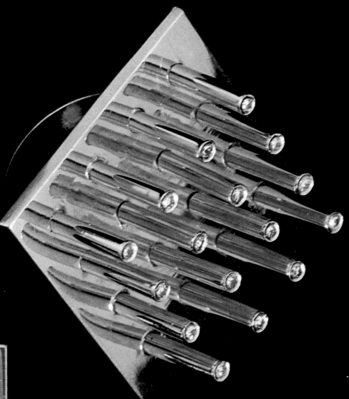
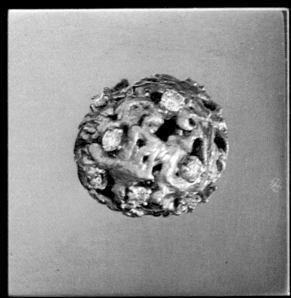

Royal Regalia
and Other Great Collections

Because of the intrinsic value of the materials used in jewellery and changing fashions only a minute proportion of jewellery from the past has survived. None the less collections do exist, both public and private, which can provide the enthusiast with a taste of the glories of the past. This brief appendix does not attempt to enumerate every gallery and museum in the world where jewellery is preserved but it does give an idea where the major collections can be found. This has a special reference to the world's Royal regalia which, because of their special nature, have not been discussed in the main text except where they were the only example of the goldsmiths' art known from the period.

The problem of scarcity is further complicated by the museums' attitude towards jewels. They are difficult and expensive to display properly and they represent a considerable security problem. The basements of museums throughout Western Europe contain as many jewels as can be found in their display cases. London's Victoria and Albert Museum, which has one of the most comprehensive collections of jewels from the 15th to the 20th century, reopened their jewellery gallery in 1972

after some three years spent in overcoming the problems of display and security. The result is a forbidding turnstile at either end of the department.

The state of flux in which all museums necessarily exist makes an accurate and reliable picture of the world's displays impossible. If, for instance, you had gone to the Hermitage in Leningrad to see the Russian regalia in 1968, you would have been disappointed to find that it had been moved to Moscow to a new department at the Kremlin. You could have travelled all the way to Cairo in 1972 to wonder at the treasures of Tutankhamun – only to find that they were spending an entire year in England to celebrate the 50th anniversary of the opening of the tomb, the proceeds from the exhibition going to UNESCO to save the temples of Philae from floods. Today, you might say with great confidence that a collection of Celtic torques can be found at the top of the main staircase in the British Museum, but next week who knows?

Many of the great collections, however, do not go on tour so this summary should be of some use to readers anxious to see great treasures on their journeys to foreign countries.

Britain

Unquestionably the finest single centre for jewellery collections is London. In its various museums it is possible to follow the development of jewellery from ancient Mesopotamia to the present day. Better collections of individual periods do exist but nowhere can the subject be studied in such breadth.

The first port of call for most visiting enthusiasts would not, however, be the British Museum or the Victoria and Albert, nor the Goldsmiths' Company, but the Tower of London which houses the most valuable and breathtaking regalia in the world. Unfortunately it is far from the oldest. If it had not been for the vandalism of the 17th century Commonwealth government we might still be able to gaze at the crowns of Alfred the Great and Edward the Confessor, but in 1659 Cromwell ordered the entire regalia to be melted down and used for currency. Only one minor piece, the Gold Ampulla, escaped. When the new Royal regalia was made for the coronation of Charles II by Sir Robert Vyner in 1661, however, many of the original gems were recovered and incorporated into the new collection. And it is these

jewels, made hurriedly by the new
Court jeweller, which form the basis of
the collection which can now be seen
at the Tower of London. The design of
the individual pieces is neither particularly varied nor impressive, but the
stones incorporated in them are the
most fabulous in the world.

The most important crown is the St.
Edward's Crown, made for Charles II
(so-called because Edward the Confessor's crown was the one traditionally
used for coronations before its destruction). The crown is a gold band surmounted by alternate crosses and fleurs-
de-lis, and above this rise two arches
symbolizing heredity and independence
of the monarchy. The arches dip in the
middle to denote royalty, whereas the
Imperial crown arch, an emblem of
Imperial authority, does not. Topping
the arches are an orb and cross. The
entire piece is liberally encrusted with
sapphires, diamonds, rubies, emeralds
and pearls. It is extremely heavy,
weighing almost five pounds, and has
seldom been worn for the entire coronation ceremony; during the latter part
it is generally replaced by the Imperial
State Crown, made for Queen Victoria
in 1838, which is now used by the
reigning monarch on all state occasions.

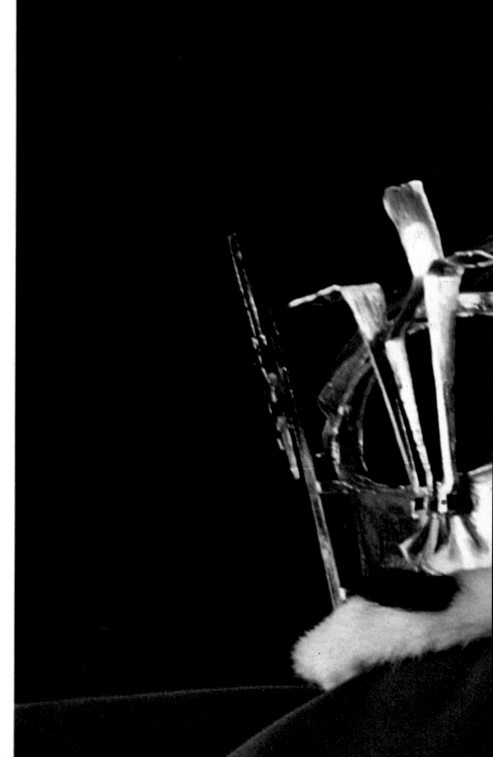

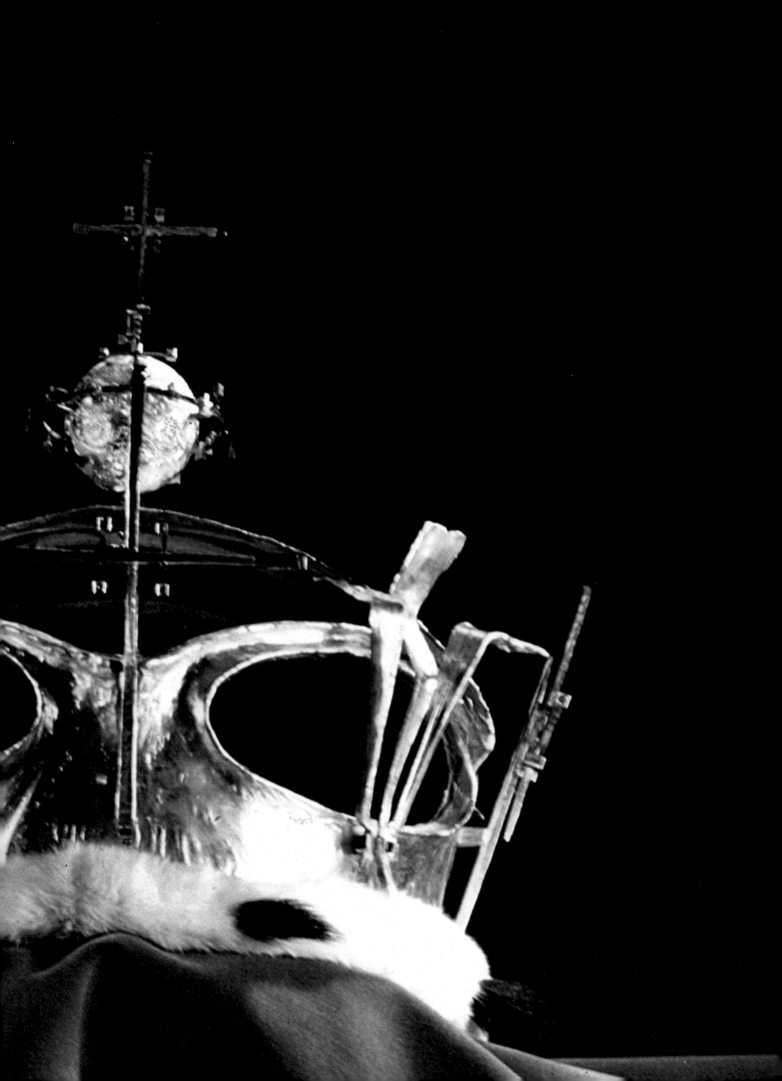

Left: the Imperial State Crown made for Queen Victoria in 1838. In the centre of the front is set the legendary Black Prince's ruby and on the band the second largest diamond in the world – known as the Lesser Star of Africa, one of the massive stones cut from the Cullinan diamond. (Crown Jewels, Tower of London) Right: Vyner's Orb, and the Royal Sceptre (made for Charles II in 1661) which houses the largest cut diamond in the world – the Great Star of Africa (also cut from the Cullinan). The pear-shaped stone is set to enable it to be removed and worn as a pendant. (Crown Jewels, Tower of London)

This Crown of State, the second most important crown, contains several stones of great historical interest. The most famous of these is the Black Prince's ruby (actually a spinel measuring about two inches by one and a half) which is supposed to have been given to the Black Prince after the Battle of Navarrete in 1367 and later worn in the helmet of Henry V at Agincourt. In the cross of the crown is set St. Edward's sapphire, a stone which is reputed to have come from the coronation ring of Edward the Confessor. The Stuart sapphire, which once occupied the front of the band, has been replaced by the Lesser Star of Africa, cut from the legendary Cullinan diamond. Apart from these, the crown contains 2,783 diamonds, 277 pearls, 17 sapphires, 11 emeralds and 5 rubies.

Another magnificent crown is the Imperial Crown of India which was made for George V when he became Emperor of India in 1912. Originally it was intended to use the Imperial State Crown for the ceremony, but it was discovered that the law forbade any piece of the regalia to leave the country and a new piece had to be made. It is of the same basic contruction as the Imperial Crown and set with more

than 6,000 diamonds and other stones.

Several smaller crowns, made for various queens consort, are included in the collection. The most impressive of these, made for Queen Mary (wife of George V), was set entirely with magnificent diamonds, including two of the Stars of Africa and the Koh-i-noor. The Koh-i-noor was later (1937) put into Queen Elizabeth the Queen Mother's crown, and the two Stars of Africa have been made into brooches.

The most recent addition to the Royal regalia is the crown which was commissioned for the investiture of the Prince of Wales in 1969. The crown was made by Louis Osman and is a superb example of harmony between traditional and modern design as well as techniques. It was made by electroforming which allowed a great expanse of metal to be used without the object becoming excessively heavy. The overall form observes traditional lines, the band, crosses, fleurs-de-lis, orb, cross and even the ermine headband are all there, but interpreted with a new freedom. It is perhaps the most encouraging sign for modern jewellers that so great a commission was entrusted to an artist-craftsman rather than the traditional crown jewellers. The Palace's

confidence in Osman was well placed.

While crowns are the most important emblems of royalty, the Crown Jewels contain some other magnificent pieces. The King's Orb, or Vyner's Orb, symbolizes the dominance of the Christian religion. It is a ball of pure gold with borders of pearls housing emeralds, sapphires and rubies in diamond settings. The cross above is encrusted with diamonds and in the front and back displays, respectively, a magnificent sapphire and emerald. A second smaller orb was made for the coronation of Queen Mary and is of almost identical construction but lighter.

The Royal Sceptre is the symbol of royal power and justice and is held in the right hand during the coronation. There are five sceptres in the Royal regalia but this is the most impressive. It was first made for Charles II but follows a tradition established in medieval times (witness the Alfred jewel). Since then it has been altered from time to time, the most recent addition being the Great Star of Africa, which like the lesser Stars was cut from the gigantic Cullinan diamond. At 516.5 carats it is by far the largest cut diamond in the world and is absolutely flawless. The stone is set on the sceptre

331

Right: two Coronation Rings. Queen Adelaide's (wife of William IV) has a large, facet-cut ruby surrounded by diamonds, with smaller rubies set round the shank. The 'ring of kingly dignity', originally made for William IV, is traditionally worn by the Sovereign on the third finger of the right hand. It is set with a large sapphire surrounded by diamonds, the gold Cross of St. George being set with rubies. (Crown Jewels, Tower of London)

to enable it to be removed and worn as a pendant.

The other important sceptre is the rod of Equity and Mercy, which is surmounted by a dove with outstretched wings and is presented to the monarch with the exhortation to guide his people. A second sceptre with a dove was made for the coronation of William and Mary (1689) but has never since been used.

Other pieces in this magnificent if somewhat gaudy collection include the five Swords of State, the gold bracelets of Charles II and Elizabeth II, and the coronation rings of Queen Victoria and King George V, both of which are diamond-set sapphires superimposed with a ruby-set gold Cross of St. George.

The entire collection, because of historical associations, is obviously priceless, but a recent assessment of its strict commercial value was more than £30,000,000. Nowhere in the world can so many magnificent stones be found in a single room – as they are at the Tower – which measures less than 16 feet in diameter.

No less valuable are the treasures of the British Museum. It is unfortunate for those interested in jewellery that they are scattered throughout the ram-

bling building, unlike the Victoria and Albert where they are preserved in a single department. The different collections give the most complete picture of the history of jewels from the 3rd millennium BC to the 16th century.

Jewels from the Ancient World are a tribute to the British archaeologists of the late 19th and early 20th centuries, and include the treasures of the Royal Tombs at Ur, and the Oxus treasure. The Greek and Roman Life room has a fine collection of jewels from the Minoan and Mycenaean civilizations, from Hellenistic and Classical Greece, Rome and Etruria. The Egyptian rooms have a fair collection of jewels but are so overshadowed by those in the Cairo Museum that it would be wrong to be too enthusiastic about them. At the top of the main staircase there is a display of Celtic gold which includes such pieces as the gold cape from Mold in Flintshire and a fine collection of torques, bracelets, clothes-fasteners.

Medieval jewels are there in abundance, notably the Sutton Hoo ship burial, which is the most important collection of jewels from that period thus far discovered.

The British Museum is also strong in Gothic and Renaissance jewels, but

for this period it is best to pay a visit to the Victoria and Albert Museum in South Kensington, London, which has one of the greatest collections of 16th, 17th, 18th and 19th century jewels anywhere in the world. The re-organized jewellery gallery has such masterpieces as the Canning jewel on show to the public. Lately, the Museum has acquired a collection of more recent jewels and in fact has sponsored exhibitions by contemporary jewellers. Other particularly strong areas include cut steel jewels, Berlin ironwork, Victorian sentimental, and Art Nouveau, jewels.

Also in London, at Goldsmiths' Hall is the Worshipful Company of Goldsmiths. Here the largest and most comprehensive collection of contemporary jewels has been assembled under the guidance of its artistic director, Mr. Graham Hughes. It includes examples of work by important goldsmiths from every country in the world. In addition to this impressive permanent collection, Goldsmiths also sponsor exhibitions by domestic and foreign goldsmiths.

Outside London there are several public collections which are worth mentioning, notably the Ashmolean Museum in Oxford which has some of the pieces found by Sir Arthur Evans in Crete and one of the most famous single pieces, the Alfred jewel.

In Ireland the Dublin National Museum displays the finest collection of pre-Celtic goldwork, such as torques, gorgets and lunulae.

In Edinburgh, there are two notable collections – at Edinburgh Castle where the remnants of the Scottish Crown Jewels are on display, and the Scottish National Museum of Antiquities where the jewels of the 4th century apostle St. Ninian are housed.

France

The first port of call in Paris for any art lover must be the Louvre, and it is here that the remaining pieces of the one-time great French Crown Jewels are preserved. France was perhaps the first country to establish a collection of crown jewels as State property rather than the Sovereign's personal property under François I in 1530. The collection was greatly increased in the course of successive reigns, but in 1792 the revolution brought about its virtually total destruction.

There are three crowns in the *Louvre* today. The oldest is a votive circlet, and

*Above: 13th century votive crown given by St. Louis to the Dominicans of Liège
Right: crown made for Louis XV by Laurent Ronde in 1722. At one time it contained the legendary Sancy and Regency (Pitt) diamonds but these have long since been replaced by paste. (Both at Louvre, Paris)*

dates from the mid-13th century. It is supposed to have been presented to the Dominicans of Liège by St. Louis. It is made up from eight foliated plaques of silver gilt, each plaque being surmounted by a fleur-de-lis and separated by an angel with outstretched wings. It must have been richly set with stones, but today most *cloisons* are empty.

The only pre-revolutionary crown of the French royal family to have survived, or partially survived, is also in the *Louvre*. It was made for the coronation of the young Louis XV by Laurent Ronde in 1722. It must have been one of the most expensive and glamorous jewels produced in the 18th century, and, though the goldwork miraculously

Below: crown made for the coronation of Napoleon in 1804. The cameos reflect the renewed interest in Classicism. (Louvre, Paris)

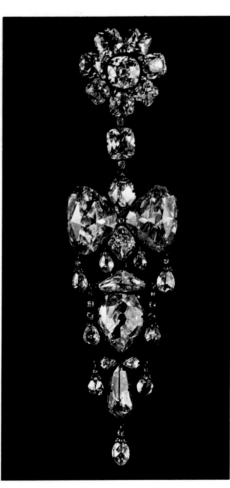

Above: diamond-encrusted sword made for the coronation of Charles X in 1824 by the French Court Jeweller, Charles Bapst. (Louvre, Paris)
Below: diamond pendant brooch made for the Empress Eugénie in 1855 by Alfred Bapst. (Louvre, Paris)

urvived, the great gems have long ince been replaced by paste. It is ormed as a circlet bordered with pearls nd set with diamonds and precious tones. Above this there are eight mall and eight large fleurs-de-lis. From hese rise eight arches which meet at he top and are surmounted with a hree-dimensional fleur-de-lis of un-acked diamonds. The crown once con-ained scores of enormous diamonds ncluding the legendary Sancy and Regent, together with other coloured ems; the cap beneath the arches was lso set with 24 large diamonds. The alue of materials alone was colossal.

When Napoleon was crowned in 1804 e wanted to use the Crown of Charle-nagne. Unfortunately for him it was ot recovered in time from its hiding lace in Vienna so a new crown was ommissioned. It is a piece of moderate uality – a simple circlet surmounted vith eight laurel leaves leading into rches. Above this there are an orb and ross. The lower part of the crown is ecorated with cameos reflecting the enewed interest in Classicism.

Perhaps the finest jewel in the *Louvre* the reliquary brooch made for Em-ress Eugénie in 1855 by Alfred Bapst. is an articulated pendant of some 35

diamonds, three of them being huge.

Among the other isolated jewels in the *Louvre* mention must be made of the sword designed by Evrard Bapst and made by Charles Bapst for the coronation of Charles X in 1824. The entire hilt and guard are decorated with *pavé*-set diamonds.

Other jewels include a modest collec-tion of Renaissance pieces and a fleur-de-lis brooch of the 14th century.

The three other major collections in Paris are at the *Bibliothèque nationale*, the *Cluny* Museum and the *Musée des arts décoratifs*. The *Bibliothèque* has a particularly good collection of cameos; the *Cluny* has some of the Merovingian royal treasure described on page 110; the *Musée des arts décoratifs*, on the other hand, specializes in jewels from the 19th and 20th centuries with a par-ticularly fine collection of French Art Nouveau, including examples by La-lique, Vever and Fouquet. A private collection in Paris also noted for Art Nouveau is that of Michel Périnet.

Elsewhere in France the only jewels of any stature are votive and belong to the Church, as Cathedral treasures. One of the most interesting of these is at Rheims Cathedral where the talis-man of Charlemagne is preserved.

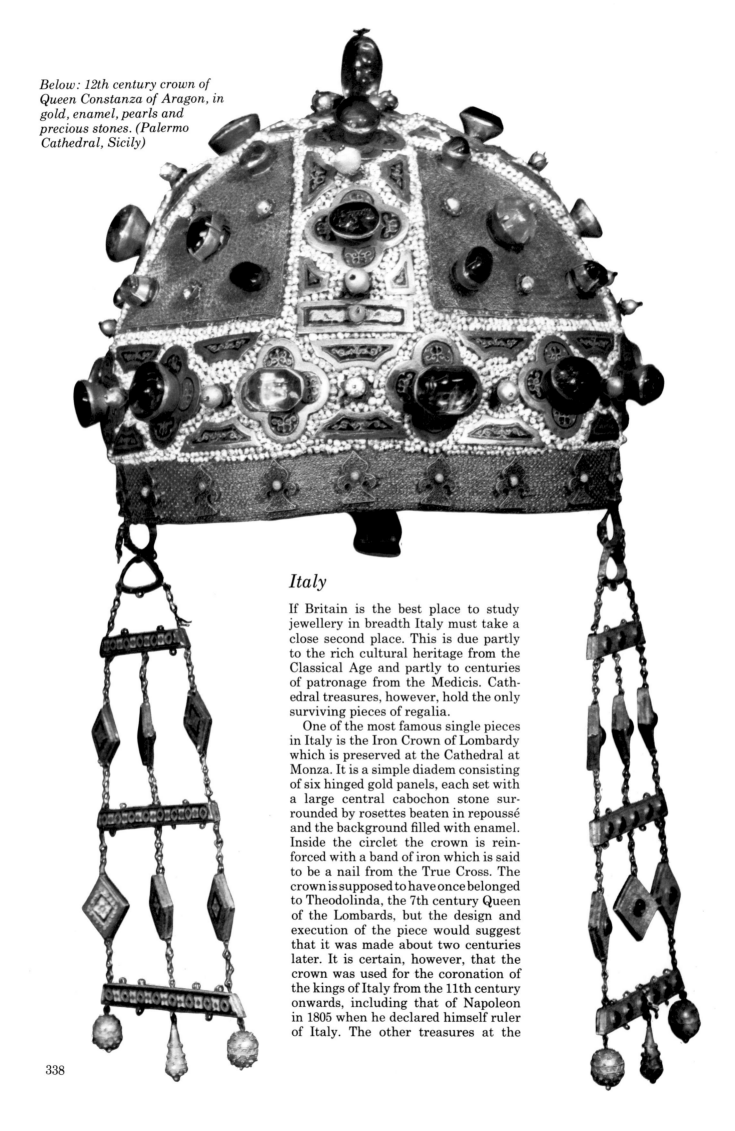

Below: 12th century crown of Queen Constanza of Aragon, in gold, enamel, pearls and precious stones. (Palermo Cathedral, Sicily)

Italy

If Britain is the best place to study jewellery in breadth Italy must take a close second place. This is due partly to the rich cultural heritage from the Classical Age and partly to centuries of patronage from the Medicis. Cathedral treasures, however, hold the only surviving pieces of regalia.

One of the most famous single pieces in Italy is the Iron Crown of Lombardy which is preserved at the Cathedral at Monza. It is a simple diadem consisting of six hinged gold panels, each set with a large central cabochon stone surrounded by rosettes beaten in repoussé and the background filled with enamel. Inside the circlet the crown is reinforced with a band of iron which is said to be a nail from the True Cross. The crown is supposed to have once belonged to Theodolinda, the 7th century Queen of the Lombards, but the design and execution of the piece would suggest that it was made about two centuries later. It is certain, however, that the crown was used for the coronation of the kings of Italy from the 11th century onwards, including that of Napoleon in 1805 when he declared himself ruler of Italy. The other treasures at the

Above: the Iron Crown of Lombardy, reputed to have belonged to Theodolinda, the 7th century Queen of the Lombards. The crown of gold, is inlaid with precious stones. (Monza Cathedral, N. Italy) Right: a second, smaller crown in Monza Cathedral treasure

Cathedral are mostly votive – magnificent crosses, jewelled bible covers, etc.

At Palermo Cathedral in Sicily is another crown of great beauty which was once the property of Queen Constanza of Aragon, wife of Emperor Frederick II (1215–1250). The crown, made towards the end of the 12th century, is a skull-cap of heavy gold mesh decorated with coloured stones set in high cabochon collets, surrounded with stylized floral panels decorated with enamel. Much of the background is covered with a bed of seed pearls which form three bands, one encircling the base, the other two forming arches which meet at the crown. Round the headband there are 16 fleurs-de-lis, and from each side hang two complex geometric pendants of gold links decorated

with enamel. The basic construction of the piece, its technical virtuosity and style of decoration show a definite Byzantine influence.

The museums in Italy have the most exciting examples of Etruscan, Roman and Hellenistic jewels – after over two centuries of ceaseless excavations. There are several collections particularly worth mentioning. For Etruscan treasures the *Museo Nazionale di Villa Giulia* in Rome and the *Museo Etrusco Gregoriano* also in Rome must be the best. For Hellenistic the *Museo Nazionale*, Taranto, has some of the most exciting pieces ever discovered. The *Museo Nazionale* in Naples also has a collection of Etruscan and Hellenistic jewellery, but is perhaps better noted for its Roman jewels. In Milan, the *Museo Poldi-Pezzoli* has a smaller collection of jewels from the Ancient World, but it covers similar ground to the Victoria and Albert Museum in London with an excellent display of jewels stretching from the Renaissance to the 19th century. Other museums worth visiting include the *Museo Archeologico* and the *Museo degli Argenti* in Florence, the *Museo Civico* in Verona, and the *Museo dell'Alto Medio Evo* in Rome.

Russia

One of the most complete and spectacular of all regalia is that of the Tsars of Russia, housed at the Kremlin in Moscow. In the Kremlin armoury, together with thrones, coaches and other jewelled extravagances of eight centuries of Russian rulers, is an extraordinary collection of crowns. Fortunately the Bolsheviks, unlike revolutionaries in both England and France, decided that the Royal regalia should be kept for posterity. Perhaps this was intended to demonstrate the evils and inequities of the old regime, but glitter-starved Moscovites queue to see the treasure and plainly enjoy what they see.

The Byzantine influence in all these crowns is obvious. The cap style, however, has been adapted to incorporate the Russian love of fur and the result is a series of beautiful crowns shaped like cossack hats with jewelled, gold domes.

The earliest crown in the collection is believed to have belonged to Vladimir II Monomakh (1053–1125), Grand Duke of Kiev. The cap is constructed in eight panels decorated with filigree and cabochon stones. Other crowns belonging to Ivan the Terrible, Tsar Michael

Theodorovich, Ivan V and Peter I are of the same basic form: gold caps with fur circlets, with a jewelled cross, but the style of decoration varies considerably. *Opus interrasile*, filigree, cabochon-cut coloured stones and facet-cut diamonds all reflected the fashions.

The later crowns of Catherine I (1724) and Anna are of a different type, shaped like a bishop's mitre, not unlike the Imperial Crown in Vienna. The most magnificent regalia, however, did not belong to these early Tsars and Tsarinas but to Catherine the Great who was crowned in 1762. Her jewels were originally preserved in the Hermitage in Leningrad (the old Winter Palace), but were moved to a new department of the Kremlin in 1967. The star piece of this collection is the Russian Imperial Crown made for her coronation. It was originally designed and made by the great Swiss jeweller Jeremy Pauzier, but it appears not to have been grand enough for the ostentatious Catherine and she had it remade. So, while the goldwork is original, it is now buried beneath more than 5,000 stones.

The other great collection in Russia is at the Hermitage in Leningrad which includes a breathtaking display of gold from Scythian and Sarmatian tombs.

This seemingly endless array includes not only pure Scythian 'animal style' but also examples of the Greek and Etruscan pieces either commissioned or plundered by Scythian leaders.

Germany

There are many outstanding collections of jewellery throughout Germany. The *Bayerisches Nationalmuseum* in Munich has an excellent display ranging from the early Middle Ages to the 18th century with a particularly fine collection of Barbarian pieces. It is the *Schatzkammer der Residenz* in Munich which offers the most exciting display with its three magnificent medieval crowns, the remnants of the Bavarian regalia. The earliest of these, made in the early 11th century, is believed to have belonged to the Empress Kunigunde, daughter of Siegfried, Count of Luxembourg. It is not dissimilar to the Iron Crown at Monza, a simple circlet of five hinged panels set with large cabochon-cut coloured stones, but, unlike the Monza Crown, the back plates are decorated with filigree rather than repoussé. A second, made for Margaret of Holland (wife of Louis IV) in about 1350, looks French,

a silver gilt circlet surmounted with eight fleurs-de-lis and a cross, decorated with gold filigree, coloured stones and pearls. But it is the crown of Princess Blanche which provides the most impressive spectacle. The crown, made for the daughter of Henry IV, is Gothic jewellery at its very best (pages 344–5).

The treasure of the 11th century Empress Gisela, found in a cellar at Mainz during the 19th century, was later stolen but a few pieces are preserved in the *Mittelrheinisches Landesmuseum* of Mainz and the *Hessisches Landesmuseum* at Darmstadt. The treasure at Aachen includes yet another medieval crown worn by Richard of Cornwall for his coronation as King of the Romans in 1257. It is a simple, uncluttered piece – a circlet surmounted with eight fleurs-de-lis, decorated with cabochon stones and Classical cameos. Other medieval jewels can be seen at the *Landesmuseum*, Saarbrucken, W. Germany.

Jewels from the Ancient World can be seen at the *Stattliche Museen* in Berlin, and excellent medieval collections at the *Museen der Stadt Köln* (Cologne) and the *Germanisches Nationalmuseum* at Nuremberg.

Pforzheim, the centre of the German

Pages 344–5: the crown of
Princess Blanche, daughter of
Henry IV, made in 1402 –
perhaps the greatest example of
Gothic jewellery.
(Schatzkammer, Munich)

The Schatzkammer in Vienna
houses two of the most exciting
royal jewels anywhere in the
world
Left: the Imperial Crown made
for Rudolf II when he became
Holy Roman Emperor in
1576. It demonstrates the
staggering level of
craftsmanship of the Prague
workshops in the 16th century.
(Schatzkammer, Vienna)
Right: the crown of
Charlemagne (also called the
German Imperial Crown or the
Nuremberg Crown) is believed
to have been made during the
10th century at the workshops
of the monastery at
Reichenau. There is no definite
evidence to connect the piece
with Charlemagne but it was
certainly used in the coronation
ceremony of later German kings
as Holy Roman Emperor.
(Schatzkammer, Vienna)

jewellery trade, has a good collection of modern jewels. The *Schmuckmuseum* there covers a considerable period, including Hellenistic, and European 17th and 18th century works.

Austria

In the old Hapsburg Palace in Vienna is the *Schatzkammer Kunsthistorisches Museum*, which houses one of the most stunning displays of royal jewels anywhere in the world. It represents the essence and embodiment of the Holy Roman Empire.

The most famous of single pieces, indeed the oldest, is the Crown of Charlemagne. The crown (which is also known as the German Imperial Crown and the Nuremberg Crown) is believed to have been made at the Reichenau Abbey during the 10th century, and, while there is no concrete evidence to connect the crown with Charlemagne, it was used by many German kings when they were crowned Holy Roman Emperor by the Pope. It was originally housed in Nuremberg but was removed when Napoleon was advancing against the city. His search for the crown continued for many years. He identified strongly with Charlemagne and wished

to use it for his own coronation but he never discovered its hiding place in Vienna. In 1938 Hitler insisted on its return to Nuremberg and some time between then and the end of the war the crown was hidden in a salt mine but was discovered by Allied troops and restored to Vienna.

It is a colourful piece of great beauty and technical virtuosity. Eight arched panels of gold are hinged and form the basic circlet. Four of these are decorated with coloured stones set in high relief and elaborated with coarse filigree; the remaining four have panels of *champlevé* enamel depicting religious scenes and surrounded with borders of stones set in filigree; a cross and arch which surmount this circlet are executed in an identical style but are believed to have been added later.

Later crowns commissioned by the Archdukes of Austria are also in the Vienna collection, ending with the Imperial Crown made for Rudolf II who became Emperor of Austria in 1576. The crown, however, is thought to date from 25 years later. It was made in the workshops of Prague and displays an astonishingly high level of craftsmanship. Once again it is constructed from a basic circlet set with a

geometric arrangement of table-cut stones in *pavé*-set borders, interspersed with pearls in floral settings. This display is contained within borders of pearls. Above the circlet rise eight gem-set fleurs-de-lis topped with huge pearls; a single arch stretches from it over the crown. The most unusual features are the two panels inside the circlet which bend in towards the arch like a bishop's mitre, and it is these panels which demonstrate the workmanship of the Prague goldsmiths to best advantage. Four scenes involving incidents in the Emperor's life are depicted in incredibly delicate repoussé; these are bordered with bands of enamelwork showing birds and flowers, and outside this is a border of perfectly matched pearls. It is undoubtedly the finest surviving crown anywhere in the world.

Rudolf's successor obviously appreciated the piece since he had an orb and sceptre made in the same style. These are also preserved at the same museum, together with a wealth of robes and other relics of the Holy Roman Empire.

The collection also includes a few fine pieces from the collections of the Dukes of Burgundy, and, more recently, some of the treasures of Napoleon and his wife Marie-Louise.

In the Middle and Nea
there are numerous ite
regalia, many of them
religious and made in
and 19th centuries. As
display of colour and
they are impressive bu
examples of the jewell
somewhat short of per
Above: 19th century b
crown in gold and pr
stones, Ethiopian. (St
Catherine's Monaster

Northern Antiqui
etets Samling av N
that keeps a good
barian pieces. A p
velopment of one w
Nouveau to today
Georg Jensen Silve
tion in Copenhagen

Greece

Understandably G
finest collection of
civilizations of the A
al Museum in Ath
examples of Myce
where in the wor

In Eastern [E...]
are two othe[...]
of royal rega[...]
St. Wencesl[...]
Cathedral o[...]
Prague (onl[...]
display), an[...]
crown
Above: St. [...]
This 11th ce[...]
been the sub[...]
internationa[...]
World War [...]
whereabout[...]
secret, and [...]
photograph[...]

348

cabochon stones and *champlevé* enamel panels depicting religious figures, bordered with rows of pearls; two arches, similarly decorated, are surmounted by a lop-sided cross. There are various conjectures about this cross: some say it was so designed, others claim it was the result of damage. The remainder of the Hungarian Royal regalia appears to have been broken up or sold.

It is sad that these two classic pieces are not on show to the public in their right setting, but, as compensation, both cities boast fine collections of jewels from the early Middle Ages.

It is in Romania, however, that the finest selection of Barbarian treasure is housed. This includes the fabulous Petrossa treasure, with its extraordinary bird brooches of gold and *cloisonné*-set stones, at the National Museum of History in Bucharest.

The East

The Middle East, the cradle of civilization, not unnaturally has some fine treasures. They would be finer had not the authorities been so slow to appreciate the results of excavations – resulting in works leaving the country. The Egyptian Museum in Cairo is one of the most famous in the world. Through the medium of jewellery it is possible to trace more than 4,000 years of the Nile civilization, their star attraction being the contents of Tutankhamun's tomb.

The Iranian government at last relented and put the Royal jewels on public show in 1960 at the National Bank in Tehran. They offer a glittering spectacle of oriental extravagance. The Archaeological Museum, also in Tehran, has an enormous collection of jewels and the extraordinary Ziwiye treasure found in Kurdistan in 1947.

Turkey has two fine collections, the Archaeological Museum in Istanbul where jewels can be found from Troy to Byzantium; and the legendary Topkapi treasure of the great Sultans.

In Baghdad, like Cairo, thousands of years of Mesopotamian history can be traced from the Iraq Museum jewels.

Other smaller collections can be found in the capitals of virtually every Middle Eastern country. In Karachi there is a display of jewels from Taxila and in Delhi National Museum the best collection of Mogul pieces in the world. Unfortunately, because of a recent theft the majority of these are kept in the basement and can only be seen by special arrangement.

In the USA

In America a number of important collections of an exceptionally high quality are housed in major museums. The Boston Museum of Fine Arts and Cleveland Museum of Art, for instance, have admirable Hellenistic pieces. The Baltimore Museum of Art and the Smithsonian Institution in Washington, D.C. own very fine Renaissance jewels; while Egyptian jewels are strongly represented in the Metropolitan Museum in New York.

For modern jewellery in New York the Owen Cheatham Foundation has a superb display including the entire Dali collection made in 1958, and the Cultural Center a good international collection of contemporary pieces.

South America

In South America there are two superb collections, both of pre-Columbian gold. The larger is at the Gold Museum in Bogotá but more enjoyable is the magnificent private collection of Miguel Mujica Gallo which is displayed at his home in Lima, Peru. It contains more than 2,000 pieces from Chavin, Mochica, Nasca and Chimu civilizations.

351

Gemstones
Their Physical Properties and Occult Significance

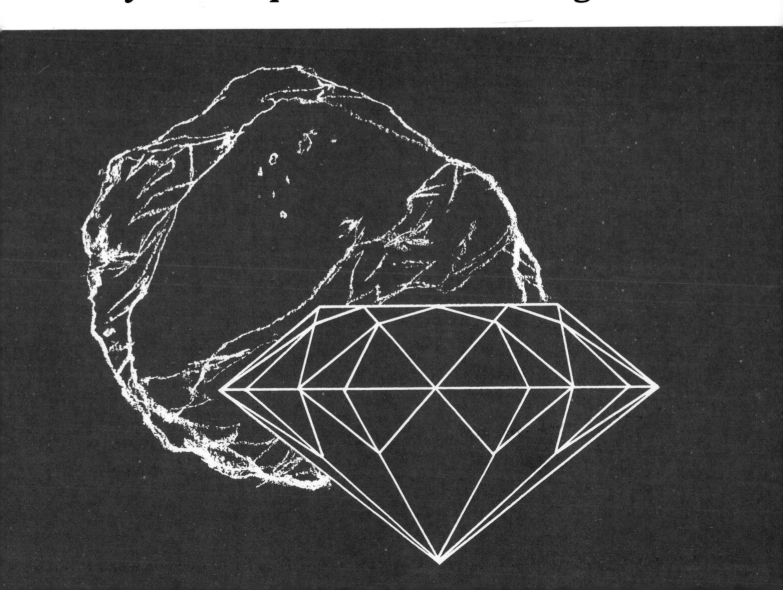

One of the few constants in the history of jewellery has been the use of gold as the basic material for the jeweller's art. From the 3rd millennium BC it has been, for both aesthetic and practical reasons, the favoured metal. Gemstones, however, have played an equally important, if less constant, role in the development of jewellery.

Initially stones were chosen for their availability and the ease with which they were cut; later harder and rarer stones gained popularity; today literally hundreds of minerals rank as gemstones. This appendix sets out to describe the gemstones available now, and to define their physical properties and magical significance.

The only two gems not included in this chapter are **diamonds** and **pearls** which, because of their enormous effect upon one particular period of jewellery design, are introduced chronologically (pages 194 and 178 respectively). Others are grouped under the headings of their mineral types.

The terms 'precious' and 'semiprecious' stones are now so commonly used as to be acceptable. A more correct definition of all the stones described here is gemstones – regardless of their commercial value.

Beryl Group

The beryl group includes several gemstones – **aquamarine**, **morganite** and **heliodor** are all used, but it is **emerald** which goes unchallenged as the most distinguished member of this family.

EMERALD: at its best an emerald is a dark green, velvety colour, and, though considerably softer than the diamond (7.75 on Mohs scale) and with a lower refractive index, it has long been one of the most precious materials known to man.

Pliny ranked it inferior to diamonds and pearls but superior to all other gems. Nero, who was very short-sighted, had an emerald lens through which he could watch the gladiatorial games. It has been attributed many different magical properties by different civilizations – to look upon an emerald was considered to improve your eyesight, others believed that an emerald would change colour in the presence of treachery.

It was probably the Chaldeans, the great astrologers and magicians of ancient Mesopotamia, who first gave the stone its occult significance. They associated it with Venus, the goddess of

Emeralds have been used as gemstones since the 3rd millennium BC, *usually polished but uncut. All members of the beryl group are comparatively soft (7½–8 on Mohs scale) which affects the way in which they are cut. The brilliant-cut is unsuitable since they would be liable to fracture. These three cut emeralds of gemstone quality show the lapidary methods most favoured*
Top: the step-cut which, because it is so widely used for emeralds, is also called the emerald-cut
Centre: the cabochon-cut. This gives the stone less sparkle but makes more of its colour
Bottom: engraved cabochon from India

Below: large crystal of Brazilian aquamarine (6 in. by 3 in.). While much less valuable than emerald, top quality aquamarine is much sought after for use in jewellery. (School of Mining, Paris)

love, and announced it the birth stone for Geminis.

A Graeco-Egyptian rite involved concentrating on an emerald scarab which was worn round the neck on a string. Beneath the beetle was inscribed the image of the goddess Isis; on relevant days the wearer would say an incantation over the stone: 'Come to me thou that art under the earth, rise up to me thou great spirit.' Another emerald talisman belonging to the Great Mogul of Delhi was inscribed: 'He who wears this charm shall be especially protected by God.'

Classical references to emeralds of an enormous size are quite common. One Egyptian Pharoah is reported to have received a gift of a single stone which measured 4 cubit by 3 cubit (a cubit being approximately 18 inches). And other writings describe statues carved from a single piece of emerald. These stories are clearly inconsistent with the conditions under which emeralds are found, but one must remember that the word emerald was used to describe all sorts of green stones, a practice which persists to this day.

Until the 19th century a green variety of corundum (the family which includes rubies and sapphires, see pages

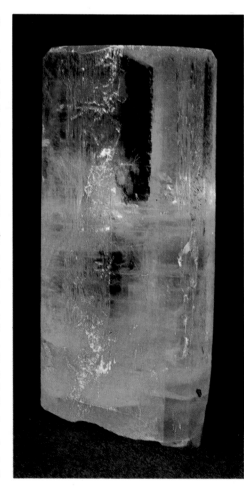

359–60) was known as an 'Oriental emerald; other descriptions persist such as 'Brazilian' emeralds (**tourmaline**); 'Uralian' emeralds (**green garnets**); 'evening' emeralds (**peridot** 'mother of emeralds' (**green quartz** and 'false' emeralds (**green fluor-spar**

To complicate matters further, method has been discovered to produce synthetic emeralds and, while these are identical in chemical structure they can be identified by their slight cloudiness caused by the inclusion of tiny air bubbles. Another method of imitating them is achieved by using layer of green gelatin, sandwiched between two pieces of quartz. This is surprisingly effective, but can be identified by putting the stone in a glass of water, when the layers become easily discernible.

True emeralds are a silicate of beryllium and aluminium and the green colour is caused ●by the traces of chromium oxide. Their rarity makes them extremely valuable: in fact a perfect emerald will fetch a higher price than a diamond of the equivalent carat weight.

The best source of supply is Colombia in South America, but other deposits exist in Russia, Austria, Norway, North

Three coloured beryls, facet-cut for jewellery. While of the same basic construction as emerald and just as vulnerable, beryl is often brilliant-cut

Below: large crystal of morganite from Pala, California. (School of Mining, Paris)

Carolina and South Africa. Mines undoubtedly existed in Ancient Egypt but they have long since been worked out, as have the great mines of India.

Their comparative softness makes the brilliant-cut difficult and emeralds, therefore, are generally step-cut. In fact, the step-cut is often referred to as the 'emerald-cut' when it is being used on other stones. Alternatively they can be cut in a smooth cabochon and while this reduces the sparkle of the stone it allows you to appreciate the full richness of the colour.

When found, emerald crystals are hexagonal and, to reduce wastage, they are generally cut square or oblong with facets polished diagonally across the corners.

The most famous emerald still in existence is probably the Devonshire Emerald which was given to the Duke of Devonshire by Pedro II, Emperor of Brazil, in 1851. The stone, which originally weighed 1,347 carats, was cut to produce a single stone of 16 carats, and, while the quality is good it falls short of being perfect. The largest perfect stone is probably that belonging to Nicholas II, the late Tsar of Russia, at 30 carats it is quite modest but its colour is superb.

AQUAMARINE: the other beryl most commonly used by jewellers is aquamarine, appropriately named because of its pale blue watery colour. Like emerald, it has a hexagonal crystalline structure, and is found in rock matrixes in various parts of the world as far apart as Siberia and Northern Ireland. It shares two other properties with the emerald, its low refractive index and softness, and is also usually step-cut or cut 'en cabochon'. It has one unusual quality – its colour and brightness are greatly enhanced when seen in artificial light. The stone was used by jewellers from the 17th century onwards and has always been popular in times of war, since it is said to endow courage in the wearer. It is also the birth stone for Arians (21 March–19 April).

The other three stones in the beryl family which are less common in jewellery are **morganite** which is pink, **heliodor** which is golden-yellow and **goshenite** which is translucent white.

Corundum Group

Rubies and **sapphires**, the two remaining 'precious' stones, are both members of the corundum family. It is questionable which is the most precious of all stones but the ruby must be a leading contender; in the 1950s a single stone of eight carats fetched £20,000 at a sale in London.

RUBY: the deep crimson colour which is characteristic of the true rubies is caused by chromium oxide, a property it shares with emeralds.

Again, the word ruby has been used very loosely in historical documents. The most common misnomer was the **balas ruby**, which is, in fact, a **spinel** (page 372). Henry VIII's great 'ruby' collar designed by Hans Holbein was in fact made from red spinels. So once again the reports of huge stones must be treated with a certain amount of sceptcism. The largest single stone discovered in America in recent times was in several pieces weighing a total of 3,421 carats, the largest fragment weighing 750 carats, but even this of no gem quality.

The ruby was considered to harness the creative power of the sun and is thus associated with the sun sign Leo (22 July–22 August). Robert Flood, the 17th century mystic, likened the ruby to the red earth or flesh, of which Adam was formed. In Burma, where the finest

359

Topaz is one of the few gemstones to fall outside mineral groups. It is generally golden in colour but, like sapphire, it can come in a wide range of other colours from colourless to blue-green or brown
Right: three facet-cut topaz. The stone in the centre weighs more than 600 carats

specimens are to be found, the stone has long been considered sacred, and offered the wearer freedom in times of war.

Physically, ruby is harder than emerald (9 on Mohs scale) and second only to diamond. Despite this, the stone tends to be brittle and is generally step-cut. 'Star' rubies, however, are generally cabochon-cut (being stones which, because of their crystalline structure, display a six-pointed star of light when viewed from above). Another fashionable use for rubies is to cut them as beads and string them. It is wise to remember that the colour improves in artificial light and therefore when buying a ruby you should view it in daylight. Many artificial rubies are made but lack the lustre of the real thing.

SAPPHIRE: if you were to ask anyone but an expert what colour sapphires are, nine times out of ten the answer would be blue. This, however, is only one type. Sapphire is the collective title for all colours of corundum other than the deep red ruby, and when describing a sapphire you should always prefix it with the colour – which can range from clear white, through yellow to green or deep blue. The structure of sapphire is identical to that of

the ruby; it has the same hardness and refractive index and logically it is cut in the same way.

'Star' sapphires, with the same six-pointed light, are rather commoner than 'star' rubies. They are generally blue-grey in colour and rather opaque but are much sought after, and, when they are cut 'en cabochon', extremely beautiful. They are sometimes referred to as the stone of fate. The three intersecting lines that form the star are called fate, hope and happiness, and are supposed to protect the wearer against poison; poisonous insects or reptiles shut in a room with a star sapphire are supposed to be killed by the rays emitted.

In ancient India they ascribed fertility to the stone; the goddess Lalita is described thus, in an ancient text: 'The sapphire devi [goddess], whose slender waist, bending beneath the burden of the ripe fruit of her breasts, swells into jewelled hips heavy with the promise of infinite maternities.'

The 19th century occultist, Madame Blavatsky, tells us that the Buddhists attributed to the sapphire 'a sacred magical power which every student of psychological mesmerism will understand, for its polished and deep blue

Right: the colour most commonly associated with topaz – amber. This is a magnificent specimen of the stone in its natural crystalline form. (Natural History Museum, Milan)

Below left: crystal of transparent blue Siberian topaz in its mother rock. (School of Mining, Paris)

surface produces extraordinary somnambulic phenomena.'

To the astrologer, the star sapphire epitomizes the absence of darkness and is associated with Saturn the ruling planet of the sign of Libra (23 September–23 October).

Very large sapphires are far from common, and legend is to be mistrusted. The largest cut stone, now in the American Museum of Natural History, weighs 565 carats and is probably a freak.

The finest deep blue sapphires come from the Vale of Kashmir, but other deposits of varying quality exist in Ceylon (Sri Lanka), Burma, Thailand, Australia, Montana (USA), Madagascar (Malagasy), the Urals and Bohemia (Czechoslovakia).

TOPAZ

One of the most beautiful gemstones after the great four is undoubtedly topaz. Though not as highly valued, it is a rich warm stone which makes it particularly suitable for jewellery.

Again, as with sapphires, it is a popular misconception to think that topaz is always the sherry colour with which it is normally associated. It can in fact range from totally colourless to blue-green. The finest specimens come

Opal is one of the most exciting gemstones in the jeweller's repertoire. It has been used sparingly since prehistoric times but established its popularity in the 19th century. It is fairly soft and fragile (about 6 on mohs scale) and is therefore inevitably cut 'en cabochon.' There are three different types of opal: black, precious and fire
Top right: black opal from Australia
Centre: precious opal, also from Australia
Bottom: fire opal from Mexico

Below right: rich red fire opal in its mother rock, from Zimapán, Mexico. (Natural History Museum, Milan)

Turquoise is one of the oldest gemstones used by jewellers, and was widely favoured in Dynastic Egypt. The main sources of turquoise are Iran, Turkestan and Tibet. It is comparatively soft (5–6 on Mohs scale) and is, therefore, cut 'en cabochon'. At its best it is a vivid, opaque sky-blue but other colours are found, ranging from apple-green to brown
Right: two turquoise cabochons from Iran. The dark inclusions in the top stone are veins of the mother rock or matrix

from the mines of Brazil where it is known as *pingos d'agoa* (drops of water). As with the other precious stones, there are various other minerals which are referred to as topaz: 'Scottish' topaz, for instance, is really **citrine-yellow quartz**, attractive but commercially worthless; 'Oriental' topaz is really **sapphire**, a much more valuable stone.

The birth stone of Sagittarians (21 November–21 December), topaz has been attributed with many occult powers. It is supposed to have a cheering effect and to drive out insomnia; like emeralds it is supposed to change colour in the presence of poisons, to cure baldness and to render the wearer invisible in an emergency.

It has one strange physical property: when heated, a sherry-coloured topaz will change colour to pink and it is this hue which has proved particularly popular in recent years. Rather less desirable is the tendency for topaz to lose its colour if exposed to intense light for prolonged periods.

OPAL

This is one of the most unusual of all gemstones. Unlike those mentioned before, opals are not crystalline but amorphous, a dehydrated jelly of silica. No other stone has the variety and brilliance of opal, which at its best flashes all the colours of the rainbow. When the stone is being formed the silica shrink and crack and it is these minute cracks which break up the light passing through the stone and produce an effect like oil on water or a soap bubble. Opals come in several types: black opals have a greyish-white background colour, white opals are milky and fire opals are red or orange in colour.

A delicate and unstable material, opal is easily chipped or cracked and damaged by heat. It is for this reason that opals are generally cut 'en cabochon'. The surface is porous and in time will absorb dirt and grease which will reduce the stone's lustre; if placed under water it will give off gas.

The birth stone of Scorpions (23 October–21 November), it has been attributed with the power of Mercury – to lead the possessor into strange and unknown realms.

As with emeralds, the doublets (imitations) produced can at a glance be extremely convincing, and, again, it is a wise precaution to immerse a stone in a bath of water before purchasing it. When this is done the different layers

362

Garnets are one of the commonest gemstones widely used in jewellery. They were mentioned by Pliny but did not gain great popularity until the Victorian era. Colours vary from cinnamon-yellow through fiery-red to green. Their hardness is about 7½ on Mohs scale and they can be facet-cut or cut 'en cabochon'
Right: three cut garnets
Top: high cabochon of semi-opaque pink grossular
Centre: facet-cut Brazilian spessartite
Bottom: low cabochon of green grossular
(School of Mining, Paris)

Garnet deposits are scattered throughout the world but one of the finest sources of hessonite, the much sought after red variety of the mineral, is Italy
Below right: hessonite crystals in their mother rock, from Val d'Ala, Piedmont, Italy. (Natural History Museum, Milan)

of the substitute stone will become immediately apparent.

TURQUOISE
Like opal, turquoise is an unstable material which requires both care and experience by the purchaser. No stone has been more effectively imitated – in glass, porcelain and chemical composition. Turquoise was highly prized in both Egypt and pre-Columbian America. At its best the stone should be vivid blue and opaque, but this colour is unstable and contact with water or grease can reduce it to a dull green which detracts considerably from its value. Many attempts have been made to rejuvenate turquoise by rubbing it with wax, dyeing it etc., but the effect wears off very quickly. It is also comparatively soft (6 on Mohs scale) and should always be set with an eye to protection.

The great turquoise mines have always been in Persia (Iran) but the stones have been traditionally marketed in Turkey, hence the name.

It is the birth stone of Capricorns (21 December–21 January) and is supposed to bring luck and money. In ancient Persia and Turkey headstalls of horses were set with turquoise which was intended to protect the rider from injury.

GARNET
This is the collective title for a family of half a dozen silicate minerals and, while they are not all of gem quality, they are all of the same basic structure. The most commonly used in jewellery is the blood red **pyrope** garnet which at its best could be mistaken for a ruby. It is because of this red colouring that it got its name (derived from the Latin for pomegranate – *granatum*).

The stone was considered to have offered protection from injury in Western civilizations, but in the East they were used as bullets with the belief that they would inflict a more terrible injury on opponents.

Almandine is a purple garnet which is usually cabochon-cut and hollowed beneath; this is called a **carbuncle** and legend has it that Noah used carbuncles to illuminate his ark. Other varieties of garnet which are used less frequently in jewellery are **grossularite** (green), **demantoid** (a brighter green, and resembling an emerald), **topazite** (yellow), **hessonite** (orange) and **melanite** (black).

Garnet is the birth stone of Aquarians (21 January–21 February), but this is generally considered to apply only to the red pyrope.

The quartz group covers an enormous variety of stones used by jewellers. These come in widely different colours and can be opaque, translucent or clear. The varieties most commonly used are: amethyst, rose quartz, aventurine, jasper, chalcedony, cornelian, agate, onyx and chrysoprase
Left: a cavity lined with the stunning purple crystals of amethyst, from the Rio Grande do Sul, Brazil. (Natural History Museum, Milan)
Right: eight facet-cut quartz gemstones show the variety of colours in the different types of transparent quartz. (School of Mining, Paris)

Quartz Group

The quartz group provides us with the majority of semi-precious stones of gem quality. They are all basically the same structure: silex with various metallic oxide impurities.

Silex or **rock crystal** is transparent and colourless and was frequently used in the 18th and 19th centuries as a substitute for diamonds. Its comparatively low refractive index, however, lacks fire and it has not retained its popularity. Rock crystal has always had supernatural connections, particularly with clairvoyants, and the enormous size of the crystals allows comparatively large objects to be fashioned from it, including crystal balls, cups, seals and other functional objects.

AMETHYST: the most popular gemstone from the quartz family is without doubt amethyst, which has a royal purple colour caused by traces of magnesium oxide. It is no harder than rock crystal nor any different optically, but it has always been much sought after. It derives its name from the Greek word *ametho* which means sobriety and is supposed to protect the wearer from drunkenness and ensure his chastity. Legend has it that Bacchus, the god of wine, was deserted by his favourite nymph Amethyst in favour of Diana, the protector of chastity. Bacchus set his lions on the unfortunate girl, but before they could reach her Diana turned her into a pure white stone. Bacchus, remorseful, poured wine on the stone and swore that those who wore it should be protected against drunkenness. In classical Greece, cups carved from amethyst were believed to allow the owner to drink unlimited quantities of wine without ill effect.

It is also the traditional stone for the Bishop's ring, which, when worn on the third finger of the right hand, was supposed to be: 'the jewel of the High Priest, of one who is not confused, distracted or overwhelmed by the intense fascination of external phenomena.' Its magic was also useful to gain political power. In the Middle Ages, the very colour assumed a magical significance and was copied for fabrics which, when worn, were considered to offer the same benefits.

Early in this century, the discovery of large amethyst deposits in South America brought the price down considerably and established amethyst as one of the most popular of semi-precious stones. Like rock crystal it is found in hexagonal crystals which have been recorded anything up to three feet in diameter. Care should be taken when purchasing a stone, however, because they are prone to lose their colour if subjected to any intense heat or light for a prolonged period. They are traditionally the birth stone of Pisceans (21 February–21 March).

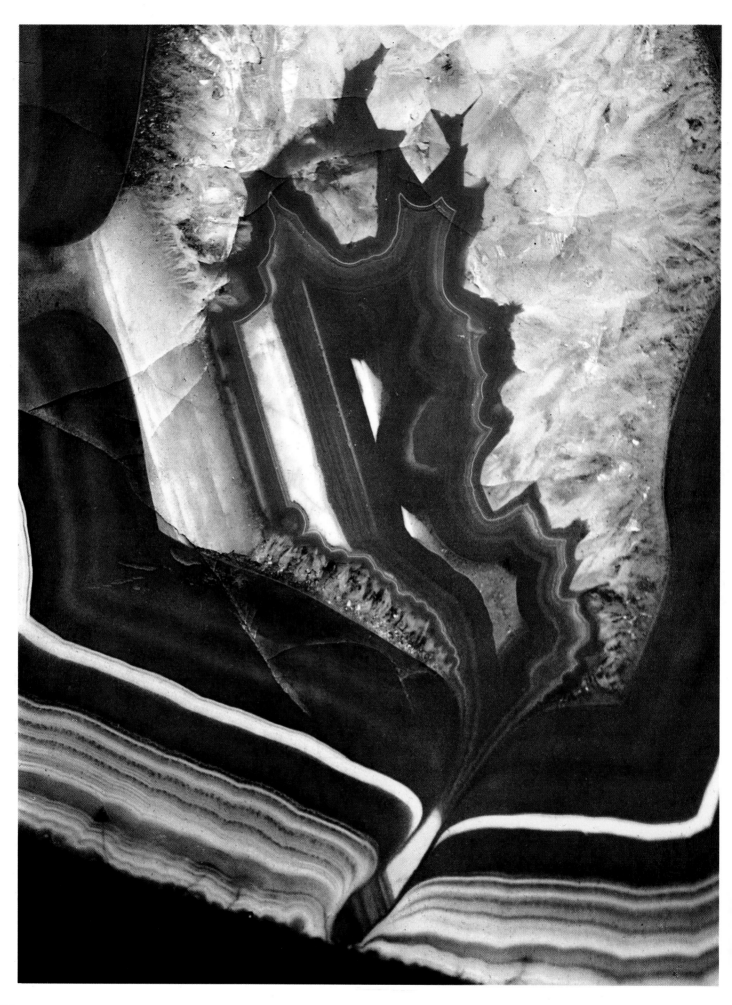

Agate is perhaps the most popular of all the opaque quartz gems
Left: agate chalcedony with a cornelian nucleus, from Brazil. (Natural History Museum, Milan)
Right: six varieties of translucent and opaque quartz gems. All are cut 'en cabochon' to display their colour rather than optical qualities. (School of Mining, Paris)
Below: crystal of smoky quartz sometimes known as cairngorm stone, from Val Giuf, St. Gotthard, Switzerland. (Natural History Museum, Milan)

OTHER QUARTZ GEMS: there are four other transparent quartz minerals used in jewellery: **citrine**, which is bright yellow and often used as a substitute for topaz, **rose quartz** which is pink and sometimes referred to as 'Bohemian' ruby, **smoke quartz** which is deep bronze caused by the presence of sodium, and **cairngorm** which is reddish in colour.

The remaining quartz gems are either translucent or completely opaque. These are of cryptocrystalline structure, i.e. composed of microscopic crystals. There is **chalcedony**, usually translucent and ranging in colour from white to blue-grey; **chrysoprase**, translucent apple-green; **jasper**, opaque and of red, yellow or brown colouring, sometimes banded with a mixture of all these colours; **agate**, a banded opaque version of chalcedony which is normally made up of parallel stripes of different colours and much favoured by contemporary jewellers; **onyx** and **sardonyx** are forms of agate with parallel even stripes, the first of black and white and the latter of red and white.

Perhaps the most popular of opaque quartz stones is **cornelian** which has been widely used for jewellery

367

Lapis lazuli is one of the oldest gemstones known to man, extensively used throughout Dynastic Egypt and the Sumerian civilization, often alongside turquoise. Its rich, deep blue colour with gold flecks is caused by the inclusion of iron pyrites
Top right: unpolished chunk of raw lapis mineral
Bottom right: oval polished disc of lapis. (Both at School of Mining, Paris)

The feldspar group is even larger than the quartz group but does not provide as many gemstones. The two most commonly used are moonstones and amazonite. All are translucent or opaque with a hardness of 6 on Mohs scale, and they are cut 'en cabochon'
Top right: blue opalescent moonstone from Ceylon (Sri Lanka)
Centre right: blue labradorite from Ceylon. (School of Mining, Paris)
Bottom right: green amazonite from Brazil. (School of Mining, Paris)

for more than 5,000 years; this glowing orange-red stone is also known as **sard**.

There are innumerable sub-groups of quartz which are far too numerous to describe, some bearing several names and some names being used to cover several stones, but the ones already described cover those which are likely to be used for jewellery.

LAPIS LAZULI

Another opaque stone which has been used by jewellers since the dawn of civilization is lapis lazuli. Good lapis is deep ultramarine with gold flecks and makes a dazzling contrast when set alongside turquoise, a fashion which was popular with lapidaries of the Ancient World. The structure of the stone is extremely complex, made up from a number of different minerals, the most important of which are **calcite** and **lazurite**. The metallic flecks are caused by the inclusion of particles of **iron pyrites** (**marcasite**). It is quite soft (5 on Mohs scale), which made it particularly suitable for the *cloisonné*-inlay technique favoured by the Ancient Egyptians; such pieces as the sarcophagus of Tutankhamun show lapis lazuli used to its greatest effect.

Astrologers connect the stone with Jupiter and, together with turquoise, it is the birth stone of Capricorns (21 December–21 January). It has also been held to have sexual powers; it was the stone of Laz, the Babylonian goddess of love, and in statues of Ishtar, the Sumerian goddess of battle and love, it was sometimes used to depict the sexual organs.

Again, care must be taken when purchasing lapis since many convincing substitutes have found their way on to the market, notably opaque blue glass with copper flecks.

Feldspar Group

There are even more varieties of feldspar than there are of quartz, but they do not contribute as many gemstones.

MOONSTONE: the best known, however, is the moonstone, which, despite its beauty, is one of the cheapest translucent stones available to the jeweller. Its milky, blue-white sheen led to an association with the moon and it was thought to absorb the moon's rays and banish nightmares. Moonstone is the second choice of birthstone after the pearl for Cancers

(21 June–21 July) and is supposed to enable the wearer to predict the future.

Of other feldspars, **amazonite** is also used by jewellers. Like moonstone it is an aluminium silicate combined with other oxides and when polished is a rich green. **Sunstone** or **aventurine** is speckled bronze caused by the inclusion of flakes of **haematite**; and **labradorite**, the least commonly used, is a blue-grey, and flashes other colours when the direction of the light passing through it is altered.

All the feldspars are fairly soft ($6-6\frac{1}{2}$) and are always cut 'en cabochon.'

CHRYSOBERYL

From Ceylon (Sri Lanka) comes an unusual stone of considerable value, **alexandrite**. The stone was so named because it was first discovered in the Ural mountains on Tsar Alexander's birthday. It is a hard, clear stone, which in daylight has a greenish hue but turns to deep red when viewed under artificial light. The novelty of this phenomenon combined with the fact that these were the Imperial colours in Russia, made the stone immediately fashionable.

Cymophane (or **chrysoberyl cat's-eye**), another form of chrysoberyl, is

The chrysoberyl group contains two important gemstones – alexandrite and chrysoberyl cat's-eye. With a hardness of 8½ on Mohs scale and good refractive qualities, chrysoberyl can be facet-cut
Top right: facet-cut alexandrite which is green in daylight but turns vivid red when seen in artificial light. (School of Mining, Paris)
Bottom right: brilliant-cut yellow-green chrysoberyl from Ceylon. (School of Mining, Paris)

Below: amazonite crystal group measuring 8 inches across, from Colorado, USA. (School of Mining, Paris)

also emerald green but does not change and is thus considered less valuable. It is much sought after and commands a considerable price. A yellow variety of the stone, not unlike citrine, was popular during Victorian times.

JADE

Jade is a loose description covering two entirely different minerals: **jadite** and **nephrite**. It is a material which we immediately connect with the East but it was from South America that jade first reached Western Europe. In the 16th century the Spanish Conquistadores were presented with jade beads which the Aztecs held precious above all other materials including gold. They named it *piedra de ijada* (stone of the loin) because of the healing properties it was supposed to have. The Indians had taught them that if a piece of the stone were placed on the skin outside an affected area of the body it would be cured; and they particularly recommended it for curing ailments of groin and kidney (hence the word nephrite, which is derived from the Greek word for kidney). Fifty years later European physicians were prescribing it to be taken internally, crushed and mixed with water.

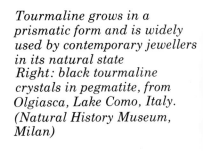

It is fortunate that these doctors were dishonest, and substituted worthless green powder, since a comparatively small dose could well prove fatal.

Jadite is the more precious of the two minerals and comes in various colours including red, brown, white and black, but it is the bright emerald green which is most sought after. This is generally found in Burma and a good piece can fetch an enormous price. Despite its comparative softness ($6\frac{1}{2}$ on Mohs scale) it has a very sound structure with intertwining crystals and is ideal for carving, an art form which was perfected by the Chinese.

Like the South Americans, the Chinese believed it to be the most precious of all materials, containing the five great virtues – charity, courage, modesty, justice and wisdom. They too believed that it had medicinal powers, particularly for those with weak blood or affected by asthma. They also considered that it helped slow down the decomposition of a body, and corpses were fitted with small jade amulets in all nine orifices of the body. The Emperor would wear jade sandals and carry a jade sceptre and badges of office were made from the material.

In the remote parts of New Zealand the Maoris still make talismanic pendants of nephrite which are formed as human figures, ensuring the wearer long life and fertility.

TOURMALINE

One of the latest additions to the jewellers' repertoire is the tourmaline. This stone, which is mined in Brazil, comes in a wide variety of colours controlled by the different metallic content. The most sought-after is the deep emerald-green, often known as 'Brazilian emerald.' A greeny-yellow variety is also known as 'Brazilian peridot'; a colourless one as **achroite**; red or pink – **rubellite**; violet – **siberite**; dark blue – **indicolite** and black – **schorl**.

The stone is formed in thin pencil-like crystals and perhaps the most beautiful examples are those which contain more than one colour, bright green at one end moving towards pink at the other.

One of the oddest things about tourmaline is that it conducts electricity, and, while the stone is too young to have a long mythological significance, modern astrologers associate it with Mercury and offer it as an alternative birth stone to opals for

*Zircon is another transparent gemstone which is widely favoured for jewels. The clear variety is one of the most popular substitutes for diamonds. It has good refractive properties but with a hardness of only 7½ on Mohs scale it is susceptible to wear and damage when brilliant-cut
Right: blue, yellow and green facet-cut zircons
Below: zircon crystal from Zlatoust, Urals, USSR. (Natural History Museum, Milan)*

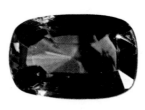

*Peridot is used infrequently as a gemstone but is extremely beautiful. Generally emerald-green, it has a hardness of 7 and can be facet-cut
Right: peridot crystal and facet-cut stone from the Island of St. John in the Red Sea. (School of Mining, Paris)
Below right: prismatic crystals of peridot in mother rock, from Mt. Summa, Naples, Italy. (Natural History Museum, Milan)*

those born under the sign of Scorpio (23 October–21 November).

ZIRCON

Another transparent gemstone which comes in a wide variety of colours is the zircon. The most sought after variety, however, is the 'Matura diamond', a clear variety which is used widely as a diamond substitute. It has a high refractive index which gives it considerable fire but its hardness is only 7½, and this makes it susceptible to damage and wear. None the less, it is the most effective non-synthetic alternative to a diamond which has thus far been discovered.

All colours of zircon are of the same basic construction – a silicate of zirconium, but contain different metallic oxides: **jargon** is yellow, **hyacynth**, orange; **malacon**, brown, and the term 'zircon' itself should be used only to describe the green variety.

Various supernatural properties have been attributed to this stone since the Middle Ages. For instance, it was considered to cure wasting diseases, prevent insomnia and help at child birth; while the Catholic religion used the stone as a symbol of humility. Astrologers consider it, with lapis and turquoise, to be the birth stone of Capricorns (21 December–21 January).

One of the most unusual physical properties of all zircons is their instability. They are mildly radioactive and their structure is in a constant state of flux; eventually all zircons will turn green and opaque, though not in the lifetime of a single owner.

PERIDOT

One of the least known gemstones, peridot can range in colour from yellowy-green to deep bottle-green and is found in Australia, Burma and the Island of St. John in the Red Sea. It is a magnesium-iron silicate with a hardness of 7 and when cut shows considerable fire.

Astrologers name it as the birth stone of Virgo (22 August–21 September) and consider that it offers the wearer happiness in marriage, the power of eloquence and freedom of insecurity both emotional and physical.

SPINEL

Spinels are another group of minerals which have been extensively used as gemstones. The range of colours, together with their hardness and high refractive index, have made them

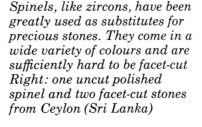

Spinels, like zircons, have been greatly used as substitutes for precious stones. They come in a wide variety of colours and are sufficiently hard to be facet-cut Right: one uncut polished spinel and two facet-cut stones from Ceylon (Sri Lanka)

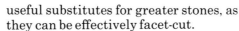

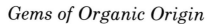

useful substitutes for greater stones, as they can be effectively facet-cut.

Most spinels come from Burma, Ceylon (Sri Lanka) and Thailand and have, over the centuries, acquired various nicknames: the crimson variety is generally called **spinel ruby**; the rose-red – **balas ruby**; orange – **rubicelle**; blue – **spinel sapphire**; purple – **almandine spinel**; and brown – **celonite**; and the single word spinel is generally reserved for the blue-green variety.

In the past, particularly during the 15th and 16th centuries, royal inventories described items of jewellery set with 'rubies' or 'sapphires.' Yet it has been discovered since, notably with Henry VIII's great 'ruby collar,' that the stones used were in fact spinels (see page 153). Whether this was because they had been fraudulently misrepresented or the difference was considered irrelevant will never be known.

Gems of Organic Origin

The mineral kingdom supply jewellers with the majority of their materials but there are various products of the animal and mineral kingdom which have been used for centuries. The most distinguished of these materials is, of course, the pearl (see page 178); the other three worth mentioning are coral, jet and amber.

CORAL: It was not until the 18th century that it was realized that coral was not in fact a form of marine vegetation, but the skeleton remains of marine animal. The mistake was understandable when you look at its tree-like formation. Coral has been used by jewellers since the Bronze Age. The Egyptians used it for making scarabs; the Hellenistic Greeks and Etruscans made seals from it. It was not, however, until the 17th century that it was used on any scale for decorative jewellery and the great coral jewellery was mostly produced in the 19th century.

Coral can be found on the ocean bed in many parts of the world but the bright red variety of gem quality comes mainly from the Mediterranean, off the coast of southern Italy where it is dredged from a depth of approximately 250 feet.

JET: this is merely the black fossil of wood, very hard coal or **lignite** which can be cut and polished like a mineral

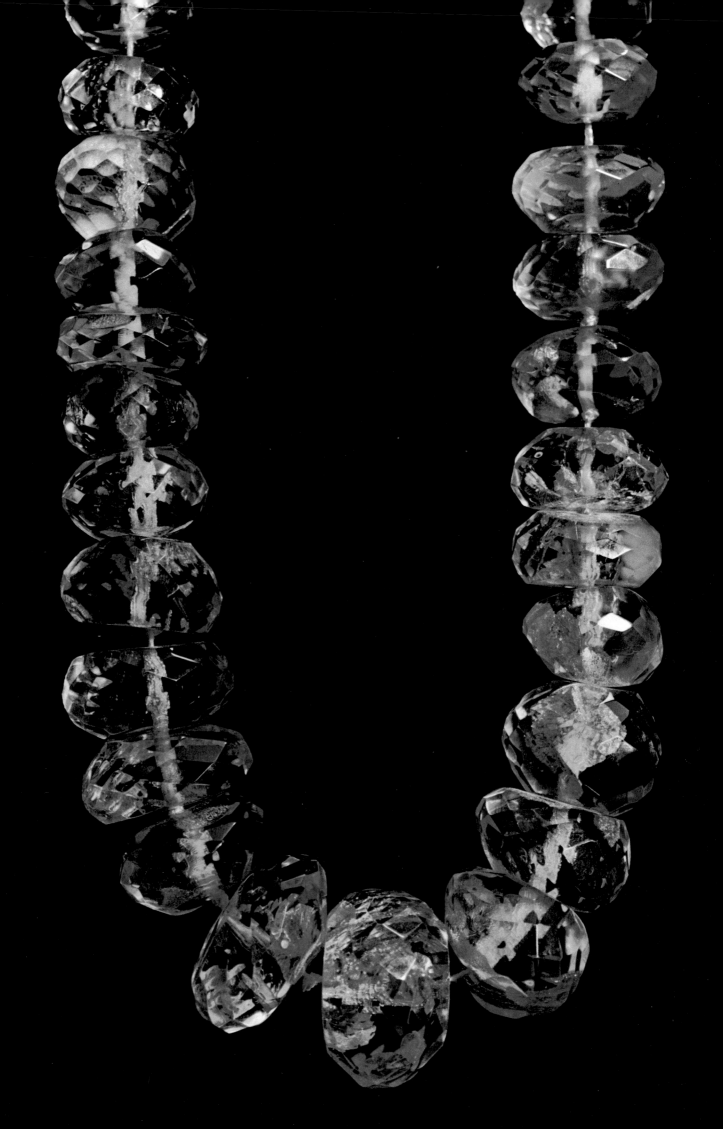

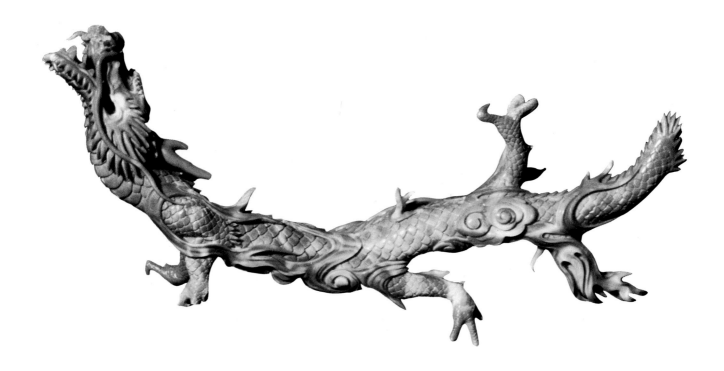

Four organic materials are often used to introduce polychromatic effects by jewellers – amber, coral, jet (see also page 253) and pearls (described on page 178) Left: necklace of facet-cut Baltic amber. Amber is the fossilized resin of wood and despite its softness (2½–3 on Mohs scale) it takes a fine polish and can be facet-cut. It wears extremely quickly and periodic repolishing is necessary
Above: a branch of coral – the skeleton remains of a marine animal – is carved into the shape of a dragon

yet will burn quite readily on a normal household fire. Like coral it was used by Bronze Age civilizations but again it did not come into its own until the 17th century when there was a vogue for memorial jewellery. This fashion then died out but was revived in the 19th century and jet came back into popularity with it. Today, facet-cut beads are used with other stones by contemporary jewellers. The best supplies of jet come from Whitby in Yorkshire, England, where, at one time, cutting and polishing the material was a thriving local industry (see page 253). It is supposed to have the power to protect against the evil eye and cure toothache and migraine.

AMBER: the substance which has the longest and most fascinating history of the organic gems is amber. It is the fossilized resin of an extinct pine tree, *pinus succinifer*, which flourished in north-eastern Europe about 40,000,000 years ago. Apart from being extremely beautiful, it has been an invaluable source of information to biologists since it is quite common for leaves, feathers and even extinct insects to be trapped in amber and perfectly preserved.

Most amber is now found washed up on the shores of the Baltic. It can range in colour from bright yellow to muddy brown and while generally translucent it can be opaque or occasionally completely transparent. Its softness (2½) makes it extremely easy to cut and polish, and it was highly prized by the Romans and Hellenistic Greeks for carving small statues. Pliny once complained that a small figure in amber cost more than a healthy slave. In classical times it was also considered to have potent medicinal powers, particularly for those troubled by headache or toothache. To cure these ailments amber was crushed and taken internally with honey.

Today amber is quite rare in the West and several substitutes have been produced which at a glance are indistinguishable but there are two very simple tests which can be applied. Real amber is incredibly light and will float in salt water: none of the fakes will achieve this. Amber is also capable of storing an electrical charge: rub a piece of amber against rough fabric and it will pick up a fragment of paper like a magnet. It was for this property that electricity derived its name from the Greek word for amber – *elektron*.

Glossary of Techniques and Technical Terms

Acanthus
Foliated ornamental style based on leaf formation (as used on Corinthian columns etc.).

Aigrette
Jewelled ornament often fashioned like a spray of feathers, designed to be worn in the hair.

A jour
Open, like lacework.

Alloy (see also **Electrum**)
Metallic substance formed from two or more metals. All metals found in their natural state are alloyed with other metals in the form of impurities. Prehistoric man learned the advantage of combining copper and tin to form bronze. Other alloys have been produced throughout history for economy, to produce different working properties and change the appearance.

Amulet (see also **Talisman**)
Ornament or gem worn to ward off evil spirits or to attract good luck; usually a jewel, coloured stone or piece of metal inscribed with magical signs. Amulet jewellery is known to have been produced since the 3rd millennium BC. In the 20th century charm bracelets fulfil this purpose.

Annealing
Process by which metal is returned to a malleable state after hammering. With continual beating metal becomes brittle and must be re-heated and quenched before work can continue. This must have been one of the first processes discovered by craftsmen of the Ancient World.

Annular
In the form of an unbroken circle.

Anthemion
Neo-Classical decorative form of a

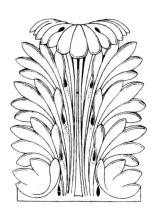

Acanthus

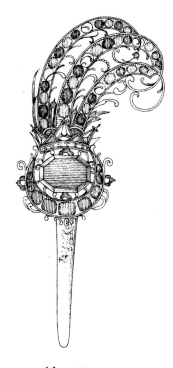

Aigrette

stylized honeysuckle which became fashionable at the end of the 18th century after the excavation of Herculaneum and Pompeii.

Appliqué
Attached to the surface.

Assay
Test of purity of a metal. In all countries of the developed world gold and silver wares are punched with an assay mark which is proof of the purity of the material used. With purity at 1,000, standards are counted as a fraction of 1,000 (920, 840 etc.). In Britain and USA gold is gauged in carats (22 ct, 18 ct, 14 ct and 9 ct being the most common levels of purity used).

Assay marks also identify the date when a piece was made, the location and name of the manufacturer. The idea of assaying gold dates back to the 1st Dynasty of Ancient Egypt. Bars of gold from Classical Rome (now in the British Museum) are marked, but the systematic marking was not introduced in Western Europe until AD 1300.

Baguette-cut: see **Cuts**

Baroque
Term used to describe all branches of the arts of the 17th century. Originally a term of abuse (in French, *baroque* means exaggerated or grotesque).
Baroque pearl: irregular or misshapen pearl, widely used and to great effect in jewellery in the late 16th century.

Base metal (see also **Pinchbeck**)
Any metal, other than gold or silver, used for jewellery. The fashion for base metal jewels came with the approach of the Industrial Revolution.

Basse taille (see also **Champlevé**)
More refined form of *champlevé* enamelling. Graded colour effect is achieved

Bulla

Cartouche

by varying the depth of cut in the surface of the metal.

Berlin ironwork
Jewellery produced in Germany during the first half of the 19th century. The fashion was encouraged by the lack of precious metals.

Bezel
Flange of metal used to hold a gemstone in position. Term often used to describe the whole upper part of a finger-ring.

Blue-white
The purest white seen in a diamond.

Borax (see also **Flux**)
Common name for acid borate of sodium, the most common substance used as a flux for soldering.

Brazing
Soldering with hard solder.

Brilliant-cut: see **Cuts**

Bronze (see also **Alloy**)
Alloy of copper and tin widely used in the Ancient World for the manufacture of tools.

Bulla
Lentil-shaped pendant hanging from a broad loop. Originally an Etruscan form but later adopted as an amulet by the Romans (who knew it as *Etruscum aurum*).

Burnishing
Method of polishing metal by rubbing with a flat piece of a harder material. In ancient times agate or bloodstone was favoured; today high-carbon steel is employed.

Cabochon (see also **Cuts**)
Term describing a gemstone cut in a smooth, convex curve without facets.

Cameo
Design or portrait cut in relief on hard gemstone or shell. The stones chosen frequently have different coloured layers, the lower serving as a background for the relief. Later, artificial methods of casting cameos were developed, the best exponent being Josiah Wedgwood in the 18th century. Glass cameos were made during the reign of Alexander the Great, and again in the 19th century.

Cannetille
The matt gold and filigree jewellery mass produced in the 19th century.

Cape
The pale yellow colour sometimes seen in diamonds.

Carat (**karat** in USA)
Measure of purity of gold (see **Assay**). The word is also used in the measurement of precious stones, when one carat equals 200 milligrams. The name and method of measuring stones derives from ancient times when the seeds of the carob tree were used as a unit of weight.

Cartouche
Decoration in the form of a scroll.

Cast chasing (see also **Chasing**)
Chasing work on the surface of a cast object to highlight details.

Casting (see also **Cire perdue**)
Process of producing an object by pouring molten metal into a mould. This is one of the oldest metalwork techniques known to man. Many different variations are used.

Champlevé
Method of enamelling in which a design is carved into the surface of a metal object and enamel poured into the recesses.

Chasing

Design inscribed on a piece of metal from the front with chisels or punches. Unlike engraving, no metal is actually taken away, it is pushed to one side. This, together with repoussé, is the oldest decorative technique known to man.

Chatelaine

Decorative plaque worn on the belt from which any number of items were suspended by chains, such as watches, scissors, needle cases, perfume bottles etc. Chatelaines were particularly popular during the late 18th and early 19th centuries.

Chinoiserie

Art derived from Oriental influences, particularly popular in the 18th century.

Cire perdue (lost wax casting)

The object, first modelled in wax, is coated (with clay or plaster of Paris) except for one vent. When the coating is hard the wax is melted out and metal forced in to make a cast.

Cleavage

The plane along which a stone will readily split. Knowledge of the structure of crystals is essential to a stonecutter. A diamond, for instance, is the hardest mineral known to man but it can be split cleanly with a single blow of a chisel once the point of cleavage has been established.

Cloisons

Compartments (or 'cells') on the surface of a piece of goldwork formed by soldering walls onto a backplate. These were originally designed to house cabochon stones.

Cloisonné

Method of enamelling in which the 'cells' are filled with enamel. Either

Chatelaine

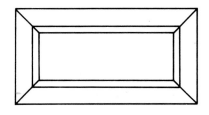

Baguette-cut

part of, or the whole, surface is covered with areas of enamel with thin gold strips between, giving a stained glass window effect. The art of *cloisonné* enamel was at its height during the early Byzantine and Barbarian times.

Collet

Encompassing band, flange etc. holding a gemstone.

Croix à la Jeannette

Traditional French jewel, usually a cross suspended from a heart.

Crown: see **Cuts**

Cupellation

Method of refining. The metal is wrapped in lead and placed in a porous block; the lead is melted and carries with it – into the block – all the base metal impurities.

Cuts

Facets (flat planes) are cut on a gemstone so that the reflecting planes allow for the light entering from above also to be reflected back through the top, thus exploiting its reflective and refractive properties. The top of a faceted stone is called the crown, the larger face on the top, the table, and the bottom, the pavilion.
Baguette-cut: used for small diamonds, generally in the form of side stones around a larger one.
Brilliant-cut: method of cutting diamonds the invention of which is attributed to a Venetian lapidary, Vincenzo Peruzzi, at the end of the 17th century. The stone is cut with 56 facets, making the most of its optical property.
Cabochon-cut ('en cabochon'): there are several styles of the domed cabochon-cut. The stone may be rectangular, oval, round, square, octagonal etc. with a low, double, or even flat table, domed top.
Emerald-cut (or **step-cut**): simple

parallel facets on crown and pavilion.
Rose-cut (or **Mazarin-cut**): triangular facets cut over whole surface of stone. The cut sponsored by Cardinal Mazarin in the mid-17th century had 16 facets and two tables.

Demi-parure: see **Parure**

Diadem
Head-ornament, ranging from a simple band of gold sheeting worn round the brow to an elaborate crown.

Dot repoussé: see **Repoussé**

Doublet
Artificial stone made in layers, the top being genuine, the bottom of glass or onyx.

Drawplate
Steel plate used for making wire. The metal is drawn through progressively smaller holes in the plate until it is uniform and of the dimension required.

Electro-forming
One of the newest techniques to affect jewellery, whereby an electric current deposits a layer of gold onto a resin mould. The technique has many advantages since the thicknesses are consistent and controllable. The crown made by Louis Osman for the investiture of Prince Charles in 1969 was made by this method.

Electro-plating
This process was patented in 1840 and is similar to the electro-forming technique, but on this occasion the metal deposit will adhere only to another metal and the two cannot be separated afterwards. The object to be plated is placed in a bath of gold potassium cyanide, and acts as a cathode. When an electric current is passed through the bath, gold atoms are attracted to the cathode and adhere to it, until

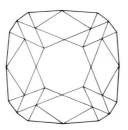

Brilliant-cut, 17th century

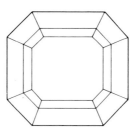

Emerald-cut

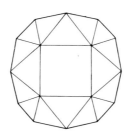

Rose-cut (or Mazarin-cut)

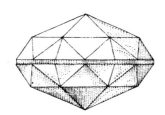

Doublet

eventually the whole object is coated with a thin film of gold.

Electrum
Alloy of gold and silver (in roughly equal proportions), much used in ancient times. The alloy is found naturally.

Email en résille sur verre
Enamelling technique developed in France during the 17th century. Design is engraved on the reverse side of a piece of glass or crystal, the cavities lined with foil and filled with low melting point enamel.

Emerald-cut: see **Cuts**

Enamelling
Glass is powdered, suspended in water and placed in a metal cavity before firing in a furnace to re-fuse it. Colours are added to the glass by mixing in various metallic oxides.

Engraving
Design is gouged out of a piece of metal with a sharp tool and, unlike chasing, metal is actually cut away. This allows a much cleaner, more precise line. The art of engraving was not used in the Ancient World since they had no metal sufficiently hard to retain a cutting edge.

En ronde bosse
Enamel applied to the surface of a design modelled in high relief or completely in the round. The technique was invented in the 15th century and produced an effect much like cameo.

Enseigne
Brooch worn in the cap, extremely popular in the Early and High Renaissance.

Equipage
A chatelaine carrying an *étui*.

Eternity ring
Simple band of metal with stones set all round, so called because of its traditionally sentimental connections.

Etui (see also **Chatelaine**)
Small decorated case which was suspended from a chatelaine and used to carry a number of small objects, such as scissors, needles and pencils. An *étui*, together with a chatelaine, was known as an *équipage*.

Facet (see also **Cuts**)
Flat plane cut on a gemstone to make it reflect light.

Faience
Process, not unlike enamel, for producing artificial stones. The body of the material is powdered quartz, covered with a coloured glaze of soda-lime glass and then fired. The process was widely used in Ancient Egypt when there was a shortage of genuine gemstones.

Ferronnière
Band or chain encircling the head, with a central jewel over the forehead (so called after Leonardo's portrait of 'La belle ferronnière').

Fibula(e)
Clasp generally used to fasten a cape or cloak, formed like a modern safety-pin. Earliest examples found in the Greek lands date from 14th century BC and are fairly simple. The Etruscans used them as a platform to demonstrate their extraordinary technical skill.

Filigree
Decorative technique dating from the Ancient World. Initially it consisted of fine wires soldered onto a background but later open filigree was developed where the backplate was eliminated. The finest filigree work was probably made by Hellenistic Greeks.

Eternity ring

Ferronnière

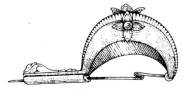

Fibula

False filigree: name given to a technique developed by the pre-Columbian Americans. The object was modelled in wax with a decoration resembling filigree and then cast by the *cire perdue* method.

Filigree enamelling: same technique as *cloisonné*, but using the compartments formed by the wires of the filigree as 'cells' for the enamel.

Flint glass
Heavy, high quality glass developed in the 17th century. Because of its hardness and high refractive index, it was extremely popular in the production of imitation gemstones or paste stones.

Flux
Material used to help metal to flow when soldering (by preventing oxidation on the surface when heated).

Foil
Thin sheet of coloured metal alloy, frequently placed behind a gemstone to improve its colour. The practice was banned at various times but it went on none the less throughout the Middle Ages, the Renaissance and the 18th and 19th centuries.

Frit
Glass-like material used as substitute for coloured stones in the Ancient World.

Garter, Order of
Senior Order of English Knighthood, instituted by Edward III, *c*.1346. The insignia of the Order consists of the jewelled garter (worn below the left knee), the star with St. George's cross, and the collar with a badge of St. George and the Dragon.

Gilding
This process was the forerunner of electro-plating. Gold sheet, beaten extremely thin, is bonded either by heat

or glue to an object made from another material, usually a base metal. It is a process which was widely used by the Egyptians, particularly for tomb furnishings.

Gimmal (or gimmel) ring
Finger-ring made to divide into two or three rings, by means of interlinking hoops. They were generally used as betrothal rings. The earliest examples are Byzantine.

Girandole
Form of pendant ear-ring fashionable in the late 17th and the 18th centuries. Each ear-ring was fitted with three drop stones which were designed to vibrate with each movement of the head and so catch the light.

Glass: see Flint glass; Frit; Paste; Strass

Golden Fleece
Order of Chivalry, instituted by Philip the Good, Duke of Burgundy in 1429–30 to commemorate his wedding to Isabella of Portugal. The badge of the Order was a jewelled plaque with a golden fleece suspended from it. Some surviving examples of these badges demonstrate the jeweller's art at its highest, particularly from the 18th century.

Gorget
type of neck-ornament characteristic of Bronze Age Ireland.

Granulation
One of the most elaborate metalwork techniques devised in Ancient Greece, perfected by the Etruscans and then lost for 2,000 years. Tiny granules of gold are soldered to a solid backplate to form figurative or geometric designs. In some cases the granules used were so small (1/1000 of an inch) that they looked like a texture on the surface of the gold.

Girandole ear-ring

Golden Fleece badge

British hallmarks

Hallmarks (see also Assay)
Stamps struck on a piece of gold or silver ware when it has been assayed, showing: the maker's mark (initials), the standard mark denoting the minimum gold or silver content, Assay Office mark, and the date of manufacture (code letter).

IHS
Monogram – *In Hac* [*Cruce*] *Salus* (In this [Cross] is Salvation), used as a motif for devotional pendants and brooches in the 16th and 17th centuries.

Inlay
Method of polychromatic decoration, the forerunner of *cloisonné* enamel. Instead of the *cloisonné* being filled with enamel and fired, individual pieces of stone or faience were cut to the shape of the 'cell' and burnished into place.

Intaglio
Design cut into the surface of a stone (exactly the reverse to cameo). This method was widely adopted for seal-cutting.

Labrets
Lip plugs worn by primitive African tribes.

Lapidary
Person who cuts or polishes gemstones.

Lavallière
Pendant with singly-mounted stones, also called *negligé*.

Lost wax casting: see Cire perdue

Lunula(e)
Crescent-shaped object made from thin sheet gold and chased with geometric designs. Lunulae were made by the pre-Celtic Irish and are presumed to have had some talismanic significance. Whether they were worn or carried, however, is uncertain.

Macaroni
Chatelaine (without a hook) used for carrying a watch.

Mannerism, Mannerist
Style which affected all branches of the arts in the 16th century, characterized by a degree of distortion or exaggeration, using of harsh colours.

Matrix
Rock in which gemstones are formed.

Mazarin-cut: see **Cuts**

Mêlée
Assortment of very small diamonds.

Memento mori
Mourning jewellery, particularly fashionable in England during the late 17th and 18th centuries. Some examples are very macabre, with coffins, skulls and skeletons, and are thought to have originated at the death of Charles I.

Mohs scale of hardness
Named after the German mineralogist Friedrich Mohs who originated this standard scale in 1812. Ten minerals are arranged in order of their hardness, diamond being the hardest; all other stones fall between Nos. 1 and 10. The scale is used to measure the hardness of stones for lapidary purposes.

1 talc	6 feldspar
2 gypsum	7 quartz
3 calcite	8 topaz
4 fluorspar	9 corundum
5 apatite	10 diamond

Monture illusion
Stone-setting technique developed in the second half of the 19th century. It cut the use of metal to the minimum in an effort to produce greater force from inferior stones.

Moresque
Moorish in style or design.

Nef
Pendant in the shape of a ship. These were originally worn in Venice but were later popular in England when the English were so proud of their prowess at sea in the late 16th century.

Negligé
Pendant of singly-mounted stones, also known as a *lavallière*.

Niello
Black compound used to decorate gold-work in the same way as enamel; usually applied by the *champlevé* method and used to highlight a linear design. The technique was developed by the Romans.

Opus interrasile
Open-work technique invented by the Romans and perfected during the Byzantine civilization. The design was chiselled from a sheet of metal in the manner of fretwork.

Orient
The lustre of a pearl.

Ouches
14th century cameo brooch which was sewn onto clothing.

Parure
Matching set of jewels, fashionable from the late 16th to the early 19th centuries, made up of three pieces or more.
Demi-parure: less elaborate set, of two or three pieces only.

Paste
Lead glass, facet-cut and used to imitate precious stones. Introduced on a large scale during the 18th century as an economical substitute for diamonds.

Pavé
Setting of small facet-cut stones butted together like paving stones.

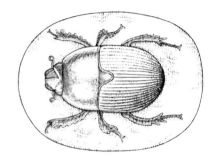

Scarab

Pavilion: see **Cuts**

Pectoral
Jewel or plaque worn on the chest.

Pelta
Etrusco-Hellenistic ear-ring design in the form of a cone hanging from a crescent-shaped shield.

Penannular (see also **Annular**)
Almost circular in shape.

Periamma
Hellenistic medallion, circular with open-work, filigree and inlay.

Piercing
Decoration achieved by cutting a design in a sheet of metal, a finer version of *opus interrasile*.

Pinchbeck
(83 per cent copper/17 per cent zinc.) Base metal substitute for gold invented in the 18th century by Christopher Pinchbeck, a London watchmaker.

Plique à jour
Open-work filled with enamel. Unlike *cloisonné* enamel, the 'cells' have no backs and the light can pass through as in a stained glass window.

Poissardes (fishwives)
Long pendant ear-rings.

Pomander
Spherical container for perfume, usually worn at the belt, frequently made from precious metal and jewelled.

Refining (see also **Assay**; **Cupellation**)
To remove base metal and impurities from a precious metal.

Reliquary
Jewelled container for a sacred relic.

Repoussé
One of the earliest decorative techniques. The design is punched in relief from behind. Probably the finest example of repoussé work is the famous helmet from the Royal tombs at Ur (**c**.2500 BC).
Dot repoussé: pattern composed of dots hammered onto a sheet of metal with a punch.

Rivière
Style of necklace in the form of a chain of individually set stones; introduced during the 18th century.

Rocaille
A style of the rococo period – characterized by asymmetry and forms deriving from flowers and shells.

Rolled gold
Base metal covered with thin layer of gold, forerunner of electro-plating.

Rose diamond
Small, rose-cut diamond.

Rose-cut: see **Cuts**

Scarab
Stone cut in the shape of a scarab beetle; an Ancient Egyptian talisman which was adopted by several of the Mediterranean and Aegean civilizations. The belly of the beetle was usually engraved with a signature, or talismanic symbols.

Sévigné

Schiller
The sheen in a moonstone.

Sévigné
Bone-shaped jewel with pendant drops, named after Madame de Sévigné in the mid–late 17th century.

Shank
Band (of ring) encircling the finger.

Silk
White flash in rubies and sapphires.

Soldering
Process of joining two or more pieces of metal with an alloy (solder) of a lower melting point than the metals being joined.

Solitaire
Finger-ring set with a single stone.

Stamping
Similar process to repoussé. A metal tool is engraved with the whole design which can then be transferred to a sheet of gold with a blow of a hammer. The first move by ancient civilization towards mass production.

Step-cut (or **emerald-cut**): see **Cuts**

Stomacher
Corsage brooch fashionable in the 18th century.

Strass
High quality lead glass, developed by Joseph Strasser in the 18th century, suitable for imitating gemstones.

Table: see **Cuts**

Taille d' épargne
Design engraved into the face of a piece of gold, the recesses being filled with enamel until flush with the surface.

Talisman (see also **Amulet**)
Object made, or carved, at a time considered astrologically favourable and thus possessing magical properties.

Torque
Celtic, penannular neck-ornament, usually made from hollow gold tubing.

Touchstone
Type of quartz or jasper used in testing gold and silver alloys (by the colour of the streak produced by rubbing them on the stone).

Tresson
Jewelled head-ornament.

Troy weight
Unit for measuring the weight of precious metals.
1 lb (16 oz) avoirdupois = 12 oz Troy
1 oz Troy = 20 pennyweight
24 grains = 1 pennyweight (dwt)

Verre églomisé
Glass or rock crystal decorated from behind in enamel and gold leaf.

Volute
Spiral scroll design.

Votive jewels
Jewels designed to serve a religious function.

Wrigglework
Engraving with a zig-zag effect.

Selected Book List

General and Contemporary

Jewellery by C. J. H. Davenport, Methuen, London 1905.

Jewellery by H. Clifford Smith, Methuen, London 1908.

The Story of Jewelry by Marcus Baerwald and Tom Mahoney, Abelard-Schuman, London and New York 1960.

Jewels and Gems by Mona Curran, Arco, London 1961; Emerson, New York 1962.

A Book of Jewelry by Vladislav Kuzel, Allan Wingate, London 1963.

Jewellery by L. Giltay-Nijssen, Merlin Press, London 1964.

Jewelry by Graham Hughes, Studio Vista, London 1966; Dutton, New York 1966.

A Book of Jewels by J. & A. Bauer, Hamlyn, London 1966.

Jewellery by Peter Hinks, Hamlyn, London 1969.

Jewellery through the Ages by Guido Gregorietti, Hamlyn, London 1970; McGraw-Hill, New York 1970.

The Art of Jewelry by Graham Hughes, Studio Vista, London 1972; Viking Press, New York 1972.

Silverwork and Jewellery by Harry Wilson, J. Hogg, London 1903, 1912.

Antique Jewelry by A. Darling, Century House, New York, 1953.

Antique Jewellery by E. Steingräber, Thames & Hudson, London 1957; Praeger, New York 1957.

Ornament and Jewellery by Klement Benda, Hamlyn, London 1967; Tudor, New York 1967.

Gems and Jewelry Today by Marcus Baerwald and Tom Mahoney, Marcel Rodd, New York 1949.

The Design and Creation of Jewelry by Robert von Neumann, Chilton, Philadelphia 1949, 1961; Pitman, London 1962.

Contemporary Jewellery and Silver Design by E. D. S. Bradford, Heywood, London 1950.

Design in Jewellery by Peter Lyon, Peter Owen, London 1956; Hillary, New York 1956.

Modern Jewelry: an International Survey 1890–1963 by Graham Hughes, Studio Vista, London 1963, 1968; Crown, New York 1963.

Investing in Antique Jewellery by Richard Falkiner, Barrie & Jenkins, London 1968; Potter, New York 1968.

Ancient Times to 19th Century

The Anvil of Civilization by Leonard Cottrell, N.A.L., New York 1957; Faber & Faber, London 1958.

Primitive Art by Douglas Fraser, Thames & Hudson, London 1962; Doubleday, New York 1962.

The Arts and Crafts of Ancient Egypt by W. M. Flinders Petrie, Foulis, London 1909.

Ancient Granulated Jewelry by Charles Densmore Curtis, American Academy Memoirs, Rome 1917.

The Art of the Goldsmith in Classical Times by Christine Alexander, Metropolitan Museum of Art, New York 1928.

Ur Excavations by Leonard Woolley, Oxford University Press, London 1927.

The Development of Sumerian Art by Leonard Woolley, Faber & Faber, London 1935.

Jewels of the Pharaohs by Cyril Aldred, Thames & Hudson, London 1971; Praeger, New York 1971.

Egyptian Jewelry, the Treasure of El Lahun by Herbert E. Winlock, Metropolitan Museum of Art, New York 1934.

Egyptian Jewellery by Milada Vilimkova, Hamlyn, London 1969.

Ancient Egyptian Jewellery by Alix Wilkinson, Methuen, London 1971; Methuen/Barnes & Noble, New York 1971.

Metallurgy in Archaeology by R. F. Tylecote, E. Arnold, London 1962.

Cylinder Seals of Western Asia by D. J. Wiseman, Batchworth Press, London 1959.

Western Asiatic Jewellery by K. R. Maxwell-Hyslop, Methuen, London 1970.

Crete and Mycenae by S. Marinatos, Thames & Hudson, London 1960; Abrams, New York 1960.

The Palace of Minos by Sir Arthur J. Evans, Macmillan, London and New York 1921.

The Bull of Minos by Leonard Cottrell, Holt, Rinehart & Winston, New York 1958; Pan Books, London 1969.

The Histories by Herodotus, Penguin Books, London and Baltimore 1971.

The Medes and Persians by William Culican, Thames & Hudson, London 1965; Praeger, New York 1965.

Greek Pins and their Connexions with Europe and Asia by Paul Jacobsthal, Oxford University Press, London 1956.

Greek and Etruscan Jewelry by Christine Alexander, New York 1940.

Greek and Roman Jewellery by Reynold A. Higgins, Methuen, London 1961; Methuen/Barnes & Noble, New York 1962.

Jewellery from Classical Lands by Reynold A. Higgins, British Museum, London 1969.

Greek and Roman Jewellery by Filippo Coarelli, Hamlyn, London 1971; Tudor, New York 1971.

Engraved Gems of the Greeks, Etruscans and Romans by Gisela Richter, Phaidon, London 1968, 1971; Phaidon/Praeger, New York 1968, 1971.

Treasures from Scythian Tombs by M. I. Artamonov, Thames & Hudson, London 1969.

The Celts by T. G. E. Powell, Thames & Hudson, London 1958; Praeger, New York 1958.

Anglo-Saxon Jewellery by R. Jessup, Faber & Faber, London 1950; Transatlantic, Florida 1951.

Byzantine Enamels from the 5th to the 13th Century by Klaus Wessel, New York Graphic Society, Greenwich, Conn. 1968; Irish University Press, Dublin 1969.

English Jewellery from the 5th Century AD *to 1800* by Joan Evans, Methuen, London 1921; Dutton, New York 1922.

Magical Jewels of the Middle Ages and Renaissance, particularly in England by Joan Evans, Oxford University Press, London and New York 1922; Argonaut, Chicago 1968.

A History of Jewellery 1100–1870 by Joan Evans, Faber & Faber, London 1953, 1970; Boston Books, Boston 1970.

Jewellery from the Renaissance to Art Nouveau by Claude Frégnac, Weidenfeld & Nicolson, London 1965; Putnam, New York 1965.

Engraved Gems: the Ionides Collection by John Boardman, Thames & Hudson, London 1968; Northwestern University Press, Evanston, Illinois 1968.

European Enamels by I. B. Barsali, Hamlyn, London 1969; Tudor, New York 1969.

Medieval Goldsmith's Work by I. B. Barsali, Hamlyn, London 1969; Tudor, New York 1969.

English Goldsmiths and their Marks by Sir Charles J. Jackson, Dover Publications, New York, 1964; Dover/Constable, London 1964.

Old Paste by A. Beresford Ryley, Methuen, London 1913.

Antique Paste Jewellery by M. D. S. Lewis, Faber & Faber, London 1970.

Cut-Steel and Berlin Iron Jewellery by Anne Clifford, Adams & Dart, Bath, Somerset 1971; A. S. Barnes, Cranbury, New Jersey 1971.

Victorian Jewellery by Margaret Flower, Cassell, London 1951, 1967; A. S. Barnes, Cranbury, New Jersey 1966.

English Victorian Jewellery by E. D. S. Bradford, Country Life, London 1959; Tudor, New York 1968; Spring Books (Hamlyn), London 1968.

Victorian Sentimental Jewellery by Diana Cooper and Norman Battershill, David & Charles, Newton Abbot, Devon 1972.

The Story of Whitby Jet, its Workers from Earliest Times by Hugh P. Kendall, Whitby, Yorkshire 1936.

English Posies and Posy Rings by Joan Evans, Oxford University Press, London 1931.

The Book of Necklaces by Sah Oved, Arthur Barker, London 1953; McClelland, Toronto 1953.

Chats on Old Jewellery and Trinkets by Maciver Percival, Unwin, London 1912.

Art Nouveau by Mario Amaya, Studio Vista, London 1966, 1971; Dutton, New York 1966, 1971.

Art Nouveau by Rossana Bossaglia, Orbis, London 1973.

The Crown Jewels and Other Royal Regalia in the Tower of London by H. D. W. Sitwell, Dropmore Press, London 1953.

A History of the Crown Jewels of Europe by E. F. A. Twining, Batsford, London 1960.

Royal Treasures of Europe by E. Steingräber, Weidenfeld & Nicolson, London 1968: Macmillan, New York 1968.

Four Centuries of European Jewellery (16th–20th century) by E. D. S. Bradford, Country Life, London 1953; Philosophical Library Inc., New York 1953; Spring Books (Hamlyn), London 1968.

Gold and Silver Treasures of Ancient Italy by Carlo Carducci, New York Graphic Society, Greenwich, Conn. 1964.

Italian Jeweled Arts by Filippo Rossi, Abrams, New York 1954.

Jewelry and Amber of Italy by Rodolfo Siviero, McGraw-Hill, New York and London 1959.

Old Hungarian Jewelry by Angela Héjj-Détári, Corvina Press, Budapest 1965; Collet's, London 1965; Heinemann, New York 1965.

Finnish Jewellery and Silverware by John Haycraft, Otava, Helsinki 1962.

Treasures in the Kremlin by B. A. Rybakov, Hamlyn, London 1964.

Treasures of the USSR Diamond Fund by Y. Duzhenko and E. Smirnova, Moscow 1969.

Gold Ornaments from the United States of Colombia by George F. Kunz, London 1887.

The Goldsmith's Art in Ancient Mexico by M. H. Saville, Heye Foundation, Museum of the American Indian, New York 1920.

The Daily Life of the Aztecs by Jacques Soustelle, Hachette, Paris 1955; Weidenfeld & Nicolson, London 1961; Macmillan, New York 1962.

The Conquest of Peru by William H. Prescott, Everyman, London 1963; Dutton, New York 1963.

The Gold of Peru by Miguel Mujica Gallo, Tandem, London 1967.

The Discovery and Conquest of Peru by Agustin de Zarate, Penguin Books, London and Baltimore 1968.

Jewellery and Personal Adornment in India by Kamala Dongerkery, Indian Council for Cultural Relations, Delhi 1970.

India of the Princes by Rosita Forbes, Gifford, London 1939; The Book Club, London 1939.

Biographical

The Life of Benvenuto Cellini by Benvenuto Cellini, Phaidon Press, London 1949; Fine Edition Press, Cleveland, Ohio 1952.

Peter Carl Fabergé by H. C. Bainbridge, Batsford, London 1949; Hamlyn, London 1966; Spring Books, New York 1966.

The Art of Carl Fabergé by Abraham Kenneth Snowman, Faber & Faber, London 1962; Boston Books, Boston 1964.

French Jewellery 19th Century, René Lalique by John Laurvik, London 1912.

A Study of his Art-in-Jewels (The Collection of the Owen Cheatham Foundation) by Salvador Dali, New York Graphic Society, Greenwich, Conn. 1959, 1965, 1970.

Foreign Language

Les Bijoux Anciens et Modernes by Eugène Fontenay, Paris 1887.

Les Bijoux Anciens by I. L. Blanchot, Paris 1929.

Bijoux et Orfèvrerie by Jean Fouquet, Paris 1930.

Amulettes Puniques by Pierre Cintas, Tunis Institut des Hautes Etudes, Paris 1946.

Le Trésor de Ziwiye, Kurdistan by André Godard, Service Archéologique de l'Iran, 1950.

Les Bijoux de Madame du Barry by Henri Welschinger, Paris 1881.

Inventaire de Marie-Josèphe de Saxe, Dauphine de France by Germain Bapst, Paris 1883.

Histoire des Joyaux de la Couronne de France by Germain Bapst, Paris 1889.

La Bijouterie Française au XIX Siècle (3 vols.) by Henri Vever, Paris 1906–08.

La Bijouterie, La Joaillerie; la Bijouterie de Fantaisie au XX Siècle by Georges Fouquet, Paris 1934.

Gli Amuleti by G. Belluci, Perugia, Italy 1908.

Argentieri, Gemmari e Orafi d'Italia by Costantino G. Bulgari, Rome 1958, 1966, 1969.

Goldschmuck der Renaissance by F. Luthmer, Berlin 1881.

Der Schmuck (Monographien des Kunstgewerbes series) by Ernst von Bassermann-Jordan, Leipzig, E. Germany 1909.

Edelsteinkunde by M. Bauer, Leipzig, E. Germany 1909.

Katalog der Goldschmiede Arbeiten by Berta Segal, Benaki Museum, Athens 1938.

Juwelen en Mensen by M. H. Gans, Amsterdam 1961.

Jagdlicher Schmuck by Renate Scholtz, Paul Perey, Berlin 1970.

Techniques, Materials and Gemstones

Jewellery Making for the Beginning Craftsman by Greta Pack, Macmillan, London 1957; Van Nostrand, Toronto 1957.

Metal Techniques for Craftsmen by Oppi Untracht, Robert Hale, London 1969; Doubleday, New York 1969.

Creative Casting by Sharr Choate, Crown, New York 1966; Allen & Unwin, London 1967.

On the Theory and Practice of Art-Enamelling upon Metals by H. H. Cunynghame, Constable, London 1899, 1901.

The Art of Enamelling by Mitzi Otten and Berl Kathe, New York 1950.

Jewelry-Making and Enamelling by Harry Zarchy, Knopf, New York 1959.

Gold by C. H. V. Sutherland, Thames & Hudson, London 1959, 1969; McGraw-Hill, New York 1959, 1969.

The World of Gold by Timothy Green, Michael Joseph, London 1968; Walker, New York 1968.

The Book of Gold by Kenneth Blakemore, November Books, London 1971; Stein & Day, New York 1972.

The History and Use of Diamond by S. Tolansky, Methuen, London 1962.

Diamonds by Eric Bruton, N.A.G. Press, London 1971; Chilton, Philadelphia 1971.

A History of Platinum by Donald MacDonald, Johnson Matthey, London 1960.

The World of Jewel Stones by Michael Weinstein, Sheridan House, New York 1958; Pitman, London 1959.

Gems: their Sources, Descriptions and Identifications by Robert Webster, Butterworth, London 1962, 1970; Archon Books, Hamden, Conn. 1970.

Gemmologists' Compendium by Robert Webster, N.A.G. Press, London 1964.

The Curious Lore of Precious Stones by George F. Kunz, Lippincott, London 1913; Dover Publications, New York 1970; Dover/Constable, London 1970, 1972.

Precious Stones; their Occult Powers and Hidden Significance by W. B. Crow, Aquarian Publishing Co., London 1968; Weiser, New York 1968.

Precious Stones and Other Crystals by R. Metz, Thames & Hudson, London 1964; Viking Press, New York 1965.

Crystals by Vicenzo de Michele, Orbis, London 1972; Crown, New York 1972.

The Retail Jeweller's Handbook by A. Selwyn, Heywood, London 1946, 1962.

Index

Page references to photographs are printed in **heavy** type.

Museums, Galleries and Collections are listed under MUSEUMS on pages 394–5.

Acknowledgments

Where no source is given in the caption, the item is privately owned or from a jewellery showroom.

G. Tomsich/Spectrum Colour Library: 12, 14 top, 15, 17 bottom.
Picturepoint Ltd.: 14 bottom.
Michael Holford Library: 16 top, 17 top, 22, 23 top, 40–41, 43, 47 bottom left, 51 bottom, 57 bottom, 61, 62, 63, 64, 65, 68, 69, 70, 72–3 top, 73 bottom, 74, 75, 76, 77, 79, 81, 82–3, 84, 85, 99 bottom, 102, 106, 112 top, 113, 115, 117, 118, 120, 121 bottom, 122, 130, 131, 133 top, 140 top, 141 top right, 147 top, 152 bottom, 156, 180, 181, 183 top, 184–5, 261 bottom, 264–5, 298 bottom, 300.
Michael Holford Library/Cameo Corner: 174 bottom left, 195 bottom left, 199, 211, 224, 230, 236, 250 top, 251 top, 255 bottom.
Michael Holford Library/M. Hakim: 189 top right, 213 right, 217 top and bottom right, 220–1 top.
Michael Holford Library/Bromet Antiques: 197 bottom.
Michael Holford Library/The Treasure Chest: 240.
Michael Holford Library/River & Co. Ltd.: 303, 304 top, 307 top left and right, 308, 311 bottom, 312–13.
Michael Holford Library/Georg Jensen (Silversmiths) Ltd.: 314, 315.
Werner Forman: 16 bottom, 31, 36, 71, 86, 87, 88, 89, 90 top and bottom left, 91, 103 bottom, 104 bottom, 105 bottom, 182, 270.
Novosti Press Agency: 18, 340, 341, 342, 343.
Mansell Collection: 19.
René Roland/J. Ziolo: 21, 28, 29, 56, 66–7, 90 bottom right, 110, 111.
Scala: 24, 25, 38, 107 bottom, 116, 119, 128 bottom, 129, 134, 145, 146, 147 bottom, 153, 158, 159 bottom, 161, 162, 163, 165 top, 170, 338, 339, 344–5.
Iain Macmillan: 26, 27, 48.
Roger Wood: 32, 33, 52, 53, 57 top, 78, 349, 350, 351.
Victoria & Albert Museum, London: 34, 35, 121 top, 128 top, 133 bottom, 138 top, 140 bottom, 141 top left and bottom, 142, 143 bottom, 148, 149 top, 150 bottom, 159 top, 160, 165 bottom, 167, 171, 172, 173, 174 bottom right, 175, 176, 195 top and bottom right, 197 top left, 200–201, 206 bottom, 214, 219, 237 bottom, 238 top, 247, 248 bottom, 266, 272, 273, 277 bottom right, 279 bottom, 283, 286 top, 287.
British Museum, London: 23 bottom, 39, 96, 126, 137 bottom.
Albert Shoucair (© Thames & Hudson Ltd. from *Jewels of the Pharaohs* by Cyril Aldred): 44, 46, 47 top and bottom right, 51 top left and right.
Carlo Bevilacqua: 45 (see also Appendix B Gemstones acknowledgments).
Peter Clayton: 47 top left.
William Macquitty: 49.
AME: 54.
Josephine Powell: 55.
Dimitrios Harissiadis (© George Rainbird Ltd.): 58–9, 60.
Giraudon: 72 bottom, 80, 135, 139, 223, 234–5.
Hirmer Photo Archiv: 92, 93, 108, 164.
Babey/J. Ziolo: 94–5.
National Museum of Ireland, Dublin: 97, 98, 99 top.
Daily Telegraph Colour Library: 100, 103 top.
Museum of National Antiquities, Stockholm: 104 top, 105 top.
F. Faillet/J. Ziolo: 107 top, 109, 112 bottom, 124, 127.
G. dagli Orti: 114.
Metropolitan Museum of Art, New York: 123.
Ashmolean Museum, Oxford: 125.
Thomas Photo Ltd.: 132.
Réunion des Musées Nationaux, Paris: 136–7 top, 334, 335, 336, 337.
Crown Copyright, reproduced by the gracious permission of Her Majesty's Stationery Office: 138 bottom, 326, 328–9, 330, 331, 332, 333.
Photo Meyer: 143 top, 149 bottom, 150 top, 151, 154 top, 155 top left and right, 191 bottom, 346, 347.
National Gallery, London: 154 bottom.

André Helo/J. Ziolo: 155 bottom.
National Portrait Gallery, London: 157, 179, 208.
Fitzwilliam Museum, Cambridge: 166.
London Museum, London: 168–9.
Museo Poldi-Pezzoli, Milan: 174 top, 177, 193, 198.
Christie Manson & Woods Ltd.: 178, 242–3, 248 top left and right, 249.
Museum für Völkerkunde, Vienna: 183 bottom.
Chris Barker: 186.
R. Todd-White/Asprey & Co. Ltd.: 187, 189 top left, 190 bottom, 191 top left and right, 194.
R. Todd-White/N. Bloom & Son Ltd.: 188, 190 top, 210, 226–7 top.
R. Todd-White/Fisher Jewels: 192, 196 bottom, 218.
R. Todd-White/Bentley & Co.: 215 top, 217 bottom left.
R. Todd-White/Gimpel Fils: 291.
A. C. Cooper/S. J. Phillips Ltd.: 189 bottom, 195 top left, 213 left, 215 bottom, 217 top left, 237 top, 244, 261 top.
Cooper-Bridgeman Library: 197 top right, 204, 212, 222, 225 bottom, 252 top left and right.
Cooper-Bridgeman Library/N. Bloom & Son Ltd.: 220 bottom, 227 bottom.
Cooper-Bridgeman Library/S. J. Phillips Ltd.: 221 bottom.
De Beers: 202, 203, 294, 323.
Robert Skelton: 205, 206 top right and left, 207 bottom.
F. Brunel/J. Ziolo: 207 top.
Hamlyn Picture Library: 216
Geremy Butler/Cameo Corner: 225 top, 233 bottom, 241, 253 bottom.
Geremy Butler/Lee Davies: 228, 231, 250 bottom, 257 top right, 285, 259 bottom.
Geremy Butler/The Treasure Chest: 232–3 top, 251 bottom, 253 top, 254, 255 top.
Robert Estall/L. Seltzer: 229, 252 bottom left, 256 bottom, 259 top.
Lauros/Giraudon: 238 bottom, 239.
Scarnati: 245, 246, 267, 268 top, 269 bottom, 277 left, 288, 289.
Clive Bubley/Cameo Corner: 252 bottom right, 256 top, 257 top left, bottom left and right, 260.
Clive Bubley/River & Co. Ltd.: 307 bottom.
Wartski Ltd.: 262, 263.
Goldsmiths' Company: 268 bottom, 269 top, 271, 274, 275, 276, 277 top right, 278–9 top, 280–1, 284, 285, 286 bottom, 296–7, 299, 301, 302 bottom, 304 bottom, 305, 306, 310, 311 top, 318 top, 320, 321 top, 322, 328–9.
Cl. Bouquignaud: 290.
Owen Cheatham Foundation (from the collection of sculptured jewels by Salvador Dali): 292, 293.
Andrew Grima Ltd.: 295, 298 top.
Jean Renet Ltd.: 302 top.
H. Zahn: 309.
Lapponia Jewellery: 316, 317.
Home & Table, Scernia Ltd.: 318 bottom, 319, 321 bottom.
Foto Marburg: 348.

Appendix B Glossary of Gemstones
Top two photographs on page 359 by courtesy of the Smithsonian Institution, Washington, D.C.; all other photographs taken by Carlo Bevilacqua by courtesy of the following:
School of Mining, Paris: 354, 356 bottom, 357 bottom, 360 bottom, 363 top right, 365, 367 top, 368, 369 all except moonstone at top left, 373 top left.
Grospiron: 356 top, 358 sapphire top right, 362 centre and bottom gems, 363 top left, 369 moonstone top left, 372 top, 375.
Compagnie Générale du Madagascar: 357 top, 360 top, 374.
Van Cleef and Arpels: 358 centre and bottom gems.
Sorbonne, Paris: 358 bottom.
Natural History Museum, Milan: 359 bottom, 361, 362 bottom, 363 bottom, 364, 366, 367 bottom, 370 bottom, 371, 372 bottom, 373 bottom.
Joz-Roland: 362 black opal at top, 370 first, second and fourth gems at top.
Pitte: 370 third gem at top, 373 top right.